Hil Byron.

£2·50

CASEBOOK SERIES

GENERAL EDITOR: A. E.

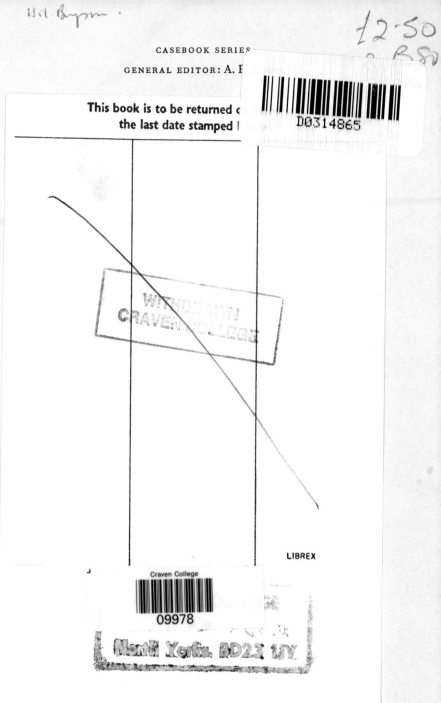

This book is to be returned on
the last date stamped

WITHDRAWN
CRAVEN COLLEGE

LIBREX

D0314865

Shakespeare
The Winter's Tale

A CASEBOOK

EDITED BY

KENNETH MUIR

M

First edition 1968
Reprinted 1973, 1977

Published by
THE MACMILLAN PRESS LTD
London and Basingstoke
Associated companies in Delhi Dublin
Hong Kong Johannesburg Lagos Melbourne
New York Singapore and Tokyo

ISBN 0 333 05094 0 (hard cover)
     0 333 08813 1 (paper cover)

Printed in Great Britain by
UNWIN BROTHERS LIMITED
The Gresham Press, Old Woking, Surrey

CONTENTS

Part I: *Some Earlier Comments*

Part 2: *Recent Studies*

ACKNOWLEDGEMENTS

Georg Brandes, *William Shakespeare* (William Heinemann Ltd); Lytton Strachey, *Books and Characters* (the Literary Estate of Lytton Strachey, Chatto & Windus Ltd, W. W. Norton Inc.); Robert Bridges, *The Influence of the Audience on Shakespeare's Drama* (The Clarendon Press); John Masefield, *William Shakespeare* (The Society of Authors as the literary representative of the Estate of the late late Dr John Masefield, O.M., Crowell-Collier & Macmillan Inc.); Ellen Terry, *Four Lectures on Shakespeare* (the author's Executors); Harley Granville-Barker, '*The Merchant of Venice*', from *Prefaces to Shakespeare* (the Executors of Harley Granville-Barker); Sir Arthur Quiller-Couch, *Shakespeare's Workmanship* (Curtis Brown Ltd); Sir Edmund Chambers, *Shakespeare: A Survey* (Sidgwick & Jackson Ltd, Crowell-Collier & Macmillan Inc.); Mark Van Doren, *Shakespeare* (Holt, Rinehart & Winston Inc.); Harold C. Goddard, *The Meaning of Shakespeare* (The University of Chicago Press); Arthur Sewell, *Character and Society in Shakespeare* (The Clarendon Press); Donald A. Stauffer, '*The Winter's Tale*', from *Shakespeare's World of Images* (© W. W. Norton & Co. Inc. 1949); E. M. W. Tillyard, 'The Tragic Pattern', from *Shakespeare's Last Plays* (Miss Angela Tillyard and Chatto & Windus Ltd); Ernest Schanzer, 'The Structural Pattern of *The Winter's Tale*', from *A Review of English Literature* (Apr 1964); Inga-Stina Ewbank, 'The Triumph of Time in *The Winter's Tale*', from *A Review of English Literature* (Apr 1964); S. L. Bethell, 'Antiquated Technique and the Planes of Reality', from *The Winter's Tale: A Study* (Mrs M. R. Bethell); G. Wilson Knight, 'Great Creating Nature', from *The Crown of Life* (Methuen & Co. Ltd); Harold S. Wilson, 'Nature and Art in

The Winter's Tale' (The Shakespeare Association of America Inc. and Mrs Harold S. Wilson); Derek Traversi, 'The Final Scenes', from *Shakespeare: The Last Phase* (Hollis & Carter Ltd); Northrop Frye, 'Recognition in *The Winter's Tale*', from *Essays on Shakespeare and Elizabethan Drama in Honour of Hardin Craig*, ed. Richard Hosley (Routledge & Kegan Paul Ltd, The University of Missouri Press; © the Curators of the University of Missouri 1962); Professor Nevill Coghill, 'Six Points of Stage-Craft in *The Winter's Tale*', from *Shakespeare Survey 8* (Cambridge University Press); M. M. Mahood, *Shakespeare's Word Play* (Methuen & Co. Ltd); Louis MacNeice, 'Autolycus', from *The Collected Poems of Louis MacNeice*, ed. E. R. Dodds (Faber & Faber Ltd, Oxford University Press Inc.; © The Estate of Louis MacNeice 1966).

GENERAL EDITOR'S PREFACE

EACH of this series of Casebooks concerns either one well-known and influential work of literature or two or three closely linked works. The main section consists of critical readings, mostly modern, brought together from journals and books. A selection of reviews and comments by the author's contemporaries is also included, and sometimes comments from the author himself. The Editor's Introduction charts the reputation of the work from its first appearance until the present time.

What is the purpose of such a collection? Chiefly, to assist reading. Our first response to literature may be, or seem to be, 'personal'. Certain qualities of vigour, profundity, beauty or 'truth to experience' strike us, and the work gains a foothold in our mind. Later, an isolated phrase or passage may return to haunt or illuminate. Where did we hear that? we wonder – it could scarcely be better put.

In these and similar ways appreciation begins, but major literature prompts to very much more. There are certain facts we need to know if we are to understand properly. Who were the author's original readers, and what assumptions did he share with them? What was his theory of literature? Was he committed to a particular historical situation, or to a set of beliefs? We need historians as well as critics to help us with this. But there are also more purely literary factors to take account of: the work's structure and rhetoric; its symbols and archetypes; its tone, genre and texture; its use of language; the words on the page. In all these matters critics can inform and enrich our individual responses by offering imaginative recreations of their own.

For the life of a book is not, after all, merely 'personal'; it is more like a tripartite dialogue, between a writer living 'then', a reader living 'now', and whatever forces of survival and honour link the two. Criticism is the public manifestation of this dialogue, a witness to the continuing power of literature to arouse and excite. It illuminates the possibilities and regards of the dialogue, pushing 'interpretation' as far forward as it can go.

And here, indeed, is the rub: how far can it go? Where does 'interpretation' end and nonsense begin? Why is one interpretation superior to another, and why does each age need to interpret for itself? The critic knows that his insights have value only in so far as they serve the text, and that he must take account of views differing sharply from his own. He knows that his own writing will be judged as well as the work he writes about, so that he cannot simply assert inner illumination or a differing taste.

The critical forum is a place of vigorous conflict and disagreement, but there is nothing in this to cause dismay. What is attested is the complexity of human experience and the richness of literature, not any chaos or relativity of taste. A critic is better seen, no doubt, as an explorer than as an 'authority', but explorers ought to be, and usually are, well equipped. The effect of good criticism is to convince us of what C. S. Lewis called 'the enormous extension of our being which we owe to authors'. A Casebook will be justified only if it helps to promote the same end.

A single volume can represent no more than a small selection of critical opinions. Some critics have been excluded for reasons of space, and it is hoped that readers will follow up the further suggestions in the Select Bibliography. Other contributions have been severed from their original context, to which some readers may wish to return. Indeed, if they take a hint from the critics represented here, they certainly will.

A. E. DYSON

INTRODUCTION

The Winter's Tale was one of a group of plays written at the end of Shakespeare's career. It is a group which includes *Pericles*, *Cymbeline* and *The Tempest* and, in the opinion of most recent critics, part of *The Two Noble Kinsmen*. *Henry VIII*, written probably last of all, does not share the characteristics of the other late plays. These differ in certain respects from Shakespeare's early comedies. They are tragi-comedies, plays which contain tragic situations and happy endings. They are not, of course, in this respect unique. The murderous hatred of Shylock, the villainy of Don John the bastard in *Much Ado about Nothing*, and Angelo's attempted seduction of Isabella in *Measure for Measure* were all potentially tragic. Nor are the Romances (as they are often called) unique in being concerned with reconciliation and forgiveness, for the theme of *Measure for Measure* might almost be so described. The late romances are nevertheless different from the early comedies, from which they are separated by a series of eight tragedies from *Hamlet* to *Coriolanus*. There is a deliberate juxtaposition of scenes from different historical periods or belonging to different conventions. In *Cymbeline*, for example, we move from the historical to the pastoral, from the pastoral to folk-tale, from Boccaccio to the Rome of the Caesars; and in *The Winter's Tale* a renaissance painter is mentioned and there is an allusion to the betrayal of Christ, despite the pre-Christian setting. Then, in the last plays, there is a more flagrant flouting of probability than there had been before, and the introduction of oracles, gods, spirits, magic, and even 'resurrections'. There are oracles in *The Winter's Tale* and *Cymbeline*; Jupiter appears in *Cymbeline*, and Diana in *Pericles*; the whole plot of *The Tempest* depends on Prospero's white magic; Prospero boasts that he has

raised people from the dead; in *Pericles*, Thaisa is restored to life
after being buried at sea; Imogen recovers from a drug which
makes her seem dead to her brothers; and in *The Winter's Tale*
all except Paulina believe that Hermione is dead and buried.

In three of the last plays there is a gap of some sixteen years
between the tragic events and the happy ending; and in *The
Winter's Tale* and *The Tempest* the reconciliation of the parents
is cemented by the marriage of their children. The audience,
moreover, is invited to watch events through the eyes of the
parents and not, as in the earlier comedies and in *Romeo and
Juliet*, through the eyes of the children – a shift partly explicable
by Shakespeare's advancing years.

Pericles is separated from his wife and daughter through no
fault of his own, and reunited to them after fifteen years of needless grief. But in *The Winter's Tale* Leontes is morally responsible for the tragedy that befalls him, and his wife and daughter
are restored to him after sixteen years of penitence: by this means
Shakespeare avoided the accidental disasters of *Pericles*, and the
jealous husband is not allowed the excuse of Othello and Posthumus that they were deluded by Italianate villains into believing
that their wives had committed adultery.

Dr Forman saw a performance of *The Winter's Tale* on 15 May
1611 (see p. 23 below); and the play was probably written not
long before this date. It was performed at Court two years later
when the Princess Elizabeth's betrothal to the Elector Palatine
had aroused interest in Bohemia. It is possible that they play was
revised for this performance. It was revived again in the reign of
Charles I; but after the Restoration it was condemned for its
violation of the unities and for its alleged absurdities. Pope even
denied Shakespeare's authorship of the play and, later in the
eighteenth century, Garrick tried to remedy Shakespeare's errors
by making the whole action of *Florizel and Perdita* take place in
Bohemia, to which country, years before, Paulina had conveyed
Hermione after her supposed death. As late as 1822, Garrick's
adaptation was printed by Mrs Inchbald in preference to the
original.

Despite this, it was left to the actors to show that the coming to life of Hermione's statue could be remarkably effective on the stage, as the accounts of performances by Mrs Siddons and Helen Faucit reveal. But most of the criticism of the play during the nineteenth century was devoted to an analysis of the main characters. It will be observed that the descriptions of Hermione and Perdita were apt to be disfigured by sentimental and pious moralising. Shakespeare's biographers rhapsodised over the way the poet, after his retirement to Stratford, was induced to create idealised young heroines because of his paternal feeling for his own two daughters. But, it may be noted, Susanna and Judith were some ten years older than Marina, Perdita and Miranda.

The attitude of Victorian biographers, and their assumption that Shakespeare's personal feelings were directly reflected in his plays, led to a reaction. Lytton Strachey, in a famous essay, argued that Shakespeare was not 'serene' in his final period, but bored with life, bored with drama, bored with everything except poetry. Strachey made the same mistake as the critics he was ridiculing – of assuming that Shakespeare's personal feelings were expressed in the plays – and in one respect he was more wrong-headed than Dowden and Furnivall, who had at least recognised the atmosphere of forgiveness and reconciliation that pervades the last plays.

Those critics who believed that the Romances were greatly inferior to the tragedies welcomed the theory of A. H. Thorndike (1901), who argued that the characteristics of the plays of the last period may be explained by the influence on Shakespeare of the popular tragi-comedies of Beaumont and Fletcher. Shakespeare in these plays shares in particular with his young rivals a fondness for exciting situations, exploited at the expense of character and probability. There are certainly many resemblances between *Philaster* and *Cymbeline*, and they cannot all be fortuitous. It is on *Cymbeline*, rather than on *The Winter's Tale* or *The Tempest*, that Thorndike's case depends. But, in fact, the relative dates of *Philaster* and *Cymbeline* are not known; and the young Beaumont and Fletcher were more likely to have imitated the most popular dramatist of his time than vice versa; the Shakespearian scenes of

Pericles were almost certainly written before the tragi-comedies of Beaumont and Fletcher; and, in any case, Shakespeare used the form of tragi-comedy not merely to provide theatrical sensations, but apparently to express certain views about the nature of reality.

In recent years we have heard less about the influence of Beaumont and Fletcher and more about the influence of Day and Heywood. Certainly there are resemblances between some of their plays and *Pericles*; and Heywood, like Shakespeare in the plays of his last period, was fond of introducing sea-voyages into his work. But, here again, Shakespeare uses similar material for a totally different purpose; and the sea in Heywood's work does not have the symbolic significance it seems to have in Shakespeare's.

Even in the present century there have been some critics who have regarded the last plays as Shakespeare's 'dotages'. Although, when he wrote them, he was still in his forties, they have been described by H. B. Charlton as 'an old man's consolation for the harshness of man's lot', a turning-away from the reality he had confronted in the great tragedies. Most modern critics, however, have realised that the plays are, in their own genre, masterpieces, though to some *Cymbeline* does not quite come off. The characters, with some exceptions, are less impressively alive than Shylock or Beatrice, King Lear or Cleopatra. The audience has to swallow a good many improbable situations. The plays do not arouse the hearty laughter of the earlier comedies, nor the pity and terror of the great tragedies. But Shakespeare, in Keats's phrase, wished to devote himself to other sensations; he wanted, apparently, to show that tragic passions need not always have tragic results. The guilty ones are given a chance to redeem themselves by penitence; and those sinned against – Imogen, Hermione, Prospero – are spared, so that they can forgive the sinners.

> The rarer action is
> In virtue than in vengeance.

The Winter's Tale falls into two parts. The first three Acts are almost a tragedy complete in itself, though in the very last scene of Act III the finding of the babe Perdita prepares the way for the fulfilment of the oracle. In all Shakespeare's other plays, he refrains from keeping the audience in the dark about essential facts: we know that Ganymede is Rosalind, that Hero is not dead, that Sebastian has not been drowned. But in *The Winter's Tale* we are led up the garden path; we are led to believe that Hermione is really dead. Paulina offers to swear that her mistress has died: Hermione appears to Antigonus in a dream; and there is nothing in the oracle to suggest that she will be restored to Leontes. The dramatic purpose of this unwonted deception by the poet was so that the reanimation of the statue could surprise us like an actual resurrection, and so that we should take Leontes' grief and Paulina's scolding with proper seriousness.

The atmosphere of the Sicilian scenes is poisoned by the sick suspicions of Leontes and emphasised by the frequent use of disease imagery. In the second scene of the play these images are particularly noticeable:

> 'twas a fear
> Which oft infects the wisest.

> be cured
> Of this diseased opinion.

> were my wife's liver
> Infected as her life.

> There is a sickness
> Which puts some of us in distemper, but
> I cannot name the disease, and it is caught
> Of you, that yet are well.

> O, then my best blood turn
> To an infected jelly, and my name
> Be yoked with his that did betray the Best!

Shakespeare cheerfully perpetrated this anachronistic reference to Judas in order to emphasise that Leontes' jealousy was both a disease and a sin. Earlier in the scene, in replying to Hermione's question about his friendship with Leontes, Polixenes speaks of his boyhood as an age of innocence, uncontaminated by original sin:

> We were as twinned lambs that did frisk i' th' sun,
> And bleat the one at th'other: what we changed
> Was innocence for innocence; we knew not
> The doctrine of ill-doing, no, nor dreamed
> That any did. Had we pursued that life,
> And our weak spirits ne'er been higher reared
> With stronger blood, we should have answered heaven
> Boldly 'not guilty'; the imposition cleared
> Hereditary ours.

This age of innocence is represented again by the love of Florizel and Perdita in Act IV; and it contrasts with the jealous behaviour of Leontes in the first three Acts, and the tyrannical behaviour of Polixenes in Act IV.

The pastoral atmosphere of the scenes in Bohemia which are introduced by the bizarre death of Antigonus, so described by the Clown that we cannot take it seriously, is quite different from that of the Sicilian scenes. Yet the wonderful sheep-shearing scene is not an escape from the real world. The violent displeasure of Polixenes is a threat to the happiness of the lovers and even to the life of Perdita's foster-father; and one of the main characters in the scene, Autolycus, is a charming but disreputable confidence-trickster and pickpocket, who preys upon the pastoral innocents as the coney-catchers in Greene's pamphlets fastened upon the innocents in London. But tragedy is kept at bay. Despite the threats of Polixenes, Florizel and Perdita are faithful to each other; and Camillo is there to suggest a means of escape.

Florizel's description of Perdita, as several critics have observed, is a picture of ideal spontaneity, 'of humanity made perfect by becoming itself', of the world of innocence previously evoked by Leontes in the lines quoted above, of the transformation of the commonplace into 'phases of enchantment' by the power of love which, as Shelley put it, 'redeems from decay the visitations of the divinity':

What you do
Still betters what is done. When you speak, sweet,
I'ld have you do it ever: when you sing,
I'ld have you buy and sell so, so give alms,
Pray so, and for the ordering of your affairs
To sing them too. When you do dance, I wish you
A wave o' th' sea, that you might ever do
Nothing but that, move so, still so,
And own no other function. Each your doing –
So singular in each particular –
Crowns what you are doing in the present deeds,
That all your acts are queens.

In this scene, as it was performed in Shakespeare's day, there
was a boy acting the part of Perdita, who is actually a princess,
but is believed to be the daughter of a shepherd, and who is
acting as the mistress of the feast, dressed in the robes of Flora,
the goddess of Spring. The Whitsun Pastorals, which Perdita
mentions, were May games, celebrating the year's rebirth.
Perdita is clearly intended to symbolise the spring and, in her
speeches, there is a continual contrast between spring and winter,
love and death. She recalls the story of Proserpine who was
seized by Pluto, the god of the underworld. Later in the play,
when Perdita arrives in Sicilia, she is described in hyperbolical
terms as one who,

Would she begin a sect, might quench the zeal
Of all professors else, make proselytes
Of who she but bid follow.

Leontes goes further, addressing her as 'goddess', and saying
that she is 'welcome hither, As is the Spring to th' Earth'. Perdita,
the lost one, is found again, and restored to her parents; and
Hermione, supposed dead for sixteen years, is restored to Leontes.
It is not surprising that Shakespeare should introduce allusions
to the story of Proserpine, especially as his neighbour Leonard
Digges was shortly to publish a translation of Claudian's poem
on the subject. Digges tells us in his preface that Ceres signifies
tillage, Proserpine the seeds, Pluto the earth which receives them,

and the six months Proserpine spends with Pluto the months in which the seed is underground before the ears appear. Shakespeare, whether he knew Claudian's poem or not, was familiar with the Proserpine story from his reading of Ovid, and he knew that it was a myth of the seasons.

It is not, of course, suggested that *The Winter's Tale* should be taken as an allegory, even though we may detect intermittent allegorical undertones. Still less ought one to press the analogy between Leontes in Act v, apparently without an heir, and the Fisher King of the Arthurian legend, made familiar to us by *The Waste Land* of T. S. Eliot.

It is, perhaps, more plausible to take the three states in which we see Leontes – in the sin of jealousy, in the sixteen years of penitence, and in his joy at the reunion with the reanimated Hermione – as corresponding to hell, purgatory and paradise. But such an interpretation omits the vitally important Bohemian scenes. Nor should we assume that the statue scene is intended to be an actual resurrection or even a symbolic representation of the resurrection. As Bonjour has shown, Shakespeare calls attention to Hermione's wrinkles: she has aged during her period of sequestration. Bonjour goes on to suggest that 'The reanimation of Hermione's statue may thus be considered as a symbol of the redeeming power of true repentance which may win again a long lost love and atone for the disastrous consequences of a past crime'.

It will be observed that some modern critics – including some who are represented in this collection – go a good deal further than this in their interpretation of the last scene; and when the late Leslie Bethell declared that 'the play represents an important moment in the history of Christian civilisation', spoke of Perdita as a compound of Flora 'with an Aphrodite chastened by prayer and alms-giving', and summed up the poetic vision of the play in the following terms –

In psychology, the life of the senses and the life of the spirit; in devotion, affirmation and denial of the flesh and the world; in society, a balance of the natural agrarian life and the graces of courtly civility which are nature too; in the broad sweep of religious thought, the natural order and the supernatural, time and eternity; these are not alternatives but mutually necessary and their integration brings a foretaste of heaven into the life of earth –

one feels that he was imposing his own religious convictions on the play. At the other extreme is Professor Philip Edwards who believes that the plays of the last period were primarily entertainments and that we should beware of reading into them any intimations of immortality. If they suggest 'thoughts beyond the reaches of our souls', it is only intermittently and secondarily. But since the themes of all four plays are clearly interrelated, it seems certain that, however much Shakespeare was satisfying the taste of the age, he was also expressing convictions about the meaning of human life.

The Winter's Tale is the most successful of these plays, dramatically more exciting than *The Tempest* (in which the sin was committed sixteen years before the rise of the curtain) and poetically more consistent than *Cymbeline*. It is true that Hermione is not so compelling a figure as Imogen, and she is absent from the stage during the middle Acts of the play. But Leontes is a more rounded character than Posthumus Leonatus, and Bernard Shaw told Ellen Terry that he was a more convincing portrait of a jealous man than Othello: 'Leontes is a magnificent part, worthy fifty Othellos (Shakespeare knew nothing about jealousy when he wrote Othello), as modern as Ibsen, and full of wonderful music.' Although this has the typical Shavian exaggeration, Leontes does not need an Italianate villain to swear away his wife's character, and in this respect the character is closer to ordinary human experience than Othello or Posthumus. Florizel and Perdita have more dramatic opportunities than Ferdinand and Miranda; and Paulina and Autolycus are superb acting parts. Indeed, in *The Winter's Tale* there is none of the thinness of characterisation which some critics regard as the main defect of the plays of the last period.

If one compares the captious complaints of Robert Bridges (see below, p. 56) about the senselessness of Leontes' jealousy and the absurdity of the dénouement with the defence by Nevill

Coghill of Shakespeare's stagecraft (p. 198) or with the claim by
Dr F. R. Leavis in *The Common Pursuit* that *The Winter's Tale*

is a supreme instance of Shakespeare's poetic complexity – of the
impossibility, if one is to speak with any relevance to the play, of
considering character, episode, theme, and plot in abstraction
from the local effects, so inexhaustibly subtle in their interplay,
of the poetry, and from the larger symbolic effects to which these
give life –

one cannot but be struck by the improvement in understanding
what Shakespeare was trying to do; and Dr Leavis is surely right
when he emphasises the besetting sin of most nineteenth-century
critics and declares that 'the relations between character, speech
and the main themes of the drama are not such as to invite a
psychologising approach'. In this respect the actors of the last
century came nearer to an understanding of the play than the
critics did; and it will be observed that none of the modern critics
represented here falls into the error of the psychologising
approach.

KENNETH MUIR

PART ONE

Some Earlier Comments

SIMON FORMAN*

Observe ther howe Lyontes the kinge of Cicillia was overcom with Jelosy of his wife with the kinge of Bohemia his frind that came to see him, and howe he contriued his death and wold haue had his cup berer to have poisoned, who gaue the king of Bohemia warning thereof & fled with him to Bohemia.

Remember also howe he sent to the Orakell of Appollo & Annswer of Appollo, that she was giltles and that the king was jelouse &c and howe Except the child was found Again that was loste the kinge should die without yssue, for the child was carried into Bohemia & ther laid in a forrest & brought vp by a sheppard And the kinge of Bohemia his sonn married that wentch & howe they fled into Cicilia to Leontes, and the sheppard hauing showed the letter of the nobleman by whom Leontes sent [away] that child and the jewells found about her, she was knowen to be Leontes daughter and was then 16 yers old.

Remember also the Rog that cam in all tottered like coll pixci† and howe he feyned him sicke & to haue bin Robbed of all that he had and howe he cosened the por man of all his money, and after came to the shep sher with a pedler's packe & ther cosened them Again of all their money And howe he changed apparrell with the kinge of Bo[he]mia his sonn, and then how he turned Courtier &c. Beware of trustinge feined beggars or fawninge fellouss.

(1611)

* [*Editor's note*] Dr Simon Forman, an astrologer, described performances of several of Shakespeare's plays in a manuscript entitled 'The Book of Plaies'. He was mainly concerned with the morals to be extracted from them. He saw a performance of *The Winter's Tale* at the Globe Theatre on 15 May 1611. As he does not mention Hermione's restoration, it is thought by some critics that in the version of the play he saw, as in Greene's *Pandosto*, the heroine actually died. But it is possible that Forman's memory was inaccurate.

† Goblin.

BEN JONSON

HEE is loth to make Nature afraid in his *Playes*, like those that beget *Tales*, *Tempests*, and such like *Drolleries*, to mixe his head with other mens heeles.

(from the Induction to *Bartholomew Fayre*, 1631)

OFFICE BOOK

THE Winter's Tale was acted on Thursday night at Court, the 16 Janua. 1633, by the K[ing's] players, and likt.*

(1633)

JOHN DRYDEN

BUT the times were ignorant in which they lived. Poetry was then, if not in its infancy among us, at least not arrived to its vigour and maturity: witness the lameness of their plots; many of which, especially those which they writ first (for even that age refined itself in some measure), were made up of some ridiculous, incoherent story, which in one play many times took up the business of an age. I suppose I need not name *Pericles, Prince of Tyre*, nor the historical plays of Shakespeare. Besides many of the rest, as the *Winter's Tale*, *Love's Labour['s] Lost*, *Measure for Measure*, which were either grounded on impossibilities, or at least so meanly written that the comedy neither caused your mirth, nor the serious part your concernment.†

(from *Defence of the Epilogue* to the Second Part of *The Conquest of Granada*, 1672, in which Dryden had criticised Elizabethan Drama)

* An indication of the play's popularity some twenty-two years after its first performance.

† See Warburton's comment below.

ALEXANDER POPE

... only some characters, single scenes, or perhaps a few particular passages, were of his hand.*

(from the Preface to his edition of Shakespeare, 1725)

CHARLOTTE LENNOX

IT has been mentioned as a great praise to Shakespear that the old paltry story of *Dorastus and Fawnia* served him for a Winter's Tale, but if we compare the conduct of the incidents of the Play with the paltry story on which it is founded, we shall find the original much less absurd and ridiculous. If Shakespear had even improved the story and cleared it of great part of its inconsistencies, yet he would still have been accountable for what remained, for why, indeed, did he chuse a subject so faulty for the story of a play? ...

Shakespear seems to have preserved the queen alive for the sake of her representing her own statue in the last scene, – a mean and absurd contrivance; for how can it be imagined that Hermione, a virtuous and affectionate wife, would conceal herself during sixteen years in a solitary house, though she was sensible that her repentant husband was all that time consuming away with grief and remorse for her death: and what reason could she have for chusing to live in such a miserable confinement when she might have been happy in the possession of her husband's affection and have shared his throne? How ridiculous also in a great Queen, on so interesting an occasion, to submit to such buffoonery as standing on a pedestal, motionless, her eyes fixed, and at last to be conjured down by a magical command of Paulina. The novel has nothing in it half so low and improbable as this contrivance of the statue; and indeed wherever Shakespear

* See Warburton's comment below.

has altered or invented, his *Winter's Tale* is greatly inferior to the
old paltry story that furnished him with the subject of it.*

(from *Shakespear Illustrated*, 1753)

SAMUEL JOHNSON

IT was, I suppose, only to spare his own labour that the poet put
this whole scene into narrative, for though part of the transaction
was already known to the audience, and therefore could not
properly be shewn again, yet the two kings might have met upon
the stage, and after the examination of the old shepherd, the
young Lady might have been recognised in sight of the
spectators.

(A note on Act v, scene iii, in Johnson's edition of
Shakespeare's Works, 1765)

LAURENCE STERNE

THIS unfortunate King of Bohemia, said Trim, – Was he unfortunate, then? cried my uncle Toby, for he had been so wrapt
up in his dissertation upon gunpowder, and other military
affairs, that tho' he had desired the corporal to go on, yet the
many interruptions he had given, dwelt not so strong upon his
fancy as to account for the epithet – Was he unfortunate, then
Trim? said my uncle Toby, pathetically – The corporal, wishing
first the word and all its synonimas at the devil, forthwith began
to run back in his mind, the principal events in the King of
Bohemia's story; from every one of which, it appearing that he
was the most fortunate man that ever existed in the world – it put
the corporal to a stand: for not caring to retract his epithet – and
less to explain it – and least of all to twist his tale (like men of

* See the account of Shakespeare's alterations in Greene's story by
Thomas and by Muir, *Shakespeare's Sources*, pp. 240 ff.

lore) to serve a system – he looked up in my uncle Toby's face
for assistance – but seeing it was the very thing my uncle Toby
sat in expectation of himself – after a hum and a haw, he went
on –

The King of Bohemia, an' please your honour, replied the
corporal, was unfortunate, as thus – That taking great pleasure
and delight in navigation and all sort of sea affairs – and there
happening throughout the whole kingdom of Bohemia, to be no
sea-port town whatever –

How the deuce should there – Trim? cried my uncle Toby;
for Bohemia being totally inland, it could have happened no
otherwise – It might, said Trim, if it had pleased God*

(from *Tristram Shandy* (1767) VIII 19)

W. WARBURTON

THIS play, throughout, is written in the very spirit of its author.
And in telling this homely and simple, though agreeable, country
tale,

> 'Our sweetest Shakespeare, fancy's child,
> Warbles his native wood-notes wild.'

This was necessary to observe in mere justice to the play; as the
meanness of the fable, and the extravagant conduct of it, had
misled some of great name into a wrong judgement of its merit;
which, as far as it regards sentiment and character, is scarce
inferior to any in the whole collection.†

(1747)

---

* Sterne is satirising the critics who complain of Shakespeare's
anachronisms and geographical mistakes. As the play was written at
the time of Princess Elizabeth's betrothal to the ruler of Bohemia, it is
unlikely that Shakespeare was ignorant of that country's lack of a
coastline.

† See Pope and Dryden's comments above.

DAVID GARRICK

The five long acts from which our three are taken
Stretch'd out to sixteen years, lay by, forsaken.
Lest then this precious liquor run to waste,
'Tis now confin'd and bottled for your taste.
'Tis my chief wish, my joy, my only plan
To lose no drop of that immortal man!*

(from the Prologue to *Florizel and Perdita* (1756)
adapted from *The Winter's Tale*)

A. W. SCHLEGEL

NOTHING can be more fresh and youthful, nothing at once so ideally pastoral and princely as the love of Florizel and Perdita; of the Prince, whom love converts into a voluntary shepherd; and the Princess, who betrays her exalted origin without knowing it, and in whose hands the nosegays become crowns.

(from *Lectures*, 1811)

WILLIAM HAZLITT

WE wonder that Mr Pope should have entertained doubts of the genuineness of this play. He was, we suppose, shocked (as a

---

* Garrick's adaptation lost a good many drops of that immortal man. The substance of the first three Acts is reported in a prose dialogue between Camillo and a Gentleman, and there are many deletions and interpolations in the remainder of the play. Warburton, an editor of Shakespeare, told Garrick 'As you know me to be no less an idolizer of Shakespeare than yourself, you will less suspect me of compliment when I tell you that besides your giving an elegant form to a monstrous composition, you have in your own additions written up to the best scenes in this play, so that you will easily imagine I read the "Reformed Winter's Tale" with great pleasure.'

certain critic suggests) at the Chorus, Time, leaping over sixteen years with his crutch between the third and fourth act, and at Antigonus's landing with the infant Perdita on the sea-coast of Bohemia. These slips or blemishes however do not prove it not to be Shakespear's; for he was as likely to fall into them as anybody; but we do not know anybody but himself who could produce the beauties. The *stuff* of which the tragic passion is composed, the romantic sweetness, the comic humour, are evidently his. Even the crabbed and tortuous style of the speeches of Leontes, reasoning on his own jealousy, beset with doubts and fears, and entangled more and more in the thorny labyrinth, bears every mark of Shakespear's peculiar manner of conveying the painful struggle of different thoughts and feelings, labouring for utterance, and almost strangled in the birth. . . .

The character of Hermione is as much distinguished by its saint-like resignation and patient forbearance, as that of Paulina is by her zealous and spirited remonstrances against the injustice done to the queen, and by her devoted attachment to her misfortunes. Hermione's restoration to her husband and her child, after her long separation from them, is as affecting in itself as it is striking in the representation. Camillo, and the old shepherd and his son, are subordinate but not uninteresting instruments in the development of the plot, and though last, not least, comes Autolycus, a very pleasant, thriving rogue; and (what is the best feather in the cap of all knavery) he escapes with impunity in the end.

The Winter's Tale is one of the best-acting of our author's plays. We remember seeing it with great pleasure many years ago. It was on the night that King took leave of the stage. . . . Nothing could go off with more *éclat*, with more spirit, and grandeur of effect. Mrs Siddons played Hermione, and in the last scene acted the painted statue to the life – with true monumental dignity and noble passion; Mr Kemble, in Leontes, worked himself up into a very fine classical phrensy; and Bannister, as Autolycus, roared as loud for pity as a sturdy beggar could do who felt none of the pain he counterfeited, and was sound of wind and limb. We shall never see these parts so acted again; or if we did, it would be in vain. Actors grow old, or no longer surprise us by their novelty. But true poetry, like nature, is always young; and we still read the courtship of Florizel and Perdita, as we welcome the return of spring, with the same feelings as ever.

(from *Characters of Shakespear's Plays*, 1817)

S. T. COLERIDGE

ALTHOUGH, on the whole, this play is exquisitely respondent to its title, and even in the fault I am about to mention, still a winter's tale; yet it seems a mere indolence of the great bard not to have provided in the oracular response some ground for Hermione's seeming death and fifteen years' voluntary concealment. This might have been easily effected by some obscure sentence in the oracle, as for example: 'Nor shall he ever recover an heir, if he have a wife before that recovery'.

The idea of this delightful drama is a genuine jealousy of disposition, and it should be immediately followed by the perusal of *Othello*, which is the direct contrast of it in every particular. For jealousy is a vice of the mind, a culpable tendency of the temper, having certain well known and well defined effects and concomitants, all of which are visible in Leontes, and, I boldly say, not one of which marks its presence in *Othello*; – such as, first, an excitability by the most inadequate causes, and an eagerness to snatch at proofs; secondly, a grossness of conception, and a disposition to degrade the object of the passion by sensual fancies and images; thirdly, a sense of shame of his own feelings exhibited in a solitary moodiness of humour, and yet from the violence of the passion forced to utter itself, and therefore catching occasions to ease the mind by ambiguities, equivoques, by talking to those who cannot, and who are known not to be able to, understand what is said to them, – in short, by soliloquy in the form of dialogue, and hence a confused, broken, and fragmentary manner; fourthly, a dread of vulgar ridicule, as distinct from a high sense of honour, or a mistaken sense of duty; and lastly, and immediately consequent on this, a spirit of selfish vindictiveness.

(from the notes of a lecture, 1818)

MRS INCHBALD

THE long absence from the scene of the two most important characters, Leontes and his wife, and the introduction of various other persons to fill their places, divert, in some measure, the attention of an audience; and they do not so feelingly unite all they see and all they hear into a single story, as he who, with the book in his hand, and neither his eye nor ear distracted, combines, and enjoys the whole grand variety. Besides the improbability of exciting equal interest by the plot of this drama, in performance as in the closet; some of the poetry is less calculated for that energetic delivery which the stage requires, than for the quiet contemplation of one who reads. The conversations of Florizel and Perdita have more of tenderness, than the fervour of love; and consequently their passion has not the force of expression to animate a multitude, though it is properly adapted to steal upon the heart of an individual . . .

There are two occurrences in the drama, quite as improbable as the unprovoked jealousy of Leontes, – the one, that the gentle, the amiable, the tender Perdita should be an unconcerned spectator of the doom which menaced her foster, and supposed real, father; and carelessly forsake him in the midst of his calamities. The other disgraceful improbability is, – that the young prince Florizel should introduce himself to the Court of Sicilia, by speaking arrant falsehoods.

(from *British Theatre* (1822) XII)

THOMAS CAMPBELL

MRS YATES had a sculpturesque beauty that suited the statue, I have been told, as long as it stood still; but, when she had to speak, the charm was broken, and the spectators wished her back to her pedestal. But Mrs Siddons* looked the statue, even to literal illusion; and, whilst the drapery hid her lower limbs, it showed a beauty of head, neck, shoulders, and arms, that Praxiteles might have studied. This statue-scene has hardly its parallel for enchantment even in Shakespeare's theatre. The star of his genius was at its zenith when he composed it; but it was only a Siddons that could do justice to its romantic perfection. The heart of every one who saw her when she burst from the semblance of sculpture into motion, and embraced her daughter, Perdita, must throb and glow at the recollection.

(from *Life of Mrs Siddons*, 1834)

ANNA JAMESON

THE character of Hermione exhibits what is never found in the other sex, but rarely in our own, – yet sometimes, – dignity without pride, love without passion, and tenderness without weakness. To conceive a character, in which there enters so much of the negative, required perhaps no rare and astonishing effort of genius ... but to delineate such a character in a poetical form, to develop it through the medium of action and dialogue, without the aid of description; to preserve its tranquil, mild and serious beauty, its unimpassioned dignity, and at the same time keep the strongest hold upon our sympathy and our imagination; and out of this exterior calm, produce the most profound pathos, the most vivid impression of life and internal power: – it is this, which renders the character of Hermione one of Shakespeare's masterpieces.

* Hermione was the last role undertaken by Mrs Siddons.

Hermione is a queen, a matron, and a mother; she is good and beautiful, and royally descended. A majestic sweetness, a grand and gracious simplicity, an easy, unforced, yet dignified self-possession, are in all her deportment, and in every word she utters. She is one of those characters, of whom it has been said proverbially, that 'still waters run deep'. Her passions are not vehement, but in her settled mind the sources of pain or pleasure, love or resentment, are like the springs that feed mountain lakes, impenetrable, unfathomable, and inexhaustible. . . .

Paulina . . . is a character strongly drawn from real and common life, – a clever, generous, strong-minded, warm-hearted woman, fearless in asserting the truth, firm in her sense of right, enthusiastic in all her affections; quick in thought, resolute in word, and energetic in action; but heedless, hot-tempered, impatient, loud, bold, voluble, and turbulent of tongue; regardless of the feelings of those for whom she would sacrifice her life, and injuring from excess of zeal those whom she most wishes to serve. . . . But Paulina, though a very termagant, is yet a poetical termagant in her way; and the manner in which all the evil and dangerous tendencies of such a temper are placed before us, even while the individual character preserves the strongest hold upon our respect and admiration, forms an impressive lesson, as well as a natural and delightful portrait.

The qualities which impart to Perdita her distinct individuality are the beautiful combination of the pastoral with the elegant, of simplicity with elevation, of spirit with sweetness. The exquisite delicacy of the picture is apparent. To understand and appreciate its effective truth and nature we should place Perdita beside some of the nymphs of Arcadia, or the Cloris' and Sylvias of the Italian pastorals, who, however, graceful in themselves, when opposed to Perdita, seem to melt away into mere poetical abstractions: as in Spenser, the fair but fictitious Florimel, which the subtle enchantress had moulded out of snow, 'vermeil tinctur'd', and informed with an airy spirit, that knew 'all wiles of woman's wits', fades and dissolves away when placed next to

B

the real Florimel, in her warm, breathing, human loveliness. . . .

Perdita has another characteristic, which lends to the poetical delicacy of the delineation a certain strength and moral elevation which is peculiarly striking. It is that sense of truth and rectitude, that upright simplicity of mind, which disdains all crooked and indirect means, which would not stoop for an instant to dissemblance, and is mingled with a noble confidence in her love and in her lover.

(from *Shakespeare's Heroines*, 1833)

HARTLEY COLERIDGE

In this wild drama the comedy is excellent, the pastoral is exquisite; but of the scenes which carry on the plot, some appear to me to be harsh in the thought, and infelicitous in diction: Shakespeare throughout, but not always Shakespeare in a happy vein. The sudden jealousy of Leontes, though unaccountable, is not impossible. I am not sure that the ready soliciting of Hermione, and the easy compliance of Polixenes might not produce, in a better mind, a momentary cloud, a wish that the request had not been made, an impatience for Polixenes' departure. How slight a spark may cause explosion in the foul atmosphere of a despot's heart it is hard to say. Irresponsible power is tyranny without, and moral anarchy within. We should little wonder at the conduct of Leontes in an Eastern tale. . . . The grossness of Leontes' imaginations, his murderous suggestions, and inaccessibility to reason, remorse, or religion, is naturally consequent on the base passion, say rather the unclean dæmon, that possesses him. . . . But is it possible that one who had once fallen thus, could ever again be worthy of a restoration to happiness? In the constituted order of human progression, – surely never. Remorse, the tyrant would feel: but it would urge him to vengeance on the instruments of his crimes, – perhaps to some superstitious rite, – some self-sought atonement; but never to a heart-cleansing repentance. . . .

Except Autolycus, none of the characters show much of Shakespeare's philosophic depth. . . . Hermione is frank and noble, rising in dignity as she falls in fortune . . . in sunshine a butterfly, in misery a martyr. Paulina is an honest scold. Perdita a pretty piece of poetry. Polixenes is not very amiable, nor, in truth, much of anything. The length of time he remains witness to his son's courtship, before he discovers himself, is a sacrifice to effect. Camillo is an old rogue whom I can hardly forgive for his double treachery. The Shepherd and his son are well enough in their way; but Mopsa and Dorcas might be countrified enough with better tongues in their heads. Of the rest nothing need be said.

(from *Essays and Marginilia*, 1851)

W. WATKISS LLOYD

The Winter's Tale stands alone in the class of Shakespeare's finished plays to which it is justly assigned, in the peculiarity of its composition, made up as it is of two, for the most part, highly contrasted portions; the first highly tragic, the second as properly taking place as comedy. The contrast is still more distinctly marked by the interval of sixteen years that is announced by Time as Chorus, as elapsing at the very point of juncture, between the third and fourth acts; the babe that suffers by tragic violence in the first scenes being the fair and happy object of romantic love in the last. This balance and division seems further enforced by the tragic section of evil passion and poignant suffering, being as nearly as possible equal in length to the agreeable and amusing scenes; and happy evolution that make up the latter half. Such a division in the abstract appears like an experiment and a dangerous one; it is rare, if not unprecedented in any art, to find an effective whole resulting from the blank opposition of two precisely counter-balanced halves when not united by common reference to some declared third magnitude. Nor is such a uniting power wanting in the present instance, whatever may appear to external view. The leading masses are contrasted with a breadth and boldness that strain the very limits of coherence, but it still holds on without crack or fracture to the perfect and rounded conclusion.

The contrast of the character and jealousies of Leontes and of Othello has frequently been remarked upon; it lies between the vice self-sown, self-born, and self-developed, and that which, however springing from a native germ, is only forced and ripened to venomous germination by the heat of tending malice, and the fostering of all unlucky moral and external circumstances. The jealousy of Leontes is the headlong plunge of the beast of prey that he is named after, and thinking of him with the lightly limbed and fine-thoughted Othello, we are reminded in a general way of the difference. . . . Leontes is chiefly affected by the insult of the fate that he stupidly and groundlessly hugs to himself. . . . Desdemona, affectionate and devoted, is the object of love of a husband whose bitterest trial in jealousy, sensitive as he is in honour, is still the loss of her trusted and tender heart.

The character of Paulina is a necessity to the play; without the support derived from her constant presence, it would not be intelligible how such a mind as that of Leontes could have the force and freshness of feeling after sixteen years have elapsed, that are required to give interest to the recognition, and to satisfy our sympathies with the honour of Hermione. . . . It is the very harshness of the virtue of Paulina that gives effect to the more delicate strength and graceful vigour of the virtue of Hermione, and saves by contrast the coolness of her temperament from the thought of coldness – nay, gives to it a glow of nature's warmth; while the softening and humanising that her character has undergone, encourages our faith in the mellowing traits of Leontes, whom her care and comfort has reclaimed.

(from *Critical Essays on the Plays of Shakespeare,* 1875)

FRANÇOIS-VICTOR HUGO

WHEN Claudio leaves us to pray at the tomb of his betrothed, we never let ourselves be moved at this grief: we know the tomb is empty. . . . But, on the contrary, in *The Winter's Tale*, the poet keeps the secret to himself. . . . He wishes us to be involved in the despair of his characters; he would have us, like Leontes, believe in the death of Hermione, and to the very last he leaves us the dupes of Paulina's device. Hence it is that the dénouement is profoundly solemn. Then our anxiety is at its height; and when the statue stirs, when marble becomes flesh, when the Queen descends from the pedestal, it cannot be but that we are present at some magic invocation by a supernatural power, and at this unexpected resurrection, we feel an indescribable emotion of wonder and surprise.

(from *Œuvres Complètes* de Shakespeare, 1868)

EDWARD DOWDEN

SERENITY Shakspere did attain. Once again before the end, his mirth is bright and tender. When in some Warwickshire field, one breezy morning, as the daffodil began to peer, the poet conceived his Autolycus, there might seem to be almost a return of the lightheartedness of youth. But the same play that contains Autolycus contains the grave and noble figure of Hermione. From its elevation and calm Shakspere's heart can pass into the simple merriment of rustic festivity; he can enjoy the open-mouthed happiness of country clowns; he is delighted by the gay defiance of order and honesty which Autolycus, most charming of rogues, professes; he is touched and exquisitely thrilled by the pure and vivid joy of Perdita among her flowers. Now that Shakspere is most a householder he enters most into the pleasures of truantship. And in like manner it is when he is most grave that he can smile most brightly, most tenderly. . . . The sly knavery of Autolycus has nothing in it that is criminal; heaven is his accomplice. 'If I had a mind to be honest, I see Fortune would not suffer me; she drops booties in my mouth.'

(from Shakspere – His Mind and Art, 1875)

F. J. FURNIVALL

ITS purpose, its lesson, are to teach forgiveness of wrongs, not vengeance for them; to give the sinner time to repent and amend, not to cut him off in his sin; to frustrate the crimes he has purposed. And, as in *Pericles*, father and lost daughter, and wife and mother thought dead, meet again; as in *Cymbeline*, father and injured daughter meet again, she forgiving her wrongs; as there, too, friends meet again, the injured friend forgiving his wrongs, so here do lost daughter, injured daughter and injuring father meet, he being forgiven; so injured friend forgiving, meets injuring friend forgiven; while above all rises the figure of the noble, long-suffering wife Hermione, forgiving the base though now repentant husband who had so cruelly wronged her.

(from the Introduction to the Leopold Shakespeare, 1877)

ALGERNON CHARLES SWINBURNE

ANY one but Shakespeare would have sought to make pathetic profit out of the child [Mamillius] by the easy means of showing him if but once again as changed and stricken to the death for want of his mother and fear for her and hunger and thirst at his little high heart for the sight and touch of her: Shakespeare only could find a better way, a subtler and a deeper chord to strike, by giving us our last glimpse of him as he laughed and chattered with her 'past enduring', to the shameful neglect of those ladies in the natural blueness of whose eyebrows as well as their noses he so stoutly declined to believe. And at the very end . . . it may be that we remember him all the better because the father whose jealousy killed him and the mother for love of whom he died would seem to have forgotten the little brave spirit with all its truth of love and tender sense of shame. . . .

(from *A Study of Shakespeare*, 1879)

H. N. HUDSON

IN the delineation of Leontes there is an abruptness of change which strikes us, at first view, as not a little a-clash with nature; his jealousy shoots comet-like, as something unprovided for in the general ordering of his character. Which causes this feature to appear as if it were suggested rather by the exigencies of the stage than by the natural workings of human passion. And herein the Poet seems at variance with himself; his usual method being to unfold a passion in its rise and progress, so that we go along with it freely from its origin to its consummation. And, certainly, there is no accounting for Leontes' conduct, but by supposing a predisposition to jealousy in him, which, however, has been hitherto kept latent by his wife's clear, firm, serene discreetness, but which breaks out into sudden and frightful activity as soon as she, under a special pressure of motives, slightly overacts the confidence of friendship. There needed but a spark of occasion to set this secret magazine of passion all a-blaze. . . .

It is true Shakespeare had a course of action marked out for him in the tale. But then he was bound by his own principles of art to make the character such as would rationally support the action, and cohere with it. . . . Nor is it by any means safe to affirm that he has not done this. For it is to be noted that Polixenes has made a pretty long visit, having passed, it seems, no less than nine lunar months at the home of his royal friend. . . . What secret thoughts may have been gathering to a head in the mind of Leontes during that period is left for us to divine from the after-results. And I believe there is a jealousy of friendship, as well as of love. Accordingly, though Leontes invokes the Queen's influence to induce a lengthening of the visit, yet he seems a little disturbed on seeing that her influence has proved stronger than his own... In his seeming abruptness Leontes, after all, does but exemplify the strange transformations which sometimes occur in men upon sudden and unforeseen emergencies. And it is observable that the very slightness of the Queen's indiscretion, the fact that she goes but a little, a very little too far, only works against her, causing the King to suspect her of great effort and care to avoid suspicion. And on the same principle, because he has never suspected her before, therefore he suspects her all the more vehemently now; that his confidence has hitherto stood unshaken, he attributes to extreme artfulness on her part; for even so to an ill-disposed mind perfect innocence is apt to give an impression of consummate art. . . .

We can scarce call Hermione sweet or gentle, though she is both; she is a *noble* woman. . . . With an equal sense of what is due to the King as her husband, and to herself as a woman, a wife, and a mother, she knows how to reconcile all these demands; she therefore resists without violence, and submits without weakness. . . . And so, under the worst that can befall, she remains within the region of herself, calm and serenely beautiful, stands firm, yet full of grace, in the austere strengths of reason and conscious rectitude. . . .

The Queen's long concealing of herself has been censured by some as repugnant to nature. Possibly they may think it somewhat strained and theatrical, but it is not so. . . . For to her keen sensibility of honour the King's treatment is literally an *infinite* wrong; nor does its cruelty more wound her affection, than its meanness alienates her respect; and one so strong to bear injury might be equally strong to remember it. . . . When she does forgive, the forgiveness is simply *perfect*. . . . Moreover, with her severe chastity of principle, the reconciliation to her husband must begin there where the separation grew. Thus it was for Perdita to restore the parental unity which her being represents, but of which she had occasioned the breaking. . . .

Perdita, notwithstanding she occupies so little room in the play, fills a large space in the reader's thoughts, almost disputing precedence with the Queen. And her mother's best native

qualities reappear in her, sweetly modified by pastoral associations; her nature being really much the same, only it has been
developed and seasoned in a different atmosphere; a nature too
strong indeed to be displaced by any power of circumstances or
supervenings of art, but at the same time too delicate and
susceptive not to take a lively and lasting impress of them.

(from Introduction to *The Winter's Tale*, 1880)

HEINRICH BULTHAUPT

THE speed with which Leontes, one of the most disagreeable
men on God's earth, talks himself into a jealous madness, is
certainly in the worst sense 'more than human'. Merely because
his wife converses earnestly with his guest, his most trusted
friend, after her request had induced that guest to remain longer
in Sicilia, this horrible, bloodthirsty creature turns to a manifold
murderer. . . .

And Hermione? The royal, exalted Hermione, who in the
First Act, especially in the Trial scene, is on a level with the
grandest that Shakespeare has created, who walks in the ranks
of innocent, afflicted, injured women, whose suffering souls no
one but Shakespeare has laid so bare, this Hermione, still loving
her husband, when she is again to appear before him, consents to
this farce of a statue. Fully to realise the blemish of it all, the
impossibility of the situation, just picture Desdemona on a
pedestal.

(from *Dramaturgie der Classiker*, 1884)

ARTHUR SYMONS

The Winter's Tale is a typically romantic drama, a 'winter's
dream, when nights are longest', constructed in defiance of
probabilities, which it rides over happily. It has all the license and
it has all the charm of a fairy tale; while the matters of which it

treats are often serious enough, ready to become tragic at any moment, and with much of real tragedy in them as it is. The merciful spirit of Shakespeare in his last period ... the delicate art which that period matured in him, seen at its point of finest delicacy in this play and in *The Tempest*, alone serve to restrain what would otherwise be really painful in the griefs and mistaken passions of the drama. . . .

Anachronisms abound, and are delightful. That Delphos should be an island, Giulio Romano contemporary with the oracles, that Puritans should sing psalms to hornpipes, and a sudden remembrance call up the name of Jove or Proserpina to the forgetful lips of Christian-speaking characters – all this is of no more importance than a trifling error in the count of miles traversed by a witch's broomstick in a minute. Too probable figures would destroy the illusion, and the error is a separate felicity.

It is quite in keeping with the other romantic characteristics of the play, that, judged by the usual standard of such a Romantic as Shakespeare himself, it should be constructed with exceptional looseness, falling into two very definite halves, the latter of which can again, in a measure, be divided. . . .

The principal charm in *The Winter's Tale*, its real power over the sources of delight, lies in the two women, true mother and daughter, whose fortunes we see at certain moments, the really important crises of their lives. . . .

The end, certainly, is reconciliation, mercy – mercy extended even to the unworthy, in a spirit of something more than mere justice; as, in those dark plays of Shakespeare's great penultimate period, the end came with a sort of sombre, irresponsible injustice, an outrage of nature upon her sons, wrought in blind anger.

(from Introduction to *The Henry Irving Shakespeare*, 1890)

THOMAS R. PRICE

WHEN, not long ago, the play was put upon the stage, well-mounted and well-acted, it became, as we all remember, both in

London and in New York, the darling of the public. There were revealed in it great possibilities of dramatic effect. The very critics that had protested against the revival of a play that 'was, in their judgement, the worst of Shakespeare's plays, and the worst constructed play in the world', came forward to acknowledge their blunder. And so for us, who have seen the play played, and have felt its power, the problem of *The Winter's Tale* comes up more perplexing than ever. . . .

It is plain, I think, to each person that reads *The Winter's Tale*, plainer still to each person that sees it, in a general way, that *The Winter's Tale* is altogether different in construction from all Shakespeare's other plays. But, for greater clearness, it may be well to compare our play, line by line of structure, with the lines of some familiar play, and to see at what points the lines diverge. For this comparison of structural lines, let us put *The Winter's Tale* side by side with the perfect model of Shakespeare's perfect construction, side by side with the *Othello*.

In the first place in Shakespeare's regular drama there is, as the motive power of all dramatic action, one great emotion displayed, one single dramatic passion. . . . But in *The Winter's Tale* there is no one great passion that thus dominates the play; no single passion that stretches in close linking of scene to scene from the opening of the first act to the close of the fifth. . . .

In the second place, it is the rule of Shakespeare's regular construction that the dramatic emotion is brought by him to its decisive outbreak about the middle of the third act of each drama. . . . But, if we turn to the same point in *The Winter's Tale*, the middle of the third act, there is nothing there at all that answers to a climax. . . .

In addition to these two points of difference, there is yet a third difference that must be noticed, a difference so vital that, if we understand it rightly, we find in it the revelation of Shakespeare's artistic design. In the other dramas there comes, before the real action begins, that part of the play which is called the dramatic protasis. It is, as it were, the muster of all the characters whose combined action is to make the drama. . . . But, in *The Winter's Tale*, all is different. There is, indeed, a protasis, and a protasis

that stands in the right place, and has the right length. But . . . it
is so far from revealing all the characters of the play that it
reveals only six out of twenty-eight; and hence, if it stood by
itself, it would leave us utterly unprepared to understand the
action that is coming. But, when we read on, there comes, far
onward, in the third act, a new muster of characters, a mad rush
into the action of a crowd of new characters, who take up the
story afresh, and carry it forward into new entanglements of
intrigue and interest. . . .

From this demonstration of the play's peculiar framing we are
able to understand, for critics of dramatic art, the amazing
interest of *The Winter's Tale* . . . it has all the fascination of a
daring experiment, devised by the subtlest of artists in extending
the domain of his art. . . .

And so, in dramatic art, *The Winter's Tale* is, I think, Shakespeare's experiment in constructing a diptych. This experiment
no poet, to my knowledge, had ever tried before him, and none
that I know of has ever tried it since. Thus, received as a bold
experiment in dramatic art, *The Winter's Tale* may well stand
last in time of the works of Shakespeare's genius, the final
stretching forth of that genius to accomplish a design never
before essayed.

The play is, then, as I conceive it, a genuine diptych in construction. It is made up of two plays, the first a tragedy and the
second a comedy, so jointed together in the middle as to produce
a final result that belongs equally to each. The tragic movement
of the first part and the comic movement of the second part are
fused into the form and spirit of genuine romance. As part of this
plan, the play is framed, not like other plays on a single dramatic
emotion, but on two. In the first part, in the tragedy, the dramatic
emotion is Leontes' hatred of Hermione. In the second part, in
the comedy, the dramatic emotion is Florizel's love of Perdita.
As the passion of hatred dominates all the tragic movement, so
the passion of love dominates all the comic movement. And it is
this organic contrast between the opposing passions of hate and
love that give to the twin drama its especial charm. . . .

Thus the apparent catastrophe of the awful tragedy of hate is swallowed up in the real catastrophe of triumphant love. The sin of Leontes has been atoned by anguish and repentance; and all enter into final joy through the victory won by Florizel's faithfulness. So Shakespeare works to its conclusion, with most elaborate skill, that piece of dramatic construction which, when looked upon as an experiment in dramatic art, may fairly be regarded as among the boldest and most conspicuous feats of his genius. And the experiment, as far as I know, stands in dramatic art alone. . . . And, in truth, even Shakespeare's success was not full enough to encourage others to make the trial. For, in dramatic construction, the method of diptych-composition is found to involve immense difficulties. In the first place, to work out two plots within the limits of five acts compels an almost painful rapidity of movement. . . . In such compression there is not space enough for that loving and careful portrayal of character which forms the highest beauty of Shakespeare's workmanship. How amazing it is, for example, to find that in Shakespeare's rapid art the character of Hermione is developed in 207 lines, and the character of Perdita in only 127!

And, in the second place, the method brings about a sacrifice of simplicity and a loss in consecutive harmony of impression. For, in passing from part to part, the mind loses grasp of the artistic unity, and becomes perplexed by the introduction of new characters and the inception of a new plot. Thus the final teaching of *The Winter's Tale* may be that, in dramatic art, no lavishness of poetic charm, no artfulness of construction, can make amends for loss of direct simplicity in movement and emotion.

(from *Shakespeariana*, VII, 1890)

HELEN FAUCIT, LADY MARTIN

A SUDDEN access of madness can alone account for the debasing change in the nature of Leontes. . . . It was easy for Greene, with the greater latitude which the narrative form allows, to lead up to and explain the ultimate explosion of Pandosto's jealousy, which had been silently growing through the protracted stay of Egistus at his court, until at last he began to put a vile construction upon his wife's simplest acts of courtesy and hospitality. But drama allows no scope for slow development. Shakespeare has therefore dealt with Leontes as a man in whom the passion of jealousy is inherent; and shows it breaking out suddenly with a force that is deaf to reason, and which, stimulated by an imagination tainted to the core, finds evidences of guilt in actions the most innocent. How different is such a nature from Othello's! . . . Of the jealousy that animates Leontes, the jealousy that needs no extraneous prompting to suspicion, Emilia, in *Othello*, gives a perfect description. . . .

> But jealous souls will not be answered so;
> They are not ever jealous for the cause,
> But jealous for they are jealous; 'tis a monster
> Begot upon itself, born on itself.

This is the jealousy which Shakespeare has portrayed in Leontes, – a jealousy without cause, – cruel, vindictive, and remorseless almost beyond belief.

Paulina . . . is a woman of no ordinary sagacity, with a warm heart, a vigorous brain, and an ardent temper. Her love for Hermione has its roots in admiration and reverence for all the good and gracious qualities of which the queen's daily life has given witness. She has been much about her royal mistress, and much esteemed and trusted by her. Leontes, knowing this, obviously anticipates that she will not remain quiet when she hears of the charge he has brought against the queen, and that he thrust her into prison. Accordingly, he has given express orders that Paulina is not to be admitted to the prison, and this fresh act of cruelty she learns from the governor only when she arrives there in the hope of being some comfort to her much-wronged mistress. . . .

[III ii] This is a scene which makes a large demand upon the resources of an actress, both personal and mental. With enfeebled health, and placed in a most ignominious position, Hermione must be shown to maintain her queenly dignity, and to control her passionate emotion under an outward bearing of resigned fortitude and almost inconceivable forbearance. . . .

[v iii] I never approached this scene without much inward trepidation. You may imagine how difficult it must be to stand in one position, with a full light thrown upon you, without moving an eyelid for so long a time. I never thought to have the time measured, but I should say it must be more than ten minutes, – it seemed like ten times ten. . . .

Paulina had, it seemed to me, besought Hermione to play the part of her own statue, in order that she might hear herself apostrophised, and be a silent witness of the remorse and unabated love of Leontes before her existence became known to him, and so be moved to that forgiveness which, without such proof, she might possibly be slow to yield. She is so moved; but for the sake of the loving friend, to whom she has owed so much, she must restrain herself, and carry through her appointed task. But, even although I had fully thought out all this, it was impossible for me ever to hear unmoved what passes in this wonderful scene. My first Leontes was Mr Macready, and, as the scene was played by him, the difficulty of wearing an air of statuesque calm became almost insuperable. As I think over the scene now, his appearance, his action, the tones of his voice, the emotions of that time, come back. There was a dead awe-struck silence when the curtains were gradually drawn aside by Paulina. She has to encourage Leontes to speak. . . .

Never can I forget the manner in which Mr Macready here cried out, 'Do not draw the curtain!' and, afterwards, '*Let be, let be!*' in tones irritable, commanding, and impossible to resist. 'Would I were dead,' he continues, 'but that, methinks, already—.' Has he seen something that makes him think the statue lives? Mr Macready indicated this, and hurriedly went on 'What was he', etc. His eyes have been so riveted upon the figure, that he sees what the others have not seen, that there is something about it beyond the reach of art. . . .

You may conceive the relief I felt when the first strain of solemn music set me free to breathe! There was a pedestal by my side on which I leant. It was a slight help during the long strain upon the nerves and muscles, besides allowing me to stand in that 'natural posture' which first strikes Leontes, and which therefore could not have been rigidly statuesque. By imperceptibly altering the poise of the body, the weight of it being on the forward foot, I could drop into the easiest position from which to move. The hand and arm still resting quietly on the pedestal materially helped me. Towards the close of the strain the head slowly turned, the 'full eyes' moved, and at the last note rested on Leontes. This movement, together with the expression of the face, transfigured as we may have imagined it to have been, by years of sorrow and devout meditation, – speechless, yet saying things unutterable, – always produced a startling, magnetic effect upon all, – the audience upon the stage as well as in front of it. After the burst of amazement had hushed down, at a sign from Paulina the solemn sweet strain recommenced. The arm and hand were gently lifted from the pedestal; then, rhythmically following the music, the figure descended the steps that led up to the dais, and advancing slowly, paused at a short distance from Leontes. Oh, can I ever forget Mr Macready at this point! At first he stood speechless, as if turned to stone; his face with an awe-struck look upon it. Could this, the very counterpart of his queen, be a wondrous piece of mechanism? Could art so mock the life? He had seen her laid out as dead, the funeral obsequies performed over her, with her dear son beside her. Thus absorbed in wonder, he remained until Paulina said, 'Nay, present your hand.' Tremblingly he advanced, and touched gently the hand held out to him. Then what a cry came with, 'O, she's warm!' It is impossible to describe Mr Macready here. He was Leontes' very self. His passionate joy at finding Hermione really alive seemed beyond control. Now he was prostrate at her feet, then enfolding her in his arms. I had a slight veil or covering over my head and neck, supposed to make the statue look older. This fell off in an instant. The hair, which came unbound, and fell on my shoulders, was reverently kissed and caressed. The whole change was so sudden, so overwhelming, that I suppose I cried out hysterically, for he whispered to me, 'Don't be frightened, my child! don't be frightened! Control yourself!' All this went on during a tumult of applause that sounded like a storm of hail. Oh, how glad I was to be released, when, as soon as a lull came, Paulina, advancing with Perdita, said, 'Turn, good lady, our Perdita is found'. A broken, trembling voice, I am sure, was mine, as I said, 'You gods, look down', etc. It was such a comfort to me, as well as true to natural feeling, that Shakespeare gives Hermione no words to say to Leontes, but leaves her to assure him of her joy and forgiveness by look and manner only, as in his arms she feels the old life, so long suspended, come back to her again. . . .

My first appearance as Hermione is indelibly imprinted on my memory by the acting of Mr Macready, as I have described it in the statue scene. Mrs Warner had rather jokingly told me, at one of the rehearsals, to be *prepared* for something extraordinary in his manner, when Hermione returned to life. But prepared I was not, and could not be, for such a display of uncontrollable rapture. I have tried to give some idea of it; but no words of mine could do it justice. It was the finest burst of passionate speechless emotion I ever saw, or could have conceived. My feelings being already severely strained, I naturally lost something of my self-command, and as Perdita and Florizel knelt at my feet, I looked, as the gifted Sarah Adams afterwards told me, 'like Niobe, all tears'. Of course, I behaved better on the repetition of the play, as I knew what I had to expect and was somewhat prepared for it; but the intensity of Mr Macready's passion was so real, that I could never help being moved by it, and feeling much exhausted afterwards. . . .

In Edinburgh, upon one occasion, I have been told by a friend who was present that, as I descended from the pedestal and advanced towards Leontes, the audience simultaneously rose from their seats, as if drawn out of them by surprise and reverential awe at the presence of one who bore more of heaven than earth about her. I can account for this only by supposing that the soul of Hermione had for the time entered into mine, and 'so divinely wrought, that one might almost say', with the old poet, my 'body thought'. Of course I did not observe this movement of the audience, for my imagination was too full of what I thought was then in Hermione's heart, to leave me eyes for any but Leontes.

(from *On Some of Shakespeare's Female Characters*, 1891)

REVIEWS OF HELEN FAUCIT'S PERFORMANCE

(1) *THE SCOTCHMAN* (1847)

BUT the triumph of the performance, perhaps the crowning achievement of all Miss Faucit's performances, is the last scene. The thrill that passed through the audience on the first raising of the curtain from the seeming statue, told how intensely the spiritual beauty of Miss Faucit's attitude and expression was felt. . . . It was the realizing of a sculptor's hopeless dream. . . . The spectator became an actor in the scene, and all 'Held their breath for a time'. The turning of the head, and the earnest gaze of the full eyes by which Miss Faucit, with the skill of a great artist, breaks the transition from repose to motion, was magical in effect, and made the suspended blood to throb. And when she descended from the pedestal, with a slow and gliding motion, and wearing the look of a being consecrated by long years of prayer and sorrow and seclusion, it seemed to us (and we cannot have been singular) as if we looked upon a being almost too pure to be gazed on with unveiled eyes. What words can paint the mingled expression of wistfulness, of regret, of forgiving sadness, with which she gazed on Leontes? . . . He takes the outstretched hand, – his touch brings back all the woman into her heart, and she falls upon his neck with a tenderness exceeding that of former days. In the mingling of this strong human affection with an elevation so lofty and spiritual, there was a moral impressiveness beyond all that we have experienced. . . . The solemn tone of Hermione's feelings appeared to communicate itself to the audience, and they felt with what fitness and beauty Shakespeare confines her words to a blessing on her daughter.

(2) *DUBLIN UNIVERSITY MAGAZINE* (1848)

Anon the solemn music begins to sound, which Shakespeare

knew so well to employ in resolving one high-strung mood into another; and Hermione, turning her averted head, gazes with full, sad eyes . . . upon Leontes. Other motion were for a time too sudden. A little space, which Shakespeare has filled up with a few lines from Paulina, and Hermione descends from her pedestal, and advances, gliding, like no thing of earth, towards her awe-stricken Lord. You see she has forgiven him, and, oh, how divinely shows that forgiveness in the deep calm eyes! . . . All this we see and feel, and yet no sound has escaped these earnest lips, for Hermione is now at a point beyond words, – and, in looking at the actress here, we are grateful that it is so, – for we dare not listen yet to the voice of what has bowed us with so much awe.

(3) *GLASGOW HERALD* (1848)

Whoever has not witnessed that exquisite performance has not seen the finest combination of Grecian sculpture, Italian painting, and British acting, that has in our day been seen on the stage. It was absolute perfection. The graceful figure, motionless and pale as marble, arrayed in the finest classic folds, and displaying to the highest advantage the fine arms and beautiful contour of the actress, riveted every eye when the curtain was withdrawn. So complete was the illusion, so still the figure, so sightless the eye-balls, that you seemed insensibly to forget it was a living being who stood before you: and when amidst the melody of music, she turned her head towards the king, the whole house started as if struck by an electric shock, or as if they had seen the dead arise.

(4) *GLASGOW CITIZEN* (1848)

We really do not know what to say in order to speak worthily of the statue scene. . . . It was the most entrancing thing we ever remember to have seen, – actually suspending the blood, and taking the breath away. It was something supernatural almost; and till the descent was fully accomplished, and the stone turned to palpable woman again, something of a fine fear sat upon us like a light chilliness.

WILLIAM WINTER

By her presentment of Perdita the actress became the glittering image and incarnation of glorious youthful womanhood and fascinating joy.* No exercise of the imagination was needful to her in that. There was an instantaneous correspondence between the part and the player. The embodiment was as natural as a sunbeam. Shakespeare has left no doubt about his meaning in Perdita. The speeches of all around her continually depict her fresh and piquant loveliness, her innate superiority, her superlative charm; while her behaviour and language as constantly show forth her nobility of soul. . . .

In the thirty-seven plays of Shakespeare there is no strain of the poetry of sentiment and grace essentially sweeter than that which he has put into the mouth of Perdita; and poetry could not be more sweetly spoken than it was by Mary Anderson in that delicious scene of the distribution of the flowers. The actress evinced comprehension of the character in every fibre of its being, and she embodied it with the affluent vitality of splendid health and buoyant temperament, – presenting a creature radiant with goodness and happiness, exquisite in natural refinement, piquant with archness, soft, innocent and tender in confiding artlessness, and, while gleeful and triumphant in beautiful youth, gently touched with an intuitive pitying sense of the thorny aspects of this troubled world. The giving of the flowers completely bewitched her auditors. The startled yet proud endurance of the king's anger was in an equal degree captivating. Seldom has the stage displayed that rarest of all combinations, the passionate heart of a woman with the lovely simplicity of a child. Nothing could be more beautiful than she was to the eyes that followed her lithe figure through the merry mazes of her rustic dance, – an achievement sharply in contrast with her usually statuesque manner. It 'makes old hearts fresh' to see a spectacle of grace and joy, and that spectacle they saw then and will not forget. The

---

* Mary Anderson doubled the parts of Hermione and Perdita.

value of those impersonations of Hermione and Perdita, viewing them as embodied interpretations of poetry, was great, but they possessed a greater value and a higher significance as denotements of the guiding light, the cheering strength, the elevating loveliness of a noble human soul. They embodied the conception of the poet, but at the same time they illumined an actual incarnation of the divine spirit.

(from *Shadows of the Stage*, 1892)

BARRETT WENDELL

THE overcrowding of the style is what most distinguishes these last three plays from what precede. . . . Thoughts crowd upon him. He actually has too much to say. In his effort to say it, he disdainfully neglects both the amenity of regular form, and the capacity of human audiences. . . . In the *Winter's Tale* this trait is more palpable than anywhere else; Shakspere's style is surely more decadent than ever before. . . .

Compare, for example, the characters of Falstaff and of Autolycus: Falstaff, though presented in a more archaic manner, is drawn from the life; Autolycus, though sympathetic and amusing, is so compressed and idealized, that he is like one of those finished pictures whose every detail somehow reveals that they are drawn from memory or from sketches. Better still, compare the final enlightenment of Othello with the similar enlightenment of Leontes. . . . Tolerably effective in conception, it is at once too compressed for full effect, and perceptibly less spontaneous, less simple, less plausible, less masterly, than the greater work it instantly recalls.

This is not unduly to dispraise the *Winter's Tale*. In many traits – in composition of plot, in firm grasp and contrast of character, in variety and precision of atmosphere, in freedom and pregnancy of phrase – the *Winter's Tale* is constantly above any power but Shakspere's. Compared with his own work elsewhere, however, the *Winter's Tale* rarely shows him at his best. The only passage, indeed, which may fairly be deemed better than similar passages which have come before is the pastoral scene. Here for once, amid all the added ripeness of feeling which pervades this romantic period, we find something like Shakspere's full, spontaneous creative power.

(from *William Shakspere*, 1894)

T. S. BAYNES

IN the three dramas belonging to Shakespeare's last period, or rather which may be said to close his dramatic career, the same feeling of severe but consolatory calm is still more apparent. If the deeper discords of life are not finally resolved, the virtues which soothe their perplexities and give us courage and endurance to wait, as well as confidence to trust the final issues, – the virtues of forgiveness and generosity, of forbearance and self-control, – are largely illustrated. This is a characteristic feature in each of these closing dramas, in *The Winter's Tale*, *Cymbeline* and *The Tempest*.

(from *Shakespeare Studies*, 1896)

GEORG BRANDES

IN the mode and manner in which the relationship between Florizel and Perdita is portrayed, there are certain peculiarities which are not to be found in the work of Shakespeare's youth, but which again appear in the description of Ferdinand and Miranda in *The Tempest*, namely, a certain aloofness from the world, a certain tenderness for those who may still hope and yearn for happiness, a renunciation, as it were, by the author of all thought of happiness for himself. . . . When, in earlier days he portrayed love, the poet stood on the same level with the lovers; it is so now no longer; they are now regarded with a father's eye.

(from *William Shakespeare*, 1896)

ALFRED, LORD TENNYSON

THERE are three repartees in Shakespeare which always bring tears to my eyes from their simplicity. One is in *King Lear*. . . . And in *The Winter's Tale*, when Florizel takes Perdita's hand to lead her to the dance, and says, 'So turtles pair that never mean to part', and the little Perdita answers, giving her hand to Florizel, 'I'll swear for 'em'.

(from *Memoir* by his son, 1897)

R. G. MOULTON

THE oracle thus brought to the trial of the queen is the motive centre of the play, in which all the lines of plot meet. . . . The first part of the oracle, clear as a flash of lightning, has laid bare at a single stroke the whole wrong of Leontes. It is a six-fold woe he has incurred. He has lost the wife he adores; he has lost the friend of his bosom; he has lost his pretty son and his new-born daughter; he has lost the minister Camillo, with whom he had taken lifelong counsel; and he has lost the loyal servant, Antigonus, who so unwillingly has gone to execute a cruel doom. But in its latter clauses the oracle is the dim revelation, which can only be read by the light of fulfilment. Latent in its mystic phrase is the sixfold restoration: the wife is to be received as from the tomb, the friend to be again embraced in Sicilia; the lost babe will reappear a lovely daughter; the lost son will be replaced by a son-in-law who is the image of Polixenes as known in his youth. Camillo will return, unable to live without his king; and if Antigonus himself has been caught in the doom of which he is minister, it is his widow, the faithful Paulina, to whom has been committed the chief ministry of restoration.

The play divides at its centre: the work of wrong is balanced by the working out of restoration.

(from *The Moral System of Shakespeare*, 1903)

LYTTON STRACHEY

SHAKESPEARE, we are confidently told, passed in a moment to tranquillity and joy, to blue skies, to young ladies, and to general forgiveness.... This is a pretty picture, but is it true? It may, indeed, be admitted at once that Prince Florizel and Perdita are charming creatures, that Prospero is 'grave', and that Hermione is more or less 'serene'; but why is it that, in our consideration of the later plays, the whole of our attention must always be fixed upon these particular characters? Modern critics, in their eagerness to appraise everything that is beautiful and good at its proper value, seem to have entirely forgotten that there is another side to the medal; and they have omitted to point out that these plays contain a series of portraits of peculiar infamy, whose wickedness finds expression in language of extraordinary force. Coming fresh from their pages to the pages of *Cymbeline, The Winter's Tale* and *The Tempest*, one is astonished and perplexed. How is it possible to fit into their scheme of roses and maidens that 'Italian fiend', the 'yellow Iachimo', or Cloten, that 'thing too bad for bad report', or the 'crafty devil', his mother, or Leontes, or Caliban, or Trinculo? To omit these figures of discord and evil from our consideration, to banish them comfortably to the background of the stage, while Autolycus and Miranda dance before the footlights, is surely a fallacy in proportion; for the presentment of the one group of persons is every whit as distinct and vigorous as that of the other. Nowhere, indeed, is Shakespeare's violence of expression more constantly displayed than in the 'gentle utterances' of his last period.

(from *Books and Characters*, 1906)

ROBERT BRIDGES

IT would seem from such instances that Shakespeare sometimes judged conduct to be dramatically more effective when not adequately motived. In the *Winter's Tale* the jealousy of Leontes is senseless, whereas in the original story an adequate motive is developed. It may be that Shakespeare wished to portray this passion in odious nakedness without reason or rein as might be proper in a low comedy, when its absurdity would be ridiculed away: but if so, his scheme was artistically as bad as any third rate melodrama of today: the admixture of tragic incident creates a situation from which recovery is impossible; and it is certain that the spectators are not intended to realise the condition of affairs. In that fall and rise of the curtain it needs, one may say, even prolonged meditation to imagine the passage of sixteen tedious years, during all which time Leontes has to be pictured kneeling daily at his wife's cenotaph, while she, pretending that he has killed her, is living and hiding away from him at a friend's house in the same city. We are diverted and delighted by Autolycus and Perdita; our interests are magically shifted – the relief of the contrast almost justifies the uncomfortable distress of the earlier acts, – and we are gratified to find Hermione alive at the end. But how are Leontes and Hermione to meet? It is a situation worthy of Labiche; yet we are expected both to take it seriously and to overlook it. When Hermione descends from the pedestal into her husband's arms, the impossibility of reconciliation is passed by in silence, and Leontes busies himself in finding a husband for the aged and unattractive Paulina.

(from *The Influence of the Audience on Shakespeare's Dramas*, 1907)

P. G. THOMAS

THE changes, which Shakespeare introduced into Greene's narrative, are due in the main to the exigencies of dramatic form. The long-winded speeches and dreary monologues of the novel lack dramatic propriety. Consequently, the speeches are either omitted altogether, shortened, or converted into dialogue. At the same time, the action is concentrated in deference to the claims of dramatic unity. When, for example, the first act of the play opens,

Polixenes is already about to depart, and is only restrained by
Sicily's importunity. To dramatic causes, likewise, we owe the
creation of Antigonus, Paulina, and Autolycus, in whom re-
spectively are concentrated the nobles, ladies, and clowns of the
novel. At other times, Shakespeare enlarges from a brief hint
given by Greene. There is no counterpart in the novel of the
pathetic scene in *The Winter's Tale*, in which the character of
young [Mamillius] is developed, merely the statement that the
guards 'coming to the Queen's lodging found her playing with
her young son, Garinter'. In the same way, Greene's reference to
the storm at sea is expanded into Act III, sc. iii of *The Winter's
Tale*.

(from Introduction to Greene's *Pandosto*, 1907)

SIR WALTER RALEIGH

WHEN Shakespeare has no further use for a character, he sometimes disposes of him in the most unprincipled and reckless
fashion. Consider the fate of Antigonus in *The Winter's Tale*. Up
to the time of his sudden death Antigonus has served his maker
well; he has played an important part in the action, and by his
devotion and courage has won the affection of all spectators. It is
he who saves the daughter of Hermione from the mad rage of the
king. 'I'll pawn the little blood which I have left', he says, 'to save
the innocent'. He is allowed to take the child away on condition
that he shall expose her in some desert place, and leave her to the
mercy of chance. He fulfils his task, and now, by the end of the
Third Act, his part in the play is over. Sixteen years are to pass,
and new matters are to engage our attention; surely the aged
nobleman might have been allowed to retire in peace. Shakespeare thought otherwise; perhaps he felt it important that no
news whatever concerning the child should reach Leontes, and
therefore resolved to make away with the only likely messenger.
Antigonus takes an affecting farewell of the infant princess; the
weather grows stormy; and the rest must be told in Shakespeare's
words:

Antigonus   Farewell:
  The day frowns more and more: thou'rt like to have
  A lullaby too rough: I never saw
  The heavens so dim by day. A savage clamour!
  Well may I get aboard. This is the chase,
  I am gone for ever! [*Exit pursued by a bear.*

This is the first we hear of the bear, and would be the last, were it not that Shakespeare, having in this wise disposed of poor Antigonus, makes a thrifty use of the remains at the feast of Comedy. The clown comes in to report, with much amusing detail, how the bear has only half-dined on the gentleman, and is at it now. It is this sort of conduct, on the part of the dramatist, that the word Romance has been used to cover.

(from *Shakespeare*, 1907)

JOHN MASEFIELD

THIS play is a study of deceit and self-deception. Leontes is deceived by his obsession, Polixenes by his son, the country man by Autolycus, life, throughout by art. In the last great scene, life is mistaken for art. In the first great scene a true friendship is mistaken for a false love.

(from *William Shakespeare*, 1911)

ELLEN TERRY

THE glimpse we get of Mamillius* with Leontes is enough to make us feel that the child is puzzled by his father's attitude to him, and rather scared. He does not chatter spontaneously, but answers the questions put to him in a few mechanically dutiful words ... Leontes, tortured by jealousy, is observing Hermione

* Mamillius was Ellen Terry's first part, and her performance was warmly praised by Lewis Carroll. In her old age she played Hermione, and she found it difficult to remember her lines.

and Polixenes all the time he asks them. The suspicion his wife is unfaithful before. What if Mamillius is not his son?

The loyalty Hermione shows to the husband who has slandered her, without abating a jot of her dignity, reminds us of Katharine's to Henry. Hermione has been cruelly and falsely accused. Yet she has more pity for her accuser than for herself. She knows that jealousy has made him for the time insane, and that when he comes to his senses he will suffer agonies of remorse. . . . Dignity under a false accusation, unwavering love in spite of it, were evidently greatly admired by Shakespeare, for he exalts them again in Imogen.

(from *Four Lectures on Shakespeare*, 1932)

H. GRANVILLE-BARKER

IF before he had set out to paint jealousy as a noble passion, and his own genius had defeated the false aim, now he would write a study of jealousy indeed, perverse, ignoble, pitiable. Straightway he faced the first difficulty. Jealousy upon any foundation is less than jealousy, or more. Leontes has, as far as we can see, hardly the shadow of an excuse for his suspicion. Straightway he redeemed the blunder of Iago, redeemed it by writing this time no such character. That niche in the scheme is left vacant, but finely filled, for the wanton malice that is Iago the jealous man can only find, but finds surely, in his own heart.

The second opportunity in the play was, of course, the sheep-shearing scene. . . .

The third chance, I think, that Shakespeare saw and seized was the last scene of all, with Hermione as a statue. The crude stage effect is so good that hasty naked handling might have spoiled it. Raw material at its richest is also the hardest to work in. But Shakespeare goes about his business, with great care. He prepares the audience, through Paulina's steward, almost to the pitch of revelation, saving just so much surprise, and leaving so little, that when they see the statue they may think themselves more in doubt than they really are whether it is Hermione herself or no. He prepares Leontes, who feels that his wife's spirit might walk again; who is startled by the strange air of Hermione that the yet unknown Perdita breathes out; who, his egotism killed, has become simple of speech, simple-minded, receptive. The scene is elaborately held back by the preceding one, which though but preparation, actually equals it in length, and its poetry is heightened by such contrast with fantastic prose and fun. While from the moment the statue is disclosed, every device of changing colour and time, every minor contrast of voice and mood that can give the scene modelling and beauty of form, is brought into easy use. Then the final effect of the music, of the brisk stirring trumpet sentences in Paulina's speech, of the simplicity of Leontes' 'let it be an act lawful as eating'. Then the swift contrast of the alarmed and sceptical Polixenes and Camillo, then Paulina's happiness breaking almost into chatter. And then the perfect sufficiency of Hermione's eight lines (Oh, how a lesser dramatist might have overdone it with Noble Forgiveness and what not!) – it all really is a wonderful bit of work.

(from the preface to his acting edition, 1912)

SIR ARTHUR QUILLER-COUCH

THIS brings us to the greatest fault of all; to the recognition scene; or rather to the scamping of it. To be sure, if we choose to tread foot with Gervinus and agree that 'the poet has *wisely* placed this event behind the scenes, otherwise the play would have been too full of powerful scenes'; if, having been promised a mighty thrill, in the great master's fashion, we really prefer two or three innominate gentlemen entering and saying, 'Have you heard?' 'You don't tell me!' 'No?' 'Then you have lost a sight' – I say, if we really prefer this sort of thing, which Gervinus calls 'in itself a rare masterpiece of prose description', then Heaven must be our aid. But if, using our own judgement, we read the

play and put ourselves in the place of its first audience, I ask, Are
we not baulked? In proportion as we have paid tribute to the art
of the story by letting our interest be intrigued, our emotion
excited, are we not cheated when Shakespeare lets us down with
this reported tale? I would point out that it nowise resembles the
Messengers' tales in Greek tragedy. These related bloody deeds,
things not to be displayed on the stage.

(from *Shakespeare's Workmanship*, 1915)

SIR EDMUND CHAMBERS

PURPOSE and structure in *The Winter's Tale* are shaped alike by
the canons of romance; if indeed one is justified in using the term
canon to denote a principle which is founded on the negation of
Law. . . . Truth that will out through disguises, wrongs that in
the end become rights again, wanderings that lead homeward in
the eventide; these are things which have always been precious
to the romantic Muse. And in Shakespeare, as elsewhere, the
development of such a theme lends itself naturally to the inter-
position of strange and exciting incidents. Men set sail and are
shipwrecked on the coasts of Bohemia, where never coast was; a
bear comes opportunely to make a meal of the witness and agent
of a crime; shepherds find an infant princess with a casket of
jewels that look like fairy gold; a statue steps from its pedestal to
become a living breathing woman. Above all, the course of
human affairs is swayed and interpreted by the enigmatic
utterances of an oracle. Romance gets all the colour and novelty
that are its life-blood; and for the philosophy of the universe,
that in Shakespeare's later moods lies behind and determines
romance, the amazement is converted into the symbol and
manifestation of an overruling force working by hidden ways to
bring the ends of man to good. The justification of Providence,
that, after all, is the conscious intention which informs the
romantic theme; and the supernatural intervention of Apollo
represents, in accordance with the ordinary use of the super-

natural by Shakespeare, an acknowledgement of the ultimate mystery which, in the last resort, the conception of Providence involves.

Nor is the happy issue of the play merely one of external accident. The power that, to the eye of Shakespeare's optimism, makes for righteousness operates not only in the ordering of events, but also in the heart of man; and the material recognitions which bring the wife and daughter of Leontes back to him, but follow upon the spiritual regeneration wherein he returns from his jealous error, and devotes himself to the life-long atonement of a 'saint-like sorrow'. Romance, indeed, will not have you apply too searching a psychology. Shakespeare must needs make vital what he touches, and Greene's graceful tale becomes a different thing when the master has introduced into it the audacious roguery of Autolycus and the ripe humanity of Paulina.

> (from *Shakespeare: A Survey* (1925), which collected the introductions to the Red Letter Shakespeare, written between 1904 and 1908)

MARK VAN DOREN

SHAKESPEARE disappoints our expectation in one important respect. The recognition of Leontes and his daughter takes place off stage; we only hear three gentlemen talking prose about it (v ii), and are denied the satisfaction of such a scene as we might have supposed would crown the play. The reason may be that Shakespeare was weary of a plot which already had complicated itself beyond comfort; or that a recognition scene appeared in his mind more due to Hermione, considering the age and degree of her sufferings, than to that 'most peerless piece of earth' Perdita. In poetic justice he gave it to Hermione, and we have the business of a statue coming to life while music plays (v iii). But the poetry he actually had written required that Perdita should have it. Perhaps he could not imagine – though this itself is hard to imagine – what Leontes would say. For Leontes had done what no words, even Shakespeare's words, could utterly undo. Mamillius and Antigonus had lost their lives, an oracle had been blasphemed, a wife had been slandered, love had been defiled. The griefs of Pericles had been fate's doing, and those of Posthumus had been an Italian fiend's. Those of Leontes had been his own, and the reward he merited was a muted joy.

(from *Shakespeare*, 1939)

HAROLD C. GODDARD

THE poet was undoubtedly right in deciding that the highlight of his act should be the scene in which Hermione, posing as her own statue, returns to life and is reunited with her husband and her daughter.

It is a scene which if taken prosaically is open to a flood of objections, but if taken poetically is near perfection. It is effective on several levels. Theatrically it is a masterpiece of suspense. Dramatically it rounds out every character who participates in it. Symbolically it ties together all the play has said or suggested concerning the relation of art and nature, and so, by implication, of the worlds of reality and romance, of Sicilia and Bohemia. And last of all it is a veritable whispering gallery of literary and mythological echoes. In a way it is the story of Pygmalion and Galatea over again; in another it is a reincarnation of the great scene that concludes the *Alcestis* of Euripides in which his dead wife is restored to Admetus. How much or how little Shakespeare may have known of this scene there is no way of telling. But however that may be, here is a remarkable example of the unity of all imaginative literature wherever or whenever written. A work of art is a world unto itself, but all works of art belong to one world. We are considering Shakespeare's *The Winter's Tale*; yet only those who are acquainted with another work of another poet written two thousand years earlier are in a position to catch all the overtones and undertones of this one. Leontes, as truly as Admetus, had let his wife sacrifice her life to his selfishness.

Hermione, as truly as Alcestis, had accepted her fate with unselfishness, nobility, and calm. Paulina, as truly as Heracles, had snatched away death's prey before it was too late. Paulina, who is an example of good impulsiveness as Leontes is of bad, has been praised at length by many commentators for her honesty, her outspokenness, and her bravery, and has time and again been justly likened to Kent in *King Lear*. But perhaps the highest tribute that can be paid to her heroism is merely to point out that she is the counterpart in Shakespeare's play of Heracles in Euripides'.

The defeat of death is the main problem of humanity. That defeat may be affected either by the direct imitation of divinity by man (the way of religion) or by the indirect imitation of it through the creation of divine works (the way of art), though practically it must be by a combination of the two, for it is only the religion that speaks artistically that is articulate and only the art that is pervaded by a religious spirit that is redeeming. As Perdita impersonated the goddess Flora, so Hermione imitates an artistic incarnation of herself as a work of sculpture. Sixteen years in which to rehearse the effect of adversity on love have made her a living proof of her daughter's words in her own moment of adversity:

> I think affliction may subdue the cheek
> But not take in the mind.

(from The Meaning of Shakespeare, 1951)

ARTHUR SEWELL

In Leontes we have very good evidence of the change - it amounts almost to an impairment - in Shakespeare's vision, which is the key to our reading of the Romances. We might even feel in the early part of the play - perhaps Shakespeare felt it, too - that the writing is a little stale, because Shakespeare had done it, or something very like it, before. So much so, that there is a

c

certain morbidity in the representation of the state of jealousy, and the effect is one of *pastiche*. Shakespeare's craft was, of course, such that he was able to give to the situation dramatic authority, but much is left to the virtuosity of the actor. We are, indeed, hard put to it to recognize the earlier Leontes in the later, and the remorse is never in poetry impregnated with the memory of earlier guilt. A 'sainted sorrow' hardly becomes the man who has done what Leontes has done, and what has happened within the repentant spirit is made altogether subordinate to the mere fact of repentance. That Leontes should repent and that Hermione should forgive are deductions from the theme of the play; and while forgiveness becomes more grateful and more gracious in Hermione, we know nothing more about the mysteries of repentance in Leontes. For these reasons Leontes is an acting part, rather than a character.

(from *Character and Society in Shakespeare*, 1951)

PART TWO

Recent Studies

Donald A. Stauffer

THE WINTER'S TALE (1949)

IN the last romances, no matter how the names of the characters change, or the setting shifts from Tyre to ancient Britain to Sicily to a desert island, Shakespeare continues to write the same play. Even when there remain but a few grains of sand in the hourglass, and when he himself needs the new life of a collaborator in order to complete a play, dominant movements in his final thought stamp his work.

The first scene of *The Two Noble Kinsmen*, for example, chimes with Shakespeare's thought in developing a situation in which the hero abandons his own interests to become the instrument of the gods. The marriage of Theseus to Hippolyta – 'This grand act of our life, this daring deed Of fate in wedlock' – is delayed at the supplication of the three kneeling queens in black.

> As we are men,
> Thus should we do. Being sensually subdu'd,
> We lose our human title. (I i 231-3)

Palamon and Arcite, too, permit Shakespeare to develop ideas of honor, of patience, of self-mastery, of distilling joy in the alembic of adversity. The dialogues of Hippolyta and Emilia and of Palamon and Arcite excellently counterpoint the old comparison of friendship and love. To Chaucer's noble antique story Shakespeare adds his touches of humor, of psychological insight, of mirth mingled with sadness, of 'infinite pity', of supplications that yoke immensity to the sharp little freshnesses of this world. At the end, Shakespeare once more unclasps the mystery and finds joy within the tragic dream:

> O cousin,
> That we should things desire which do cost us

> The loss of our desire! that naught could buy
> Dear love but loss of dear love!   (v iv 109–12)

Or again:

> O you heavenly charmers,
> What things you make of us! For what we lack
> We laugh, for what we have are sorry; still
> Are children in some kind. Let us be thankful
> For that which is, and with you leave dispute
> That are above our question.   (v iv 131–6)

The Winter's Tale reworks the pattern, and is no less worthy of prolonged scrutiny. But what has been seen in detail in the other romances is true in this romance as well, and there is no need to play over minor variations on the basic melodies.

Like *The Tempest*, *The Winter's Tale* is compressed and simplified. It gets along with only fifteen scenes. Four scenes alone – of jealousy, of judgment, of feasting, and of repentance – fill three-fifths of the play. The sprawling stories of *Pericles* and *Cymbeline* give way to a piece concentrated in two equal movements; and the tighter organization here compels Father Time to apologize for the lapse of a decade or two between the halves, a lapse which in other plays Shakespeare takes as a matter hardly worth comment.

If *Pericles* and *Cymbeline* are comparable to *Lear* in their themes and ample structures, *The Winter's Tale* has parallels with *Othello*. Its dramatic economy in setting forth its ideas is notable. The first part introduces Leontes' jealousy without delay, and sets it against purity, loyalty, and integrity. After a little transitional scene in which new helpless life is protected even in the middle of a world of storms and man-eating bears, a second part is devoted to the healing of time and the light-hearted laughter of an innocent world. The stage is set for the discoveries and forgiveness of the fifth act. Throughout, the telling scenes are set off by shorter scenes that afford breathing spells; in the fifth act, Shakespeare's recurring theorem – repentance, followed by restoration – is broken into three scenes, in which he maintains the poignant gravity of the climactic moments by interjecting a middle scene that narrates reunions and recognitions instead of presenting them.

The jealousy of Leontes is as degrading as Othello's, and is even less justifiable. It strikes him suddenly and inexplicably like a pestilence, and 'infection' is Shakespeare's key-word in describing it. The blight is even more fearful in Leontes than Othello, for it is almost without external support of any kind. Hermione is spotless, and everyone in the play but Leontes knows and proclaims her innocence. Leontes poisons himself; Leontes and his counsellors reverse the rôles of Othello and Iago. Paulina brands Leontes as the sole traitor, who has betrayed 'the sacred honour of himself'. Antigonus tells his King: 'You are abus'd, and by some putter-on That will be damn'd for 't. Would I knew the villain!'

The villain is man's vile imagination, self-generating, from whose sullen embers jealousy rises like a foul phoenix. To show evil as purely subjective, the gods themselves speak flatly against Leontes' suspicion. Divine intervention here takes the form of the message from the Delphic oracle. With only enough mystification to carry on the plot for three more acts, Apollo's oracle is read aloud in the court of justice: 'Hermione is chaste; Polixenes blameless; Camillo a true subject; Leontes a jealous tyrant; his innocent babe truly begotten.' In the insane fury of his *tremor cordis*, Leontes blasphemes:

> There is no truth at all i' th' oracle! (II ii 141)

And again in accordance with the direct progress of the play, Leontes learns at once of his punishment – the deaths of the two nearest his heart – and falls immediately into self-abasement, remorse, and the desire for reconcilement. The shock opens his eyes. To that extent, his faith and love – 'that which is lost' – are found before the play is half over, though he must yet persist in his repentance and woo his dead queen for longer than Jacob sought Rachel.

Leontes' self-induced jealousy is countered by the integrity of Florizel and the simplicity of Perdita, while the compromising wisdom and good intentions of the older characters bridge the pure extremes of evil and of innocence. If the first half of the play carries out in fantasy Leontes' bitter assumption, 'Let what is dear in Sicily be cheap', the second half reacts to reveal how what is cheap in Bohemia may be dear. For this is a drama that rings changes on the theme of spiritual integrity, and insists in multiple variations that reality is mental. It is a pleasurable dance of minds when Polixenes from his experience argues that man should accept the bastard mixing of base and noble, the grafting of human sophistication upon great creating nature; and Perdita, though granting his argument, immediately answers that for her part she will have none of this streaked and pied compromise. Spring is sweetly answering to the 'flow'rs of winter' (IV iv 79). Or again, Shakespeare presents his picture of human life – observed, not argued – when Camillo tells Perdita that prosperity is the true bond of love, whose complexion and heart are altered by affliction, and Perdita answers in her young confidence:

> I think affliction may subdue the cheek
> But not take in the mind.   (IV iv 583–90)

'Yea? say you so?' Camillo retorts, and falls at once to the less controversial contemplation of Perdita's beauty.

Again, as in *Cymbeline*, the interlude of harmless pastoral must precede the forgiveness which is without a shadow of reproach. The play fills with floral patterns and dances and rustic gaiety; and after the contemplation of that which is graceful and becoming and fresh and innocent, the themes of repentance and resignation and joy mingled with sorrow lead imperceptibly to the end. Though reality is mental, it may be embodied in human beauty. *The Winter's Tale* confirms again that Shakespeare never tired of reading the eloquence of the human face. Florizel may look like truth itself; he may breathe out his life in protestations; love itself may be a statue, and that statue miraculously warm and answering to desire; and grace, though it is a spiritual gift from the gods, is to be found also in becoming actions and deportment and freedom that looks out at the eyes.

Outside the mind of Leontes, plus a casual tempest or a carnivorous bear, there is no evil in the play. Court and country alike are good. Good intentions are the rule, and like Paulina, every character can maintain that he means well, even when he does not well. Among all who try to act as physicians to Leontes' sick mind, Paulina is the most skilful. Pity never breaks in upon her until her runaway tongue has compelled Leontes to confront his fault. She knows that 'You that are thus so tender o'er his follies Will never do him good, not one of you'. Her rôle as teacher and healer parallels that of the Fool for Lear, Edgar for Gloucester, the Duke for Isabella and Angelo, Ulysses for Troilus. But though Leontes tells her that her bitter frankness strikes him sorely, he confides to her truth and goodness.

The Winter's Tale is a dream of love lost only to be restored, and of love that is never lost, and of love born afresh. Its opening line contains a hidden image of birth, its closing prayer is Hermione's

> You gods, look down,
> And from your sacred vials pour your graces
> Upon my daughter's head!

Throughout, it tells a story to 'make old hearts fresh', it deals with 'things new-born', it welcomes spring to the earth, watches some new grace born every wink of an eye, and redeems dear life from the numbness of death. 'The doctrine of ill-doing' is part of the dream, but is forgotten in a more enduring vision which was first and will be final: the interchange of 'innocence for innocence'. The reality that rules, the dream beyond dreams, is to be found in Florizel's 'I am heir to my affection', and in his 'I cannot be Mine own, nor anything to any, if I be not thine', and in Perdita's 'By the pattern of mine own thoughts I cut out The purity of his', and in the noble line of Hermione's:

> My life stands in the level of your dreams.

Florizel knows that Perdita's dignity 'cannot fail but by The violation of my faith'.

As love or the loss of love prevails, the play changes color. Hermione, having lost the crown and comfort of her life, cannot be frightened by the bugbear death in the flatness of her misery. Yet always hope rises above despair. Prayers spring from the grimmest situations. Antigonus, who is to be forewarned in a dream of his own death, prays for the helpless infant Perdita:

> Come on, poor babe!
> Some powerful spirit instruct the kites and ravens
> To be thy nurses! . . . And blessing
> Against this cruelty fight on thy side,
> Poor thing, condemn'd to loss!

The messengers pray that great Apollo may turn all to the best, that the desperate issue may prove gracious, sensing that 'something rare Even then will rush to knowledge'.

The play proceeds in its pictures: the court of justice, the reading of the oracle, the swooning of Hermione, the dancing on the shepherd's green, the unveiling of the statue with Leontes silently weeping. All is told as an old story, out of space on the seacoast of Bohemia, out of time in a pre-Christian world where nevertheless 'that rare Italian master, Julio Romano' carves statues. It is 'like an old tale', 'like an old tale still', 'like an old tale'. The young son Mamillius knows that 'A sad tale's best for winter', and has one of sprites and goblins that begins: 'There was a man dwelt by a churchyard. . . .'

The man in this play dwells not far from a church built to Aphrodite Urania, removed by every purposeful device from ordinary life. In that temple the highest thoughts are kept in an inner shrine, the image curtained from profane eyes:

> As she liv'd peerless,
> So her dead likeness I do well believe
> Excels whatever yet you look'd upon,
> Or hand of man hath done. Therefore I keep it
> Lonely, apart.

The image is silent only not to chide; it moves, is sentient, steps from its pedestal, looks with pity from those eyes that are 'Stars, stars! And all eyes else dead coals'. And Hermione never spoke to better purpose (it is her own husband Leontes who recalls the words) than when she said:

> I am yours for ever.

This was 'Grace indeed'.

To the clear unearthly beauty of the romances, *The Winter's Tale* adds an element not notable in *Pericles* and *Cymbeline* – the element of humor. These moral, almost religious, visions may be anchored to the earth by brutal realism, as in the brothel scenes of *Pericles*; or by action, as in the battle pieces in *Cymbeline*; or by fresh and smiling character sketches, as are those of Fidele and Mamillius, or by rounded and individualized portrayals like that of Paulina. The descriptions of a harmonious nature and of rustic life, however, are not in themselves enough to relate a fairy story to the actual world, for the pastoral and the idyl are blood cousins of the romance, a cave in Wales or a shepherd's green is only the antimasque to a royal court, and mountaineers and shepherdesses may easily turn into children of the king. But in *The Winter's Tale* the spirit of pure light-hearted comedy returns, almost for the first time since *Twelfth Night*. Comedy orients the temple of love and honor in a wider world, and comments spontaneously like an unconscious chorus on the moral conclusions of the main romantic action.

In that scene that serves as a fulcrum at the play's center, Antigonus has consigned Perdita to the rough lullaby of the elements. The storm begins, and Antigonus has gone to his own death. With a shock of contrast, we suddenly enter the world of the old shepherd – complaining, talking endlessly, finding good luck in a lost child. His son is ridiculously inept in expressing pity for the shipwrecked sailors and the slaughtered Antigonus: 'The men are not yet cold under water, nor the bear half din'd on the gentleman – he's at it now.' The old shepherd takes the news with the calm philosophy of Justice Shallow meditating on death and the price of bullocks at Stamford fair:

Heavy matters, heavy matters! But look thee here, boy. Now bless thyself! thou met'st with things dying, I with things newborn.

Here is the doctrine of compassion and of hopeful action played as a rollicking scherzo. On their lucky day, the loutish son can yet remember: 'I'll go see if the bear be gone from the gentle-man, and how much he hath eaten. If there be any of him left, I'll bury it.'

This motif of the country bumpkins, like an ebullient dance-movement in Beethoven, needs some element that will har-monize it and temper it with the rest of the symphony. Autolycus is the solution. He is as light-hearted as the lark he sings about. Spring is in his song, with doxies and thieves and tumbling in the hay. Gaiety and carelessness flood back in over the celestial mingling of tears and joy, as if they glanced at answers that Leontes and Hermione never knew. Autolycus has his own in-dependence, like the grave-digger or Pompey Bum. Driven into a corner, he knows 'I am a poor fellow, sir'. The little ones of the earth may sleep out the thought of the life to come, and may acknowledge that 'when I wander here and there, I then do most go right'. Let the gods reward in their own way either careless-ness or cunning! Professionally (and in this, does he differ from the lawyer, the teacher, the preacher, and the physician?), he must live on man's weakness and ignorance. 'Every lane's end, every shop, church, session, hanging, yields a careful man work.' He might say with Beowulf that Wyrd oft saves the daunt-less man. Or in his own terms: 'Sure the gods do this year con-nive at us, and we may do anything extempore. I see this is the time that the unjust man doth thrive.' If he cannot shear the sheepshearers, then 'let me be unroll'd and my name put in the book of virtue!'

Yet he is too careless – or too devoutly obedient to higher powers – even to defend his own professional rascality. He accepts the fact that 'though I am not naturally honest, I am so sometimes by chance'. He cannot lament that he was not the revealer of good tidings to the princess, for 'it would not have relish'd among my other discredits'. Goddess Fortune is his mistress, and whatever happens, ' 'tis all one to me'. Therefore, he greets again (for he may find them lucky) his victims, 'these two moles, these blind ones', whom 'I have done good to against my will'. Who can say that the shepherd and the clown are wrong in their judgment: 'He was provided to do us good'? He acts out

Florizel's counsel: 'Be merry, gentle! Apprehend Nothing but
jollity.' In the words of his own song:

> A merry heart goes all the day,
> Your sad tires in a mile-a.

With Autolycus as sympathetic midwife to bring to full birth
their 'so preposterous estate', the shepherd and his son repeat in
bumptious tempo many of the main themes of the play. The
sophistications of court life may be judged with direct seriousness, as they are by Belarius or Perdita. Or they may be attacked
even more effectively by horseplay: 'Advocate', the shepherd's
son explains to his father, 'is the court word for a pheasant. Say
you have none.' When Autolycus is 'courtier cap-a-pe' in his
insolent inquiries and threats, the two rustics marvel at his
startling costume: 'He seems to be the more noble in being
fantastical.' And when they too have acquired gentility in new
suits of fine clothes, Autolycus is the first to acknowledge blithely
that each is a gentleman born. 'Ay,' the shepherd's son reassures
himself, 'and have been so any time these four hours. But I was a
gentleman born before my father.'

Witnessing the brotherly reconciliation of their principals, the
shepherd's son tells Autolycus that 'we wept – and there was the
first gentlemanlike tears that ever we shed'. The poor have pity,
and there was gentleness in the world even when Adam delved
and Eve span. Important issues may be touched upon in
humorous vein: did Shakespeare ever reconcile pity and justice?
Did he find the highest meaning of 'truth' in loyalty to those one
loves, or in knowledge of a universal order? When are good
intentions good enough? There is compassionate laughter when
the shepherd's son handles the questions. He will swear to the
prince that Autolycus is a valiant fellow in action and that he will
not be drunk. But he knows that Autolycus is no valiant fellow
in action and that he *will* be drunk. Nevertheless, he'll swear it,
and he wishes that Autolycus would be a valiant fellow. 'If it be
ne'er so false,' he is sure, 'a true gentleman may swear it in the
behalf of his friend.'

> How blessed are we that are not simple men!
> Yet Nature might have made me as these are;
> Therefore I will not disdain.   (IV iv 772–4)

These are the words of Autolycus, and it is difficult to tell
whether he is laughing at the shepherds, or whether he is laughing at himself, or whether Shakespeare is laughing at him, or
whether both together are laughing at all of us who, but for the
grace of God, would go like simpletons. Humor, which is but
another guise for humility, has again complicated the moral
issues.

In these noble dreams of 'a world ransomed, or one destroyed',
humor sadly reminds us that Shakespeare may have known
them to be no more than bright speculations. Man may believe
those messages that happen to please him, particularly if the
ballads are 'Very true, and but a month old'. He may be over-
joyed to find that the ballad ends happily: 'Where some stretch-
mouth'd rascal would, as it were, mean mischief, and break a foul
gap into the matter, he makes the maid to answer "Whoop, do
me no harm, good man!" puts him off, slights him, with
"Whoop, do me no harm, good man!" ' It is possible that
nature may govern 'the ordering of the mind' – but the thought
is based upon an 'if'. It may be argued that 'art itself is nature',
since 'nature is made better by no mean But nature makes that
mean'. Yet the mere fact that a complicated argument is necessary
– which instinct proceeds to disregard – suggests that there is
another side, and that nature may be insentient to man's artful
choosing of the beauty that is withdrawn, the shining hope, the
ending joy.

Reality remains the undiscovered country. Even to Shakespeare, the continuance in uncertainty, the constant realization
of conflicting possibilities, was painful. 'Most miserable Is the
desire that's glorious', and April is the cruelest month. At times
it seems easier to find rest in death, and to hold with Hermione
in her despair, 'The bug which you would fright me with I seek',
or with Leontes: 'Say she were gone, a moiety of my rest Might
come to me again.' For 'While she lives, My heart will be
a burthen to me'.

Yet the creative force of love cannot be killed:

> Affection! thy intention stabs the centre.
> Thou dost make possible things not so held,
> Communicat'st with dreams! How can this be?

Whether it is a gracious instinct of truth or a blind movement of the independent will, man must make the assumption of life, must act compassionately, must trust that 'something rare Even then will rush to knowledge'. Paulina, who has done so much for others, will not be allowed to wing herself, an old turtledove, to some withered bough; she must be restored to the society of love. And for the last miracle, capable of breathing life into cold marble,

> It is requir'd
> You do awake your faith.

E. M. W. Tillyard

THE TRAGIC PATTERN (1938)

In *The Winter's Tale* Shakespeare omitted all the irrelevancies
that had clotted *Cymbeline*, and presented the whole tragic
pattern, from prosperity to destruction, regeneration, and still
fairer prosperity, in full view of the audience. This is a bold,
frontal attack on the problem, necessitating the complete disregard of the unity of time; but it succeeded, as far as success was
possible within the bounds of a single play. One difference in
plot from *Cymbeline* is, that there is little overlap between the
old and the new life. In Guiderius and Arviragus the new life had
been incubating for years while the old life held sway in Cymbeline and his court. But Perdita, chief symbol of the new life,
has not lived many hours before Leontes begins his own
conversion.

Unlike *Cymbeline*, the first half of the play is seriously tragic
and could have included Hermione's death, like Greene's
Pandosto. Leontes's obsession of jealousy is terrifying in its
intensity. It reminds us not of other Shakespearean tragic errors,
but rather of the god-sent lunacies of Greek drama, the lunacies
of Ajax and Heracles. It is as scantily motivated as these, and we
should refrain from demanding any motive. Indeed, it is as much
a surprise to the characters in the play as it is to the reader, and
its nature is that of an earthquake or the loss of the *Titanic* rather
than of rational human psychology. And equally terrifying is
Leontes's cry, when, after defying the oracle, he hears of his son's
death:

> Apollo's angry; and the heavens themselves
> Do strike at my injustice.

Hermione's character is far more firmly based on probability than Imogen's. There is nothing strained or hectic about her love for her husband: it is rooted in habit. And when at her trial, addressing Leontes, she says:

> To me can life be no commodity;
> The crown and comfort of my life, your favour,
> I do give lost; for I do feel it gone,
> But know not how it went,

we accept the statement as sober truth. While for distilled pathos no poet, not even Euripides, has excelled her final soliloquy, when she realises Leontes's fixed hostility:

> The Emperor of Russia was my father:
> O that he were alive, and here beholding
> His daughter's trial! that he did but see
> The flatness of my misery, yet with eyes
> Of pity, not revenge!

In sum, the first half of the play renders worthily, in the main through a realistic method, the destructive portion of the tragic pattern.

Now, although Leontes and Hermione live on to give continuity to the play and although the main tragic pattern is worked out nominally in Leontes, the royal person, it is not they in their reconciliation who most create the feeling of rebirth. At the best they mend the broken vessel of their fortunes with glue or seccotine; and our imaginations are not in the least stirred by any future life that we can conceive the pair enjoying together. Were the pattern of destruction and regeneration the sole motive of the play, the statue scene would have little point and be, as Middleton Murry calls it, a theatrical trick. But the continued existence of Leontes and Hermione is a matter of subordinate expediency; and it is Florizel and Perdita and the countryside where they meet which make the new life.

And here I must plead as earnestly as I can for allowing more than the usual virtue and weight to the fourth act of *The Winter's Tale*. There are several reasons why it has been taken too lightly. It has been far too much the property of vague young women doing eurhythmics at Speech Days or on vicarage lawns; and, when it is acted professionally, the part of Perdita is usually taken by some pretty little fool or pert suburban charmer. Also, it is usually thought that joy and virtue are inferior as poetic themes to suffering and vice; or that the earthly paradise taxed the resources of Dante less than Ugolino's tower. It would seem that the truth is the other way round, because convincing pictures of joy and virtue are extremely rare, while those of suffering and vice are comparatively common. Shelley succeeds in describing the sufferings of Prometheus; the earthly bliss brought on by them is, except in patches, a shoddy affair in comparison. Shakespeare never did anything finer, more serious, more evocative of his full powers, than his picture of an earthly paradise painted in the form of the English countryside. The old problem of adjusting realism and symbol is so well solved that we are quite unconscious of it. The country life is given the fullest force of actuality, as when the old shepherd describes his wife's hospitality at the shearing feast:

> Fie, daughter! when my old wife lived, upon
> This day she was both pantler, butler, cook,
> Both dame and servant; welcomed all, served all:
> Would sing her song and dance her turn; now here,
> At upper end o' the table, now i' the middle;
> On his shoulder, and his; her face o' fire
> With labour and the thing she took to quench it,
> She would to each one sip.

Yet the whole country setting stands out as the cleanest and most elegant symbol of the new life into which the old horrors are to be transmuted.

It is the same with the characters. Shakespeare blends the realistic and the symbolic with the surest touch. Florizel, who is kept a rather flat character the more to show up Perdita, one would call a type rather than a symbol; but for the play's purposes he is an efficient type of chivalry and generosity. He will not let down Perdita, but defies his father at the risk of losing a kingdom:

I am not sorry, not afeard; delay'd
But nothing altered: what I was, I am;
More straining on for plucking back, not following
My leash unwillingly.

Perdita, on the other hand, is one of Shakespeare's richest characters; at once a symbol and a human being. She is the play's main symbol of the powers of creation. And rightly, because, as Leontes was the sole agent of destruction, so it is fitting, ironically fitting, that the one of his kin whom he had thrown out as bastard should embody the contrary process. Not that Leontes, as a character, is the contrary to Perdita. *His* obsession is not a part of his character but an accretion. Her true contrary is Iago. It is curious that Iago should ever have been thought motiveless. The desire to destroy is a very simple derivative from the power-instinct, the instinct which in its evil form goes by the name of the first of the deadly sins, Pride. It was by that sin that the angels fell, and at the end of *Othello* Iago is explicitly equated with the Devil. Shakespeare embodied all his horror of this type of original sin in Iago. He was equally aware of original virtue, and he pictured it, in Perdita, blossoming spontaneously in the simplest of country settings. There is little direct reference to her instincts to create; but they are implied by her sympathy with nature's lavishness in producing flowers, followed by her own simple and unashamed confession of wholesome sensuality. The whole passage, so often confined to mere idyllic description, must be quoted in hopes that the reader will allow the profounder significance I claim for it. Perdita is talking to her guests, to Polixenes, Camillo, and Florizel in particular:

Per.   Here's flowers for you;
Hot lavender, mints, savory, marjoram;
The marigold, that goes to bed wi' the sun
And with him rises weeping: these are flowers
Of middle summer, and I think they are given
To men of middle age. You're very welcome.
Cam. I should leave grazing, were I of your flock,
And only live by gazing.

Per.　　　　　　　　　　　Out, alas!
　You'ld be so lean, that blasts of January
　Would blow you through and through. Now, my fair'st
　　friend,
　I would I had some flowers o' the spring that might
　Become your time of day; and yours, and yours,
　That wear upon your virgin branches yet
　Your maidenheads growing: O Proserpina,
　For the flowers now, that frighted thou let'st fall
　From Dis's wagon! daffodils,
　That come before the swallow dares, and take
　The winds of March with beauty; violets dim,
　But sweeter than the lids of Juno's eyes
　Or Cytherea's breath; pale primroses,
　That die unmarried, ere they can behold
　Bright Phoebus in his strength – a malady
　Most incident to maids; bold oxlips and
　The crown imperial; lilies of all kinds,
　The flower-de-luce being one! O, these I lack,
　To make you garlands of, and my sweet friend,
　To strew him o'er and o'er.
Flo.　　　　　　　　　　What, like a corse?
Per.　No, like a bank for love to lie and play on;
　Not like a corse; or if, not to be buried,
　But quick and in mine arms.

The great significance of Perdita's lines lies partly in the verse, which (especially at the close) is leisurely, full, assured, matured, suggestive of fruition, and acutely contrasted to the tortured, arid, and barren ravings of Leontes, and which reinforces that kinship with nature and healthy sensuality mentioned above. But it lies also in the references to the classical Pantheon. The gods of Greece and Rome occur very frequently in the last plays of Shakespeare and are certainly more than mere embroidery. Apollo is the dominant god in *The Winter's Tale*, and his appearance in Perdita's speech is meant to quicken the reader to apprehend some unusual significance. He appears as the bridegroom, whom the pale primroses never know, but who visits the other flowers. Not to take the fertility symbolism as intended would be a perverse act of caution. Perdita should be associated with them, as symbol both of the creative powers of nature, physical fertility, and of healing and re-creation of the mind. She is like Milton's youthful Ceres,

> Yet virgin of Proserpina from Jove,

or his Eve, mistress of the flowers of Paradise.

The health of Perdita's natural instincts not only helps her symbolic force; it helps to make her a realistic character. Other parts of her character are a deep-seated strength and ruthless common sense. She argues coolly with Polixenes about art and nature, and is not frightened by his later fulminations, saying when he has gone:

> I was not much afeard; for once or twice
> I was about to speak and tell him plainly,
> The selfsame sun that shines upon his court
> Hides not his visage from our cottage but
> Looks on alike.

At the same time she shows that she has been all the time quite without illusions about the danger she runs in loving Florizel, the Prince, and when the shock comes with the discovery of their plighted love she is prepared without fuss to accept her fate. Turning to Florizel, she goes on:

> Will't please you, sir, be gone?
> I told you what would come of this: beseech you,
> Of your own state take care: this dream of mine –
> Being now awake, I'll queen it no inch farther,
> But milk my ewes and weep.

It is through Perdita's magnificence that we accept as valuable the new life into which the play is made to issue. The disadvantage of centring the creative processes in her and Florizel is structural. There is a break in continuity; for though Perdita is born in the first half of the play, as characters the pair are new to the last half. And we have juxtaposition, not organic growth. There is no Orestes to lead from the *Choephoroe* to the *Eumenides*. On the other hand, I find this juxtaposition easy enough to accept; and it is mitigated by Perdita's parentage. She is Hermione's true daughter and prolongs in herself those regenerative processes which in her mother have suffered a temporary eclipse.

The common praise of Autolycus as a character is well justified. It is likely that he is organic to the whole country scene, and that it would collapse into an over-sweetness of sentiment without him. Though he comes and goes with the aloofness of an elf among humans, he is united with the other characters in his admirable adjustment to the country life. His delinquencies, like the pastoral realism, keep the earthly paradise sufficiently earthly without disturbing the paradisiac state; for they are anti-toxic rather than toxic, harmless to vigorous health, and an efficient prophylactic against the lotus-fruit which, as a drug, has so greatly impaired the health of most earthly paradises.

Ernest Schanzer

THE STRUCTURAL PATTERN (1964)

IN his stimulating little book, *Shakespeare's Last Plays*, E. M. W. Tillyard suggests that we may see in *The Winter's Tale* Shakespeare's attempt to compress the whole scheme of Dante's *Divine Comedy* into a single play. This is most obviously true if we make Leontes' spiritual experiences the centre of our concern. In Acts I–III we are then given the *Inferno*, the hell which Leontes builds in his own mind. Like that of Milton's Satan, it is a hell which is entirely self-created and self-sustained. Next, at the end of Act III and the beginning of Act V, we are given glimpses of the *Purgatorio*, the sixteen-year period of repentance and penance in his life. And finally, in the remainder of Act V, we have the *Paradiso* in his reunion with daughter, wife, and friend. For the broad outlines of this pattern Shakespeare turned back to what was probably his immediately preceding play, *Cymbeline*. In Posthumus he had there created a husband who mistakenly believes his wife to have been unfaithful to him, goes through a mental hell (much more briefly sketched in than in *The Winter's Tale*), which is quickly followed by a period of deep repentance and penance, until the final joyful reunion.

This tripartite division of *The Winter's Tale* into *Inferno*, *Purgatorio*, and *Paradiso* involves, however, a distortion of its structural pattern, for it takes no account of Act IV, which is almost as long as the first three acts put together. In this act Leontes does not appear at all, and instead our attention centres on Perdita. This double focus of *The Winter's Tale*, upon the father in the first three acts and upon the daughter in Act IV, is found in only one other play by Shakespeare, *Pericles*, which, in fact, provided its structural model.

In both plays the centre of the stage is held in the first three

acts by the royal father (Pericles, Leontes); between Acts III and
IV is placed the great gap of time, fourteen years in the one, sixteen in the other; in Act IV the father does not appear, while our
attention focuses on the daughter (Marina, Perdita), whom we
last saw just after her birth in the first part of the play; in the final
act the two focuses coalesce, with the reunion of father and
daughter, followed by the reunion of husband and wife (Thaisa,
Hermione), whom the husband had believed dead and buried. In
both plays the reunion of father and daughter is the result of
mere chance, while that of husband and wife is the result of
direction, its agent being in the one play the goddess Diana, in the
other Paulina.

This structural pattern of the two plays is quite unique in the
Shakespeare canon. Nowhere else is there this double focus, with
the protagonist of the first three acts of the play not appearing in
Act IV, his place being taken by a completely new character. And
nowhere else is there a similar treatment of time, with a gap of
many years placed in the middle of the play. Elsewhere in his
comedies Shakespeare either observed the most rigorous unity of
time, as in *The Comedy of Errors* and *The Tempest*, or allowed at
most several months to elapse in the course of the play's action,
as, for instance, in *All's Well* and *Cymbeline*.

In both *Pericles* and *The Winter's Tale* the relation between
the two halves of the play, which are separated by the great gap
of time, is one of contrast as well as of likeness. In *Pericles* the
likeness is found above all in the ill fortunes that befall father and
daughter. In both cases their afflictions begin with a plot to
murder them; they escape this, only to be overtaken by further
calamities. The contrast is mainly that between the losses and
separations of Acts I–III and the reunions of Act V. In *The
Winter's Tale* the contrasts are much more pervasive and important than in *Pericles*. Indeed, they constitute a principal element
in the play's thematic pattern. As these contrasts have been much
discussed by commentators, a brief outline of them will suffice.

Shakespeare has divided the play into a predominantly destructive half and a predominantly creative and restorative half; into a
winter half, concentrating on the desolation that Leontes spreads

at his court, and a spring and summer half, concentrating on the
values represented by the mutual love of Florizel and Perdita and
the reunions at the finale. Leontes, like Macbeth, creates a wintry
landscape of death and desolation around him, destroying all
happiness and good fellowship. But whereas Macbeth, the
winter-king, has to be killed before spring and new life – represented by Malcolm – can reign in Scotland, Leontes is made to
undergo a long process of purgation. This too is a desolate and
wintry period, as is brought vividly home to us by Paulina's
hyperbolical description of the penance:

> A thousand knees
> Ten thousand years together, naked, fasting,
> Upon a barren mountain, and still winter
> In storm perpetual, could not move the gods
> To look that way thou wert.   (III ii 207–11)

But this desolate period comes to an end with the arrival at
Leontes' court of Florizel and Perdita, whom he greets with the
words:

> Welcome hither
> As is the spring to th' earth.   (v i 151–2)

The scene of the sheep-shearing feast in Act IV is used by Shakespeare to present those human values which Leontes had banished
from his court: love, joy, trust, hospitality, good fellowship.
While the time of year is midsummer,* when bright Phoebus is
in his strength and 'great creating nature', the goddess which

* Some commentators have doubted this, apparently misled by
Perdita's

> Sir, the year growing ancient,
> Not yet on summer's death nor on the birth
> Of trembling winter, the fairest flow'rs o' th' season
> Are our carnations and streak'd gillyvors.   (IV iv 79)

But Perdita here is not saying that it is *now* autumn, but that the fairest
flowers of autumn are carnations, etc. Sheepshearings in Shakespeare's
day always took place around midsummer (see New Arden edition,
p. 83), and Shakespeare would not have deliberately gone counter both
to this custom and the required symbolic suggestiveness of the scene
by placing it in the autumn.

presides over this part of the play, reigns supreme, some of the
poetically most memorable allusions are to spring, the spring
embodied by the young lovers, which, in the play's symbolic
pattern, takes the place of the long wintry period established by
Leontes: there is Florizel's description of Perdita as 'no shepherdess, but Flora Peering in April's front' (IV iv 2); there is
Perdita's great speech about spring-flowers (IV iv 112); and there
is Autolycus's opening song:

> When daffodils begin to peer
>   With heigh! the doxy over the dale,
> Why, then comes in the sweet o' the year,
>   For the red blood reigns in the winter's pale.
>
> (IV iii 1–4)

'For the red blood reigns in the winter's pale', i.e. the boundaries,
the domain of winter: the line sums up the basic progression of
the play.

Between the two contrasting halves Shakespeare introduced a
transitional scene at the end of the destructive phase. Wilson
Knight says of this scene (III iii), which depicts the death of
Antigonus and the ship's crew at the very moment of the Shepherd's discovery of the babe, that it 'is a hinge not only for the
story but also for the life-views it expresses . . . we pass from
horror to simple, rustic comedy. . . . Tragedy is confronted by
comedy working in close alliance with birth.'[1] And Nevill Coghill, aptly pointing out how the horror itself is turned into
comedy by the manner in which Shakespeare makes the Clown
report it,* speaks of the scene in very similar terms:

That this scene is a kind of dramaturgical hinge, a moment of
planned structural antithesis, is certain from the dialogue; we are
passing from tears to laughter, from death to life:

---

* This device of turning horror into comedy is by no means unique.
Shakespeare employed it on at least two other occasions: in Imogen's
lament over the headless body of Cloten (*Cymbeline*, IV ii 309 ff), and
in the Capulets' and the Nurse's lament over the apparently dead body
of Juliet (*Romeo and Juliet*, IV v 43 ff).

Now bless thyself: thou mett'st with things dying,
I with things new-born.[2]

But the relationship between the two halves of the play consists not only of a series of contrasts but also of a series of parallels. As these have been largely ignored by commentators, I shall have to consider them in greater detail.

At the beginning of each half (I i and IV ii) stands a brief prose scene of almost identical length, consisting of a dialogue between Camillo and another person: Archidamus in the first half, Polixenes in the second. In this dialogue the conversation partly turns upon a happy and harmonious relationship, which is soon to be violently disrupted, that between Polixenes and Leontes in the first half and that between their children, Florizel and Perdita, in the second. In each half Shakespeare then proceeds to bring before us this relationship as it exists before its violent disruption. The friendship of Polixenes and Leontes is presented to us not only through Camillo's description in the first scene, but also in the opening dialogue of the following scene (I ii 1–27), and in Polixenes' description of their boyhood days (I ii 62). Next, in the brief dialogue between Leontes and Hermione, in which he recalls his wooing of her (I ii 88), Shakespeare sketches in the joyful and loving communion that exists between them at the play's opening. And in the same way the close and happy relationship between Leontes and Mamillius (I ii 120) and, finally, between Hermione and Mamillius (II i 1) is presented to us. Shakespeare is evidently at pains to establish clearly at the outset all that Leontes loses and destroys.

In a similar way in the second half of the play the joyful and loving relationship of Florizel and Perdita is fully brought out before its would-be destroyer, Polixenes, unmasks himself. The effect, as in the first half, is that of the sudden and violent intrusion of winter, blighting the blossoms of spring. It is in aid of this effect that Shakespeare, earlier in the scene, makes Perdita give to Polixenes flowers of winter to suit his age (IV iv 73), and has him swear 'by my white beard' (IV iv 397). Whatever its moral differences, the imaginative impact of Polixenes' cruel threats is very

similar to that of Leontes' ravings.* We need only to compare
Leontes' words to Antigonus,

> Thou, traitor, hast set on thy wife to this.
> My child! Away with't. Even thou, that hast
> A heart so tender o'er it, take it hence,
> And see it instantly consum'd with fire;
> Even thou, and none but thou. Take it up straight.
> Within this hour bring me word 'tis done,
> And by good testimony, or I'll seize thy life,
> With what thou else call'st thine. If thou refuse,
> And wilt encounter with my wrath, say so;
> The bastard brains with these my proper hands
> Shall I dash out . . .   (II iii 130–40)

with Polixenes' threats to the old Shepherd and Perdita:

>   Thou, old traitor,
> I am sorry that by hanging thee I can
> But shorten thy life one week. And thou, fresh piece
> Of excellent witchcraft, who of force must know
> The royal fool thou cop'st with . . .
> I'll have thy beauty scratch'd with briers and made
> More homely than thy state. For thee, fond boy,
> If I may ever know thou dost but sigh
> That thou no more shalt see this knack – as never
> I mean thou shalt – we'll bar thee from succession;
> Not hold thee of our blood, no, not our kin,
> Farre than Deucalion off. Mark thou my words.
> Follow us to the court. Thou churl, for this time,
> Though full of our displeasure, yet we free thee
> From the dead blow of it. And you, enchantment,
> Worthy enough a herdsman – yea, him too
> That makes himself, but for our honour therein,

* This view is supported by Derek Traversi, who declares that
Polixenes' 'brutality in separating the lovers, and more especially his
ferocious attack upon Perdita's beauty . . . form an exact complement
to Leontes' earlier behaviour' – *Shakespeare: The Last Phase* (1954)
pp. 158–9. But I cannot endorse his claim that 'they proceed from the
same impotence of aged blood'. Leontes in the first half of the play
cannot be much above thirty years old, as I ii 155 makes clear.

> Unworthy thee – if ever henceforth thou
> These rural latches to his entrance open,
> Or hoop his body more with thy embraces,
> I will devise a death as cruel for thee
> As thou art tender to't.   (IV iv 412–33)

Autolycus gives what amounts to a *reductio ad absurdum* of this
outburst in his talk with the Clown later in the scene:

He has a son – who shall be flay'd alive; then 'nointed over with
honey, set on the head of a wasp's nest; then stand till he be three
quarters and a dram dead; then recover'd again with aqua-vitae
or some other hot infusion; then, raw as he is, and in the hottest
day prognostication proclaims, shall he be set against a brick
wall, the sun looking with a southward eye upon him, where he
is to behold him with flies blown to death.   (IV iv 772)

It takes our minds back to Paulina's outcry in the first half of the
play:

> What studied torments, tyrant, hast for me?
> What wheels, racks, fires? what flaying, boiling
> In leads or oils?   (III ii 172–4)

The effect of Polixenes' tyranny is that Perdita is for a second
time committed to the mercy of the waves, as she flees with
Florizel to Sicily. In both halves Camillo plays the same rôle,
advising the victim of the King's anger and helping him to escape
from the realm to a place of safety, a parallel which is made
explicit when Florizel calls him 'Preserver of my father, now of
me' (IV iv 578).

At the end of each half stands the scene which provides its
climax: the trial-scene in the first half, the statue-scene in the
second. In each our attention centres on Hermione: Hermione
pleading eloquently in her own defence in the trial-scene; Hermione standing silent and motionless before us in the statue-
scene. The first half culminates in Hermione's death, the second in
her 'resurrection'. Structural parallel and thematic contrast are
here combined.

Our sense of the similarity, the repetition in the two halves of

the play, which we experience despite our awareness of the predominant contrasts between them, is accentuated by the Chorus-
speech of Time, which separates them and comes almost exactly
in the middle of the play. After a playful defence of the poet's
violation of the unity of time in *The Winter's Tale*,

> since it is in my power
> To o'erthrow law, and in one self-born hour
> To plant and o'erwhelm custom,

Time declares:

> Your patience this allowing,
> I turn my glass, and give my scene such growing
> As you had slept between.   (IV i 15--17)

By his gesture of turning the hour-glass Time marks the great
break between the two halves of the play, but also creates in us a
feeling of repetition. Both parts of the hour-glass look alike, and
it may not be fanciful to think that this fact enhances our sense
of the similarity of the shape and structure of the two halves of
The Winter's Tale.

It is also enhanced by its imagery. More than any other play
in the canon *The Winter's Tale* is akin to *Macbeth* in the nature
and use of its imagery, a kinship which derives, of course, from
the affinity of its themes. This is above all true of the first half,
which shares with *Macbeth* the contrast on the one hand of images
of planting and growth with images of uprooting and blight, and
on the other images of health and physic with images of sickness
and infection. In the very first scene of the play the positives in
both groups of images are introduced. Of the friendship of
Leontes and Polixenes we are told by Camillo that 'there rooted
betwixt them then such an affection which cannot choose but
branch now' (I i 21), while of Mamillius he remarks that he is 'one
that indeed physics the subject, makes old hearts fresh' (I i 36).
And in the following scene Polixenes says of his son:

> He makes a July's day short as December,
> And with his varying childness cures in me
> Thoughts that would thick my blood. (I ii 169--71)

In *Macbeth* it is the English king who is represented as a source of healing, in opposition to Macbeth, the source of infection and disease. In *The Winter's Tale* it is, significantly, above all the young who fill this rôle, and are opposed to Leontes, in whose jealous ravings disease-images abound.

Great creating nature, *natura naturans*, who presides over the scene of the sheep-shearing feast, is also twice referred to in the first half of the play, each time by Paulina, and each time in connection with the birth of Perdita (II ii 60 and II iii 103). For the birth of Perdita fills a similar rôle in the symbolic pattern of the first half as does her love for Florizel in the second half, setting the creative, fertile, and natural against the destructive, barren, and monstrous.

Imagery drawn from nature is found repeatedly in the first half of the play. Its second scene opens with Polixenes'

> Nine changes of the wat'ry star hath been
> The shepherd's note since we have left our throne
> Without a burden.

And a little later in the scene he compares his boyhood friendship with Leontes to 'twinn'd lambs that did frisk i' th' sun And bleat the one at th' other' (I ii 67). What are here poetic embroideries or figures of speech are introduced into the second part on a more literal level: we meet real shepherds, who talk of real sheep, just as the images of planting and growing, used purely figuratively in the first half, reappear in the second half on a more literal level in the horticultural debate between Perdita and Polixenes. But their symbolic suggestiveness in both halves is basically similar.

Even in their imagery, then, the two halves are linked in a variety of ways. And not only has the scene of the sheep-shearing feast, with its images of spring, of fertility, and growth, got its corresponding images in the first half of the play. The statue-scene, too, has its equivalent in the 'ceremonious, solemn, and unearthly' atmosphere of the Delphic oracle, as described by Cleomenes and Dion in the first scene of Act III, a resemblance which has been noted by several commentators.

We have seen, then, that the structural pattern of *The Winter's*

Tale consists not only of a series of contrasts between its two halves, but also of a series of parallels. They may be mainly structural parallels, as is the case with the brief prose-scene at the beginning of each half; or mainly thematic parallels, such as the sudden intrusion of the cruelly threatening king into a scene of happy relationships; or mainly plot-parallels, such as Camillo's aid to the victim of the king's fury; or mainly parallels of tone and atmosphere, such as that between the description of the Delphic oracle and the statue-scene.

But whereas the contrasts between the two halves of the play are clearly a principal means of conveying its concerns, its deeper significance, the function of the parallels is far from obvious. Though *The Winter's Tale* is full of dramatic irony – as is not unexpected in a play concerned so largely with human blindness and ignorance – the parallels, like the contrasts, are not, for the most part, ironic in nature. In *Coriolanus*, another play divided into two sharply contrasted halves, with a pattern of repetition in the action, the pervasive parallels and contrasts between the incidents of the two halves are filled with dramatic irony, an irony which is, indeed, a central effect of the play, and a chief vehicle of its significance. There is nothing of this in the parallels and contrasts of *The Winter's Tale*. Only in Camillo's rôle of preserver of Florizel from the wrath of Polixenes, the very person whom he had previously preserved from the wrath of Leontes, can an element of dramatic irony be discerned. The case of *The Winter's Tale* seems to be more like that of *Henry IV*, where there is a close parallel between the structure of the two parts – much closer, indeed, than that of *The Winter's Tale* – and yet no marked ironic relationship between the parallel scenes is apparent. The audience is not expected to be aware of the structural parallels, neither does such an awareness add appreciably to the play's significance. It is rather as if Shakespeare, in writing the second part of *Henry IV*, had used the scenario of the first part as a blueprint, a labour-saving device.

Perhaps we come a little closer to an understanding of the significance of the parallels between the two halves of *The Winter's Tale* if we compare them with Shakespeare's use of the sub-plots in *Lear* and *Timon*. The unnatural behaviour of Edmund towards his father and brother, the callous ingratitude shown by the Athenian Senators towards Alcibiades, parallel and thus universalize the action of the main plot. The parallels between the two parts of *Pericles* produce a similar effect. The sudden and violent blows of fortune which strike Marina, as they had earlier struck her father, deepen and widen the play's image of the world as a lasting storm, whirring us from our friends. In the same way the principal effect of the pattern of repetition in *The Winter's Tale* is to increase our sense of the fragility, the precariousness of human happiness. As we watch, twice over in the play's symbolic pattern, the progression from summer to winter, with the return of spring and summer at the end, the affinity between human affairs and the cycle of the seasons, which is close to the imaginative core of *The Winter's Tale*, is borne in upon us.

NOTES

1. G. Wilson Knight, *The Crown of Life* (1947) pp. 98–9.
2. 'Six Points of Stage-craft in *The Winter's Tale*', in *Shakespeare Survey 11* (1958) p. 35. This essay is reprinted in this volume, pp. 198–213.

Inga-Stina Ewbank

THE TRIUMPH OF TIME (1964)

IT is often assumed that, while Shakespeare's middle plays and many of his sonnets show a keen awareness of, and even obsession with, the power of time over man, his final plays are not concerned with the theme of time and change. In these plays we are, according to one critic, in 'a fairyland of unrealities' in which 'injurious time plays no controlling part';[1] and another critic sees Shakespeare as abandoning time-thinking in order to devote himself to 'myths of immortality'.[2] Yet *The Tempest*, for all that it celebrates values which are not subject to time, also balances these against time in its 'injurious' capacity, time which triumphs over

> The cloud-capped towers, the gorgeous palaces,
> The solemn temples, the great globe itself,
> Yea, all which it inherit.[3]

Prospero's island may be a 'fairyland of unrealities', but it is also the land of Petrarch's *Trionfi*:

> Our Tryumphs shal passe our pompes shal decay
> Our lordshyppes our kyngdomes shall all awaye
> And al thynge also that we accompt mortall
> Tyme at the length shal clene deface it al.[4]

And when Shakespeare was looking around for material for the play which was to become *The Winter's Tale*, he chose a story with the sub-title 'The Triumph of Time' and developed it in a fashion which suggests a deepening and enrichment, rather than an abandonment, of time-thinking.

The Time which triumphs on the title-page of Greene's *Pandosto* is not the dreaded *tempus edax* but the beneficent Revealer who shows that 'although by the means of sinister fortune Truth may be concealed, yet by Time in spight of fortune it is most manifestly revealed'.[5] The *Pandosto* story itself fails to work out its motto – *Temporis filia veritas* – for it puts all the emphasis on Fortune, with her wheel, as the ruling agent of human affairs. Shakespeare, on the other hand, makes the Triumph of Time into a controlling theme of his tale; and in doing so he transforms what the conventional motto suggests – a simple victory of Time, the Father of Truth – into a dramatic exploration of the manifold meanings of Time.

The chief evidence of Shakespeare's time-thinking in his middle period lies in the time allusions and time imagery of the plays and sonnets. The chief evidence for assuming a lack of concern with time in the last plays has been, it would seem, their almost total lack of time imagery. But, as I hope to show, while in *The Winter's Tale* time has largely disappeared from the verbal imagery, it is all the more intensely present as a controlling and shaping figure behind the dramatic structure and technique. It is true that certain features of the dramatic technique in *The Winter's Tale* are aimed at achieving an effect of timelessness: S. L. Bethell has shown how Shakespeare uses deliberate anachronisms to create the never-never world of a winter's tale.[6] It would be wrong, however, to conclude that the absence of the objective, social time of history which characterizes the setting of the tale, means that in the human issues of the play Shakespeare is unaware of, or uninterested in, man's subjection to time in its various aspects, injurious as well as benevolent.

The most obvious indication of Shakespeare's concern with time is the overall structure of the play. Not only does the action span a long period, so as – and this never happens in the tragedies – to give working-space to time, both as Revealer and as Destroyer; but, through the arrangement of the play into two halves separated by the 'wide gap' of sixteen years, past and present can be emphatically juxtaposed. The structure thus becomes a vehicle for the exploration of the meanings of time – in the sense of what time does to man. The intricacy and complexity of this exploration is revealed, in parts of the play, by subordinated structural features, and it is to these we must first turn if we are to see the full relevance of the larger structure.

The scene of exposition (I i) is a dialogue between Camillo and Archidamus, which proceeds via a series of references to time seen as natural growth; it places the play in a perspective of naturally ripening time, opening backwards as well as forwards. Camillo describes the span of the relations between the Kings of Sicilia and of Bohemia: from an indicative past – 'They were trained together in their childhoods' – to a present consequent upon that past – 'there rooted betwixt them then such an affection, which cannot choose but branch now' – and on to a desired (but soon to be threatened) future – 'The heavens continue their loves!' Similarly he introduces the whole span of human life by way of talking about the little Prince Mamillius: 'they that went on crutches ere he was born desire yet their life to see him a man'; and this subject is expanded to provide, as the scene closes, an ironically foreboding note: 'If the king had no son, they would desire to live on crutches till he had one.' Linking up with this introduction, the beginning of I ii is a conversation which modulates from one subject to another, with time as the shared note. It opens with the most immediate time-concern, conditioned by the plot: how long Polixenes has stayed already and how much longer, if at all, he may be prevailed upon to stay. Even this persuasion (for which there is no source in *Pandosto*) has about it a peculiar urgency, as if love could be measured in time-units:

> When at Bohemia
> You take my lord, I'll give him my commission
> To let him there a month behind the gest
> Prefix'd for's parting: yet, good deed, Leontes
> I love thee not a jar o'the clock behind
> What lady-she her lord.

Hermione's fatal victory leads naturally on to remembrances of things past, first of the two Kings' blissful childhood as 'twinn'd lambs'. Here Shakespeare deliberately juxtaposes time's destruction with things as they were: 'We were', says Polixenes,

> Two lads that thought there was no more behind
> But such a day to-morrow as to-day,
> And to be boy eternal.

Polixenes' speeches create a strong sense of time as destructive, as equalling the passing of innocence, making nonsense of the ideals of youth. The transition from this stage of the scene to the next is delicately made via the courtly banter of Polixenes and Hermione. The next remembrance is of the long-seeming courtship of Leontes and Hermione, when finally, so he tells her, after three 'crabbed months', 'then didst thou utter "I am yours forever"'. It is, I think, noteworthy that this recollection of Hermione's forward-looking statement is what triggers off Leontes' first outburst of jealousy. The 'forever' (which the rest of the play is going to prove true),* spoken in innocent remembrance, suddenly becomes tormentingly ironical to Leontes. From his next words, 'Too hot, too hot', all is feverish haste, in word and deed.

For the action centring on Leontes, from this moment until the end of Act III, is not only a vivid realization of Polixenes' words about the loss of innocence, but it is also a dramatization of the failure to trust Time the Revealer. If Leontes had given himself time to observe the behaviour of Hermione and Polixenes and to listen to his advisers, he would have discovered that his suspicions were rootless. Instead he goes, as it were, against time and is therefore blind to truth; for time, when not allowed to ripen, can only *make*, not *unfold*, error. From now on, speech-patterns, as well as the structure of individual scenes and their combination, are so devised as to bring out the unnatural haste of Leontes' thoughts and acts; and this frenzied hurry is all the more marked for being set against the references to naturally progressing time with which the play opened. The telescoped syntax and half-finished sentences of Leontes' speeches image the frenzy within. His heated imagination fabricates evidence the very nature of which adds to the sense of rush:

> Is whispering nothing?
> Is leaning cheek to cheek? is meeting noses?
> Kissing with inside lip? stopping the career

* Leontes is, in a sense, an inverted Troilus. Troilus believes that Cressida's love will last forever, and is disillusioned by Time. Leontes does not believe in Hermione's 'forever', and is converted by Time. In each case there is a failure to know the love offered for what it is worth.

Of laughter with a sigh? – a note infallible
Of breaking honesty – horsing foot on foot?
Skulking in corners? *wishing clocks more swift?*
Hours, minutes? noon, midnight?

and it repeatedly draws time itself into its scope:

> . . . were my wife's liver
> Infected as her life, she would not live
> The running of one glass.

The arrangement of events is partly responsible for the hectic
effect of these scenes. Shakespeare here greatly condenses the
sequence in the source story. For example, in *Pandosto*, Egistus
(Polixenes), having been told of Pandosto's (Leontes') intention
to poison him, waits six days for favourable winds before he sets
sail; whereas in *The Winter's Tale* the events up to the end of
Act I, when Camillo urges Polixenes 'please your highness To
take the urgent hour', would seem to happen in as little time as it
takes to act them. Camillo's function, in relation to Leontes, is
to try to brake the speed:

> Good my lord, be cured
> Of this diseased opinion, and *betimes*;
> For 'tis most dangerous;

and indeed, when brought to insight at the end of Act III,
Leontes looks back and sees Camillo as the voice of time whose
'good mind . . . *tardied* My *swift* command'. But he is not listened
to in time; and in a sense he is himself guilty of untimeliness in
urging Polixenes to leave at once. Polixenes' hasty departure
cannot but tie the knot of error more firmly by confirming
Leontes' 'true opinion' (II i 37).

In *Pandosto* Bellaria finds herself quick with child only after
Egistus is gone, and she is kept in prison, awaiting trial, till after
the child is born. In *The Winter's Tale* Hermione's lying-in is
imminent at the outset of the play (Polixenes has been in Sicilia
for 'nine changes of the watery star'), and it is in keeping with
the onrush of time in these Acts that she is *something before her
time deliver'd*. Although at least twenty-three days must have

passed during the course of Acts II and III, the structure of events is shaped so as to give the impression that Leontes has not once stopped to think – 'nor night nor day no rest'. The child is no sooner born than it is doomed to suffer (probable) death. Hermione is rushed into court,

> hurried
> Here to this place, i'the open air, before
> I have got strength of limit.

The verdict of the Oracle is no sooner announced than flaunted: 'There is no truth at all i'the oracle: The sessions shall proceed: this is mere falsehood.' Shortly before, Leontes had hailed the early return of the messengers:

> Twenty three days
> They have been absent; tis good speed; foretells
> The great Apollo suddenly will have
> The truth of this appear.

Indeed Apollo has been 'sudden' in revealing the truth, but Leontes is even more sudden in rejecting it, thereby demonstrating to the full his perversion of truth and justice.

In terms of Elizabethan thought the injustice done to Hermione is linked up with the time theme more closely than a modern reader or audience may realize. Her arraignment can be seen as the epitome of Leontes' rejection of Time, the Father of Truth, for Justice, like her sister virtue Truth, was conceived of as closely associated with Time.[7] Rosalind points to the connection in her parting words to Orlando after the mock-wooing: 'Time is the old Justice that examines all ... offenders, and let Time try' (*As You Like It*, IV ii 203). Leontes does not let Time try, despite Antigonus' warning: 'Be certain what you do, sir, lest your justice Prove violence' (II ii 127). And throughout the court scene (III ii) the word 'justice' rings ironically, coming from Leontes:

> Let us be clear'd
> Of being tyrannous, since we so openly
> Proceed in justice, which shall have due course,
> Even to the guilt or the purgation.

Significantly, no one else in this scene uses the word. Hermione never appeals to Leontes' 'justice', for all along is stressed her awareness that she and Leontes – now that time is out of joint – do not use words in the same sense: 'You speak a language that I understand not: My life stands in the level of your dreams.'

It is, I think, important to notice that it is the first actual death to happen in the play which stops the mad onrush. Previously death has been spoken of, envisaged theoretically, even planned and arranged for; but now Leontes is brought face to face with its actuality. The fact that his son is 'gone', his own issue cut off, his future in terms of the Sonnets' 'lines of life that life repair' interrupted, is what shocks Leontes into seeing in a true perspective the present and the immediate past: 'I have too much believed mine own suspicion.' Too late, this conversion and repentance. The queen is reported dead, too, and suddenly, in a deliberate contrast to what has gone before, time cannot be long enough:

> A thousand knees
> Ten thousand years together, naked, fasting,
> Upon a barren mountain, and still winter
> In storm perpetual,

could not atone for the deeds of a few hectic days of error.

This is the lowest point in the play. The sands have, as it were, rushed through the dramatic hour-glass to measure the decline in Leontes' fortune, his self-inflicted loss of wife and issue. But in the final scene of Act III the finding of the babe replaces things dying with things new-born; and so we are prepared for the visible turning of the hour-glass by 'Time, the Chorus': 'I turn my glass and give my scene such growing As you had slept between.'

If we have been aware of the insistence on, and the importance of, the time theme in the first half of the play, we are, I think, prepared to see the introduction of Father Time here as more than a mere stop-gap, a desperate attempt to tidy over the Romance breach of the unities.* He has come, at a crucial moment in the

* See the Introduction to the New Cambridge edition of the play (1931) p. xix: 'having to skip sixteen years after Act 3, he desperately

play, not merely to substitute for a programme note of something like 'Act IV: Sixteen years later',* but to provide a pivotal image, part verbal part visual, of the Triumph of Time. The last fifteen lines of his speech are indeed a *résumé* of events during the sixteen-year lapse, but they are set in the context of the first fifteen lines, where Time is presented as a principle and power: 'I, that please some, try all, both joy and terror Of good and bad, that makes and unfolds error. . . .' Far from having abandoned time-thinking, Shakespeare presses home the fact that the 'wide gap' of dramatically 'untried growth' is part of the universal process of time who 'makes and unfolds error' in his immutable onward flight. Rather than being timeless, *The Winter's Tale* is thus set in a context of *all* time.

We have seen error being made; now, it is suggested, it is to be unfolded by Time the Revealer. Of course, in a mere plot sense, error had been unfolded at the end of Act III. But truth is more than just getting the facts straight: it is not enough for Leontes to find out that he has been mistaken in his jealousy. He has to become aware of truth in a wider sense, and that can only be achieved through subjection to Time the Revealer – and through grappling with Time the Destroyer. For Time, the Chorus, reminds us of his destructive qualities, too: of his power 'To o'erthrow law and in one self-born hour To plant and o'erwhelm custom'. Above all – anticipating Prospero in his use of the very form of the work of art of which he himself is a part, as an image of transience – he reminds us that 'brightness falls from the air':

> I witness to
> The times that brought them in; so shall I do
> To the freshest things now reigning and make stale

drags in Father Time with an hour-glass. . . . Which means on interpretation that Shakespeare . . . simply did not know how to do it, save by invoking some such device.'

* I cannot agree with E. Panofsky's criticism of Father Time in this play: 'Sometimes the figure of Father Time is used as a mere device to indicate the lapse of months, years, or centuries, as in Shakespeare's *Winter's Tale*, where Time appears as Chorus before the fifth [*sic*] act' – *Studies in Iconology* (New York, 1939) p. 81.

The glistering of this present, as my tale
Now seems to it.

These lines are less haunting than Prospero's, because they are
written in a kind of pageant doggerel, and because the speaker
here is the triumphant agent, not the object; so that the element
of human nostalgia is lacking. Their effect is to establish the play's
connection with Time's triumph; and the total effect of the
choric speech is to invite a dual response to such triumph.

Needless to say, Shakespeare's audience in 1610–11 would
have been familiar with the figure of Father Time, from in-
numerable verbal and pictorial representations and from pageants
and masques.[8] Time as the Father of Truth had appeared in the
last three royal entries, and Middleton was soon going to use him
in the 1613 Lord Mayor's show, *The Triumphs of Truth*. He had
become a popular figure in the allegorical masque, because as
Revealer he could be used as an effective *deux ex machina* to solve
the central conflict and turn anti-masque into masque. Thus he
appears, for example, in the fourth of Beaumont and Fletcher's
Four Plays in One, the masque called *The Triumph of Time*: 'helping triumphantly, Helping his Master Man'. Yet, to the Elizabethan or Jacobean imagination, Time is never for long allowed
to remain a purely beneficent figure. Beaumont and Fletcher's
triumphant Time first appears 'mowing mankind down'. When
represented iconographically as the Father of Truth, he also has
his scythe and his hour-glass – an example of this is the emblem
of *Veritas temporis filia* in Whitney's *Choice of Emblemes*[9] – and
thus remains connected with transience and death. One of the
fullest catalogues of the characteristics of Time is Lucrece's
diatribe, and there we hear within one stanza that 'Time's glory'
is both 'to calm contending kings, To unmask falsehood and
bring truth to light', and 'To ruinate proud buildings with [his]
hours, And smear with dust their glittering golden towers' (*The
Rape of Lucrece*, 939–44).

Those who tried to put Father Time on the stage in his dual
significance often found themselves ending up with an unresolved
contradiction, as in Middleton's *Triumphs of Truth*, where Time,

the agent of good, suddenly and incongruously turns destructive:

TIME, standing up in TRUTH's Chariot, seeming to make an offer with his sithe to cut off the glories of the day, growing neere now to the season of rest and sleepe, his daughter TRUTH thus meekely stayes his hand.[1c]

It was easier for non-dramatic poets to combine destructive and truth-revealing Time, and perhaps the most complete fusion of the two attributes takes place when truth is seen not just as the opposite of falsehood but as, in itself, the realization of the immutable flux of time:

> When *Trewth* (*Tymes daughter*) doth owr triall touch,
> Then take the Glasse and wee shal hardly knowe,
> Owreselves therein we shalbe changed so.[11]

This is the truth connected with time in many of Shakespeare's sonnets on mutability, and indeed in the wrinkled Hermione at the end of *The Winter's Tale*. Shakespeare's choric Time is in a firm Elizabethan tradition when he insists on the multiplicity of his powers – and rather more successful than most pageant Father Times in reconciling his opposed attributes. He needs no disintegrationists or apologists for Shakespeare's 'bad poetry' to justify his appearance in the play, for he is more than a self-contained emblem: he is a concrete image[12] of the multiplicity which the play as a whole dramatizes and which is a leading theme of the second half of the play.

When Act IV opens, sixteen years of time have acted as a healer through the process of growth – natural in the case of Perdita and moral in the case of Leontes. But Leontes himself is withheld from our view till Act V, and two whole scenes precede the appearance on stage of Perdita, thus preparing our acceptance of growth and change before they are actually demonstrated. It is Camillo (just as in I i) who at the beginning of Act IV brings in the sense of time and puts the immediate action into a time perspective: 'It is fifteen years since I saw my country: . . . I desire to lay my bones there.' We are not, it should be noted, introduced at once to the positive result of the 'wide gap' – the

growth into womanhood of the child Perdita – but are first asked
to realize what the sixteen years have meant in terms of depriva-
tion for Camillo and, more importantly, of suffering for Leontes:
'that penitent . . . and reconciled king . . . whose loss of his most
precious queen and children are even now to be afresh lamented.'
This scene, then, as well as preparing for the rest of Act IV, also
forms the foundation of the whole of Act V.

The importance of the pastoral scene as an image of regeneration has often been commented on, and even seen as mythical. In
the context of the present discussion it is important that Perdita,
who is herself almost an image of time seen as natural growth,
should first appear in a world where time equals the life of nature
and the cycle of the seasons. Perdita's flower-speeches and
flower-giving become the epitome of this world. She starts in a
vein which may recall Ophelia:

> For you there's rosemary and rue; these keep
> Seeming and savour all the winter long:
> Grace and remembrance be to you both;

but while Ophelia's flowers are altogether emblematic and dis-
tributed according to the emotional significance of the situation
and the recipient, Perdita's turn out to be mainly a measure of
time and age. Polixenes at once takes her meaning thus: 'well you
fit our ages With flowers of winter'; but Perdita, whether out of
courtesy or of chronological accuracy, would assess the ages of
Polixenes and Camillo as

> the year growing ancient,
> Not yet on summer's death, nor on the birth
> Of trembling winter.

The famous discussion on Art versus Nature arises from the
'streak'd gillyvors' allegedly representing Polixenes' time of life;
and, having agreed to differ, Perdita returns to her identification
of time in nature's year with age in man, giving 'flowers Of
middle summer' to 'men of middle age' and lamenting the lack of
early spring flowers which would have typified youth, particularly Florizel. Despite their sheer lyrical beauty, these speeches

are not just decorative or just meant to create atmosphere: they not only establish a contrast between this world and the world of most of the first three Acts, but also define the contrast as being between a world where time is taken for granted as a natural progression and one where time is altogether defied.

Timeless the pastoralism in *The Winter's Tale* is not. Pastoral poets soon discovered that death and transience were in Arcadia too;[13] and the love of Florizel and Perdita in a central passage pits itself against time and change. Florizel's adoration is formulated as a desire to arrest time, to achieve permanence outside the flux of time:

> When you speak, sweet,
> I'ld have you do it ever . . .
> when you do dance, I wish you
> A wave o'the sea, that you might ever do
> Nothing but that; move still, still so.

We are reminded of Polixenes' reference, in I ii, to how he and Leontes assumed that 'there was no more behind' than to be 'boy eternal' (and indeed the joint childhood of the two kings is referred to in pastoral terms); but in Florizel's case the thinking is not naive, it is wishful, and consciously so. Both Florizel and Perdita are aware of the precariousness of their love in relation to the extra-pastoral world, and throughout the scene the audience sees the threat to it literally present, in the shape of the disguised Polixenes. Before the scene is over, Polixenes has broken up this world of natural time, as Leontes did with the one remembered at the beginning of Act I.

Up till Polixenes' intervention, this scene had presented a structural contrast with the first three Acts: long speeches – lyrical, meditative or descriptive – had set a leisurely pace, relaxed further by singing and dancing. With the King's outburst, the pursuit is on, but instead of our following the hectic activity, as we do in Acts II and III, it takes place off-stage; and we are, as Act V opens, finally brought face to face with Leontes.

In V i the emphasis is again on the past sixteen years. Time, which we know has to Perdita meant growing up in step with

nature, has to Leontes meant unceasing grief over a self-inflicted
loss. His sense of time is entirely retrospective; he looks into the
future only to lament that it does not exist to him because of

> The wrong I did myself; which was so much,
> That heirless it hath made my kingdom and
> Destroy'd the sweet'st companion that e'er man
> Bred his hopes out of.

'Heirless' and 'issueless' are thematic words in this scene, made
even more poignant (though also ironical in terms of what the
audience knows) when Florizel and Perdita arrive to emphasize
the difference between what is and what was. It is significant that
Hermione is mourned not only for her own sweetness' sake but
also as 'the sweet'st companion that e'er man Bred his hopes out
of'. Leontes has robbed himself not only of love and friendship
but also of that other means of defeating time: issue.

After the first acute reminder of loss, the arrival of the young
couple (allegedly bearing with them also the loving greetings of
Polixenes) strikes a new note in Leontes. The form of his
greeting to them – 'Welcome hither, As is the spring to the
earth' – echoes the many references to 'natural' time in the
pastoral scene, and hints at an acceptance of the possibility of
time as healing and restoring. Critics of the myth-making school
read these lines as a confirmation of the essentially mythical
nature of the play: here, they argue, is the first direct sign of the
regeneration of the King. But if we see the coming of Perdita and
Florizel into Leontes' court as altogether an archetypal situation,
then we miss some very human aspects of it which are clearly
recognized by Shakespeare. True, the pair are first of all repre-
sentatives of a second generation, of youth and innocence and
regenerative forces – and in being so, they represent to us the
beneficial effects of time. But indirectly – through other characters' reaction to her – Perdita also indicates something about
time's destructiveness. Paulina is used by Shakespeare in this
scene as a choric commentator, turning people's admiration of
Perdita into a reminder, though in a muted fashion, that time
hath a wallet at his back. Before Perdita appears, the Gentleman's

praise of her beauty provokes Paulina to a lamentation much reminiscent of some of the words of Time the Chorus, earlier in the play:

> O Hermione,
> As every present time doth boast itself
> Above a better gone, so must thy grave
> Give way to what's seen now! ...
>   'She had not been
> Nor was not to be equall'd' – thus your verse
> Flow'd with her beauty once: 'tis shrewdly ebb'd,
> To say you have seen a better ...[14]

The Gentleman's defence, as concerns Hermione, is a simple 'I have almost forgot'; and at this point it contrasts markedly with Leontes' insistence, a few lines earlier, that *he* cannot forget. But by the end of the scene, in the one possible approach to what in *Pandosto* is a fully developed and elaborated incestuous passion, Leontes himself seems to find the past dimming before the beauty of the present; and again Paulina is there to comment on the treachery:

>   not a month
> 'Fore your queen died, she was more worth such gazes
> Than what you look on now.

Perdita's return, then, becomes the occasion for several and varied insights into what time does to man. What it really means to Leontes, when her identity is known, is dramatized in the final scene; for, by letting this reunion be merely reported, Shakespeare reserves its impact to combine it with that of the ultimate reunion.

In the last scene the time themes are drawn together and acted out in a unique way. The whole scene has about it a sense of the fulness of time – pointed at the climactic moment by Paulina's ' 'Tis time; descend' – of stillness and solemnity. Speeches are short, the diction plain, the language almost bare of imagery: as if Shakespeare is anxious not to distract attention from the significance of action and movement. Characters' reactions to the statue are patterned in a fashion which approaches ritual. An unusual number of speeches are devoted just to underlining the emotions and postures of people on-stage, as in Paulina's words to Leontes: 'I like your silence, it the more shows off Your wonder'; or in Leontes' to the statue:

> O royal piece,
> There's magic in thy majesty, which has
> My evils conjured to remembrance and
> From thy admiring daughter took the spirits,
> Standing like stone with thee.

Verbal repetitions in the first three Acts imaged Leontes' obsession and frenzied hurry, as in the 'nothing' speech; here they give the effect of ritual:

> What can you make her do
> I am content to look on, what to speak,
> I am content to hear.

When the statue comes alive, it is as though we were witnessing the central movement of a masque, with music as accompaniment, Paulina as the presenter and Hermione as the main 'device'. Paulina's commands –

> Music, awake her; strike!
> 'Tis time; descend; be stone no more; approach;
> Strike all that look upon with marvel –

are in tone and phrasing very like a presenter's call for the chief figure of the masque to appear.[15]

Into this ritual and revelation Shakespeare has woven the various time-concerns of the play so closely that the scene can be said, in the widest sense, to represent a Triumph of Time. In the widest sense only, for at this stage in the play the simple identification of time as either Revealer or Destroyer has been obliterated. At first the statue seems to bring back the past so vividly that time itself is obliterated:

> O, thus she stood,
> Even with such life of majesty, warm life,
> As now it coldly stands, when first I woo'd her!

As on another, fatal, occasion Leontes harks back to his courtship. But the past is present with a difference, for Leontes'
reaction also is: 'Hermione was not so much wrinkled, nothing
So aged as this seems'; to which Paulina replies:

> So much the more our carver's excellence;
> Which lets go by some sixteen years and makes her
> As she lived now.

The intervening time has meant physical decay, symbolized as in
the Sonnets, by 'necessary wrinkles'. As the sense of the distance
between now and sixteen years ago sharpens in Leontes, it again
becomes identified with guilt and penance: he speaks of how the
statue conjures his evils to remembrance, and Camillo recalls the
sorrow 'Which sixteen winters cannot blow away, So many
summers dry'.

But the statue comes alive. Paulina's words suggest that Hermione's return is a kind of resurrection:

> Come
> I'll fill your grave up: stir, nay, come away,
> Bequeath to death your numbness, for from him
> Dear life redeems you;

and so it is, of course, to Leontes. As he stands there with Hermione and Perdita, many of the Sonnets' resolutions are fused
into one dramatic situation. Leontes has defeated time in that his
lines of life are stretching into the future. Not only is Perdita
restored, but she is in love and about to be married and is herself
the potential mother of future generations. Hermione's return
represents another form of victory over time; she is a living
proof that 'Love's not Time's fool, though rosy lips and cheeks
Within his bending sickle's compass come' (Sonnet cxvi). These
sonnet lines could perhaps also paraphrase the truth that time has
finally revealed to Leontes: paradoxically, time has at last in its
triumph brought about its own defeat. This does not efface the
human suffering that has gone before, however, and that weighs so
heavily on the play right till the very end. Rather than a myth of

immortality, then, this play is a probing into the human condition, and – as a whole as well as in details – it looks at what time means and does to man.

It would, needless to say, be wrong to think of *The Winter's Tale* as a treatise on time. The play does not state or prove anything. But through its action, its structure and its poetry, it communicates a constant awareness of the powers of time. Shakespeare, had his small Latin allowed, might well have substituted for the motto of *Pandosto* the words of St Augustine, 'Quid est ... tempus? si nemo ex me quaerat, scio; si quaerenti explicare velim, nescio'.[16]

NOTES

1. J. M. Nosworthy, New Arden ed. of *Cymbeline* (1955), Introduction, p. lxiii.

2. G. Wilson Knight, *The Crown of Life* (1947) p. 30.

3. All quotations are taken from the Globe edition of *The Works of Shakespeare*, ed. W. G. Glark, J. Glover, and W. A. Wright (1866).

4. *The Tryumphes of Fraunces Petrarcke, translated out of Italian into English by Henrye Parker knyght, Lorde Morley* (1565?) fo. M2^r.

5. Greene's *Pandosto*, ed. P. G. Thomas (1907) p. xxiii.

6. *The Winter's Tale: a Study* (1947) pp. 47 ff.

7. For a discussion of this association, see S. C. Chew, *The Virtues Reconciled* (Toronto, 1947) pp. 90 ff. An example of the close connection of Time and Justice can be seen in the last of Beaumont and Fletcher's *Four Plays in One*, the masque-play called *The Triumph of Time*. The central Everyman character here abandons false friends, to turn to Time and Justice. The function of Time in this piece is to set things right by unmasking falsehood.

8. For examples of these, see, e.g., S. C. Chew 'Time and Fortune', in *Journal of English Literary History*, VI (1939) 83–113; F. Saxl, 'Veritas Filia Temporis', in *Philosophy and History; Essays presented to Ernst Cassirer*, ed. R. Klibansky and H. J. Paton (1936) pp. 203 ff; Rudolf Wittkower, 'Chance, Time and Virtue', in *Journal of the Warburg Institute*, I (1937–8) 313–21, and D. J. Gordon, 'Veritas Filia Temporis: Hadrianus Junius and Geoffrey Whitney', in *Journal of the Warburg and Courtauld Institutes*, III (1939–40) 228–40.

9. Plate 34b.

10. J. Nichols, *Progresses of James I* (1828) II 695.

11. George Gascoigne, *The Grief of Joye*, ed. J. W. Cunliffe (1910) st LII 5–7.

12. Unfortunately in productions of *The Winter's Tale* Father Time often looks like some kind of wizard. The most successful Time I have seen was in a Munich performance in 1959, when he was acted by an octogenarian with little make-up and no paraphernalia other than an hour-glass.

13. See E. Panofsky, 'Et in Arcadia Ego', in *Philosophy and History*.

14. Cf. the Chorus lines, 'so shall I do To the freshest things now reigning and make stale The glistering of this present.'

15. Cf., to take just one example, the call for Neptune in the masque in *The Maid's Tragedy*, I i, ed. A. R. Waller and A. Glover (1905) p. 10. Various critics – e.g. Alice Venezky, *Pageantry on the Shakespearean Stage* (New York, 1951) p. 128, and T. M. Parrott, *Shakespearean Comedy* (London and New York, 1949) p. 386 – have suggested that the statue which comes alive is an adaptation of a masque-device; but I have never seen it pointed out that in fact no masque-writer had used this device before *The Winter's Tale* was first performed. Soon after *The Winter's Tale*, however, both Campion and Beaumont in their respective masques for the Princess Elizabeth's wedding made use of statues coming alive. Campion's main masque consists of eight women statues, which come to life, four at a time; but in Beaumont's masque the 'statuas' are relegated to the first anti-masque; a variation on the theme is needed by now, and so, 'having but half life put into them, and retaining still somewhat of their old nature', they give 'fit occasion to new and strange varieties both in the music and paces'. It was obviously statues used in this fashion that Bacon had in mind when in his essay 'Of Masques and Triumphs' he placed 'statuas' among the baboons, fools and other grotesques of the anti-masque. (*A Harmony of the Essays*, ed. E. Arber (1871) pp. 539–40. The essay first appeared in the 1625 edition.) It might be noted that the Beaumont masque referred to was in fact 'ordered and furnished' by Bacon.

16. *Confessions*, II 14.

S. L. Bethell

ANTIQUATED TECHNIQUE AND THE PLANES OF REALITY (1947)

IT would seem that Shakespeare's artistic judgment served him well in choosing an ancient and naïve story to carry the burden of his deepest thought, but the question still remains: Why is his dramatic technique crude and apparently incoherent? The technique of *The Winter's Tale* is commonly regarded as deficient on a number of counts. First there is that awkward gap of sixteen years between the two parts of the play. This we may justify as providing necessary material for the complex statement about time; it must have been deliberate, for *The Tempest* seems deliberately and mockingly to repudiate the suggestion that Shakespeare was incapable of preserving the unities when he wanted to. The introduction of new characters half-way through the play and the abandoning of the principal character for so long a time are faults in construction only if the play is to be regarded as primarily psychological, a study in the development of character. To begin with a preconceived notion of the nature of a play and criticize any failure to fulfil its requirements is surely apriorism of the wrong kind; the fact that Shakespeare does treat characters somewhat cavalierly must be taken as an indication that he has other dramatic fish to fry. This would explain the notoriously unmotivated jealousy of Leontes (though I shall suggest that it has a further significance), the casual disposal of Antigonus (*Exit, pursued by a bear*) and the rather tenuous characterisation of every one save Leontes in his jealousy.

The stagecraft is justifiably described as crude or naïve. We have the frequently remarked *Exit, pursued by a bear*, and there is a patch of astonishingly awkward management towards the end of Act IV, Scene iv, beginning at the point where Camillo ques-

tions Florizel and learns that he is determined to 'put to sea' with
Perdita (IV iv 509). Then we have:

> *Flo.*   Hark, Perdita (*drawing her aside*).
> (*To Camillo*) I'll hear you by and by.
> *Cam.*   He's irremoveable,
> Resolved for flight. Now were I happy, if
> His going I could frame to serve my turn.   (IV iv 517)

The conversation of Florizel and Perdita is required only to
cover Camillo's explanation of his motives and this explanation
is given to the audience in soliloquy, with more than a tinge of
direct address.[1] A little later the device is repeated; Camillo has
disclosed his plan and ends:

> For instance, sir,
> That you may know you shall not want, one word.
>   (*They talk aside.*)
> (*Re-enter Autolycus.*)
> *Aut.* Ha, ha! what a fool Honesty is!
>   etc.   (IV iv 604)

At the end of his speech we have another stage direction:
Camillo, Florizel, and Perdita come forward. There is no natural
occasion for this 'talk aside', since all three are engaged in it; its
only purpose is to allow Autolycus his direct address to the
audience on the gullibility of rustics. Worst of all is the device to
allow Camillo a last explanation to the audience in an aside.
Florizel exclaims:

> O Perdita, what have we twain forgot!
> Pray you, a word. (*They converse apart.*)
>   (IV iv 674)

We never hear what they have forgot, but Camillo steps forward
with

> What I do next, shall be to tell the king
> Of this escape . . .   (IV iv 676)

Florizel, Perdita and Camillo then go off, Autolycus has more
direct address to the audience and then we have his meeting with

Shepherd and Clown, in which the dialogue is liberally be-
spattered with asides. In the end Autolycus sends the others
ahead of him to the seaside:

> Walk before toward the sea-side; go on the right hand: I will
> but look upon the hedge and follow you.   (IV iv 855)

Shepherd and Clown go, conversing in asides about Autolycus,
and Autolycus remains to tell the audience his future plans.

I do not think anybody has tried to avoid the difficulty raised
here by calling in the usual hack assistant said to have been
responsible for Posthumus' dream in *Cymbeline* and other such
passages where it is supposed that Shakespeare has nodded – the
dialogue is too clearly Shakespearean for that. Now it is hard to
believe that Shakespeare – even if tired, bored, cynical, in
despair and dead drunk at the time – could repeat a crudely
amateur device like this 'talking aside' or 'walking before' four
times in a few minutes and not intend something by it. Before the
end of the scene it has become laughable, and the laugh is in-
creased by the reason Autolycus gives for sending the others
ahead (i.e., the necessity of relieving himself); surely this is a
deliberately comic underlining of a deliberately crude technique.
Considering now the play as a whole, are we not justified in
suspecting a quite conscious return to naïve and outmoded
technique, a deliberate creaking of the dramatic machinery? Are
there not clear indications that it is an imitation naïveté after all?[2]
Exit, pursued by a bear! How commentators have laughed at the
slumbering Shakespeare, without noticing the comedy of Antigonus' vision, in which the eyes of the supposed dead Hermione
'became two spouts' (III iii 26) in the manner of an earlier
rhetoric, and without gauging the significance of the 'gentleman'
on whom the bear had not yet half dined (III iii 108)! Perhaps we
cannot claim as an old device the conventional impenetrability of
disguise by reason of which Polixenes and Camillo move un-
recognised among the shepherds; so useful a convention had long
life on the stage. Autolycus, however, is an interesting dramatic
throw-back. He is on terms of peculiar intimacy with the
audience and so resembles the Vice of the interludes and Shake-

speare's early clowns such as Launce and Lancelot Gobbo. At his first appearance he gives a summary history of himself:

I have served Prince Florizel and in my time wore three-pile; but now I am out of service...
My traffic is sheets; when the kite builds, look to lesser linen. My father named me Autolycus; who being, as I am, littered under Mercury, was likewise a snapper-up of unconsidered trifles. With die and drab I purchased this caparison, and my revenue is the silly cheat. Gallows and knock are too powerful on the highway: beating and hanging are terrors to me: for the life to come, I sleep out the thought of it.   (IV iii 13)

This is far away from even a modified naturalism; not only is it addressed directly to the audience but a person such as Autolycus would never in reality achieve such neat and objective self-description. If, for instance, he 'sleeps out the thought' of the life to come, then he would hardly mention it; religious categories would not be in the forefront of his mind. From 'my traffic is in sheets' the speech, in effect, constitutes a 'character of a rogue' in the Theophrastan manner which had become popular, a description of a type in terms of seventeenth-century wit. It is in fact an admirable example of the blend of narrative and the representational, in which the character, as it were, tells his own story to the audience – a convention inherited from the medieval miracle plays.

Why, then, did Shakespeare return so late in his career to this old-fashioned stage technique? I have already indicated internal evidence which suggests that the return was deliberate and this is confirmed by the fact that *The Winter's Tale* does not stand alone in respect of 'technical crudity'. Among a great many other instances we have 'Gower, as Chorus' in *Pericles* and Posthumus' dream in *Cymbeline*, both which Shakespeare permitted, whether he wrote them himself or not. *The Tempest* presents a different technique but with the same suggestion of inefficiency; we have a positive flaunting of the unities, yet coupled with the mildly comic tedium of Prospero's long narrative to the drowsily obedient Miranda. Even to preserve the unities Shakespeare need

not have been so tedious – nor underlined the tedium by
Miranda's apparent inattention, Prospero's protests and her
assurances:

> *Pr.*   Thou attend'st not.
> *Mir.* O, good sir, I do.   (I ii 87)

Prospero the bore has left little for Prospero the magician to perform, for though he sends her magically to sleep he admits she is
already 'inclined' to it (I ii 185). I imagine that Shakespeare's
intention was to show that he could preserve the dramatic unities,
about which there was so much critical cant, and at the same time
mildly to burlesque the extended narrative of past events which
this classical technique required.[3] What is more significant is that
he thus draws attention to the play as play by obtruding matters
of technique upon the audience, and I believe that in the previous
romances the function of the old-fashioned technique is precisely
the same. If this should seem unlikely, we may remember that as
early as *Hamlet* Shakespeare had used a burlesque of the older
dramatists' style to distinguish the 'Mousetrap' from the dialogue
of the main play. An audience in 1611 would react to some aspects
of *The Winter's Tale* (Antigonus' vision, his '*Exit, pursued by a
bear*' and the other examples I have mentioned) pretty much as a
modern theatre audience reacts to a burlesque revival of *Maria
Martin* or *East Lynne*.

By deliberately drawing the audience's attention to technique
Shakespeare was able to distance his story and to convey a
continual reminder that his play was after all only a play. The
dialogue itself reinforces the duality of play world and real
world, as frequently in other plays of Shakespeare; there is no
need to believe this to have been deliberate, though the reminders
here seem specially insistent. Time the Chorus is aware that his
tale must seem stale to 'the glistering of this present' (IV i 14), but
this is almost a reminder from without. Within the tale itself,
Mamillius would tell a story:

> A sad tale's best for winter: I have one
> Of sprites and goblins.   (II i 25)

There is a winter's tale within *The Winter's Tale*, recalling the play's title and reminding the audience that it is a play and not reality which confronts them. The 'peripeteia' and 'discoveries' of the last act produce significant comment: 'this news which is called true is so like *an old tale* that the verity of it is in strong suspicion' (v ii 29), says the Second Gentleman. Later we have:

> *Second Gent.* What, pray you, became of Antigonus, that carried hence the child?
> *Third Gent.* Like *an old tale* still, which will have matter to rehearse, though credit be asleep and not an ear open. He was torn to pieces with a bear.   (v ii 64)

(For the soporific effect of an old tale we may compare Miranda as she suffers Prospero's long narrative.) The tone here is very delicate; there is an oblique apology for being tedious, and there is also a reminder – once again – of the play as play. Finally, in the last scene, where the 'coming to life' of the supposed statue of Hermione is markedly theatrical (it has further significance, how-ever, in addition to its function as 'obvious' technique), Paulina says:

> That she is living,
> Were it but told you, should be hooted at
> Like *an old tale*: but it appears she lives,
> Though yet she speak not.   (v iii 115)

Such internal comments upon the nature of a story always remind us of its unreality, breaking through any illusion which may have been created. Thus they combine with the deliberately old-fashioned technique to insist that it is after all only a dramatic performance that the audience have before them.

There are, I believe, a number of interlocking reasons for the unusually careful distancing of the play. I am not prepared to say how many of them may have been consciously in Shakespeare's mind as he wrote. He must have been aware that he was using old-fashioned technique, but it may be that all he intended was a pot-pourri entertainment including burlesque of the older drama. He seems always to have written for the more intelligent members of his audience and perhaps neither he nor they took

the new craze for romances very seriously; he may have set out
to produce a 'highbrow' comic version of the Beaumont and
Fletcher popular success – if Beaumont and Fletcher had had
enough successes at this time to have attracted his notice. Perhaps
he even deliberately designed that this light entertainment should
be at the same time profoundly serious, a poetic vehicle for
philosophical and religious truth. I want to make quite clear
that all this is highly speculative and is not my concern. A
dramatist or any other kind of artist may express meanings of
which he is himself only dimly aware and his methods may be
dictated by an end which he is not consciously seeking; the real
reason for his doing this or that can be discerned only when the
work is finished and understood. I do not know what Shakespeare deliberately intended in this play; no one can ever know
and the question is not important. What I am attempting to
show is what in fact he did and how he did it – the perhaps
unconscious reasons which led him to use one type of technique
and reject another.

First, then, there is the nature of the story; 'an old tale' may
have its antiquity pressed home by the employment of an outmoded technique. There are two ways of dealing with historical
material: one is to make it as realistic as possible by presenting it
in precisely the same way as one would material from contemporary sources, and the other is to emphasize its remoteness
by adopting a certain archaism in the means of presentation.
Some historical novelists, for example, write in a modern style,
while others prefer to suggest 'period' by an approximation to
the language of an earlier age – not necessarily the age they are
depicting. Shakespeare's is a double achievement: he suggests
antiquity by the methods I have just discussed, and suggests
contemporaneity of interest through the verse. Secondly, this
distancing indicates the sort of attention that the play demands.
Shakespeare had always required close attention to the verse and
the themes which it expressed; he had continually exploited the
conventions of the theatre so as to reinforce in his audience an
alert dual consciousness of play world and real world. Nevertheless, with the tragedies it must have been difficult on first seeing

them not to become wholly absorbed in character and action.
Now, by exaggerated conventions and constant reminders of the
play as play, he virtually forbids this sort of absorption; it is 'an
old tale', remote from modern concerns; it is a play almost
mockingly presented as a play, with the stage machinery
innocently visible. We find it hard to become absorbed in
characters which are dropped for a whole act at a time or which
only appear half-way through the performance, and especially
hard to become concerned over their fate when we may be called
upon to laugh at an untimely end, as with the gentleman on
whom the bear had not half dined. The course of events is too
casually unfolded, with too many interruptions and asides, for a
breathless anxiety such as we tend to feel over *Othello*. We are,
in fact, quite firmly warned to seek our pleasure elsewhere; we are
compelled to attend to the verse, to seek for 'inner meanings', to
observe the subtle interplay of a whole world of interrelated
ideas. Thirdly, as in the treatment of time, this is not only a
means of commanding a special sort of attention but is also in
itself a statement about the nature of reality.

Dr Tillyard in *Shakespeare's Last Plays* uses the phrase
'planes of reality' to describe the difference between the dream
world of Leontes' jealousy, the religious world of the reported
visit to the oracle and of the 'statue' scene, the melodramatic
vision of Antigonus and the earthy comedy of the rustics.
Before discussing this aspect of the play I should like to point out
the various planes of reality revealed in relation to the contrast
of play world and real world – a matter which Dr Tillyard comments on all too briefly in dealing with *The Tempest* but omits
from his treatment of *The Winter's Tale*. This is a subject which
must have been constantly in Shakespeare's mind and which
receives its fullest and final statement in Prospero's famous
speech, 'Our revels now are ended', after the performance of the
Masque of Ceres (*The Tempest*, IV i 148). 'On the actual stage',
says Dr Tillyard, 'the masque is executed by players pretending
to be spirits, pretending to be real actors, pretending to be supposed goddesses and rustics.' Prospero's speech then sees the
whole creation as a fading pageant (akin to the dream world –

another 'plane') and only the eternal remains as the truly real.
In *The Winter's Tale*, if there is nothing to equal Prospero's
poetic statement, there is a sufficiently complex presentation of
the planes of reality. The audience watch a dramatic performance
of an old tale whose events take place in the unreal world of
romance yet are related by literary means to their own real
world. Within the play itself characters speak of the old tale as
being 'like an old tale', which is both a reminder of the tale as just
a tale and also the opening up of a new degree of remoteness;
characters in an old tale speaking of an old tale carry a suggestion
of infinite regression. Again, there is Mamillius' reference to 'a
sad tale' which is 'best for winter' (II i 25) and he even begins this
tale within a tale: 'There was a man . . . Dwelt by a churchyard'
(II i 29) – a man suspiciously like the later Leontes. Yet again we
have examples of Shakespeare's usual stage metaphor – the plane
of thought:

> Go, play, boy, play: thy mother plays, and I
> Play too, but so disgraced a part, whose issue
> Will hiss me to my grave.   (I ii 187)

> Methinks I play as I have seen them do
> In Whitsun pastorals: sure this robe of mine
> Does change my disposition.   (IV iv 133)

> . . . it shall be so my care
> To have you royally appointed as if
> The scene you play were mine.   (IV iv 602)

> I see the play so lies
> That I must bear a part.   (IV iv 669)

> No more such wives; therefore, no wife: one worse,
> And better used, would make her sainted spirit
> Again possess her corpse, and on this stage,
> Where we're offenders now, appear soul-vex'd,
> And begin, 'Why to me?'   (V i 56)

This last is the familiar Shakespearean identification of this world
with a stage, a metaphor carrying the suggestion of a solider

reality behind the visible world. Perdita's half-bewildered remark:

> ... sure this robe of mine
>   Does change my disposition,

is interesting, especially in view of the Elizabethan convention by which disguise may alter the nature of the disguised stage-personage – a convention of which a shadowy trace may remain in Autolycus' complete change of personality with his change of garments, from pedlar-rogue to upstart courtier, though this can in fact be explained purely in terms of character criticism. We may further note that Perdita for the sheep-shearing feast is acting queen – a sort of May Queen – as for the 'Whitsun pastorals'; we have thus a characteristically Shakespearean complication, for which the formula would be 'boy acting girl who is a princess supposed to be a shepherdess acting as make-believe princess'. The elaborate interconnection of planes of reality here and throughout the play reveals Shakespeare's interest in this further metaphysical problem which is related to the problem of time. In *The Winter's Tale* the two problems intersect and it is Time the Chorus who completes the statement of relationship between the various planes (though the statement is not really complete until Prospero's great speech in *The Tempest*) by showing the relativity even of that plane upon which the audience find themselves; their fixed point disappears and they are made to look back upon themselves from the remote future as upon people in an old tale. It is necessary to be beyond time in order to be beyond the possibility of illusion.

As we have said, Dr Tillyard uses the same term, 'planes of reality', to cover shifts in the writer's presentation of his subject. *The Winter's Tale* is remarkable for the subtlety of these adjustments and they are best considered now, since they are not unrelated to the planes of reality I have just discussed and are sometimes mediated by the seemingly crude dramatic technique which in this connection gains further significance. In the first brief scene Camillo and Archidamus discuss the friendship of the two kings; and the 'unspeakable comfort' (1 i 37) which the country of Sicilia has in Mamillius, the young heir. Mamillius, says Camillo, 'physics the subject, makes old hearts fresh: they that went on crutches ere he was born desire yet their life to see him a man'. The dialogue continues:

> *Arch.* Would they else be content to die?
> *Cam.* Yes; if there were no other excuse why they should desire to live.
> *Arch.* If the king had no son, they would desire to live on crutches till he had one.   (I i 46)

This is quite typical, a quietly humorous statement of the ambiguity of human motives; the general devotion to Mamillius is real enough but not more real than the general devotion to a continued existence even upon crutches. From the beginning seriousness is blent with 'wit' in the seventeenth-century sense – 'tough reasonableness', as Mr Eliot has described it in an essay on Marvell. In the next scene jealousy descends suddenly upon Leontes and he is isolated in a dream world of his own projection; yet it is a dream which can be potent for evil in the real world. Hermione in her clear-eyed virtue sums up the position at her trial:

> My life stands in the level of your dreams,
> Which I'll lay down.   (III ii 82)

Meanwhile Leontes within his dream regards himself as aware of the real situation, though others similarly placed may remain in ignorance:

> ... many thousand on's
> Have the disease, and feel't not;   (I ii 206)

and

> There may be in the cup
> A spider steep'd, and one may drink, depart,
> And yet partake no venom, for his knowledge
> Is not infected; but if one present
> The abhorr'd ingredient to his eye, make known
> How he hath drunk, he cracks his gorge, his sides,
> With violent hefts. I have drunk, and seen the spider.
>   (II i 39)

Here is another problem concerning the nature of reality; ignorance may be bliss and mistaken belief may carry all the horrible consequences of objective ill. While Leontes believes Hermione guilty, his belief brings about the same consequences as if it were the truth; had she been guilty and he not known it, their married life would not have been jeopardized. Yet there *is* an objective truth – Shakespeare is no psychological relativist; Leontes is dreaming and truth will out, for the divine oracle will declare it.

Paulina is an interesting character with something of a 'morality' flavour; she symbolizes conscience, always at Leontes' shoulder to prompt him to right conduct. Yet she is a scold, presented as a comic figure, for the conscience in its nagging persistence can be both comic and serious at the same time. The third scene of Act II has some remarkable variations in tone. It begins with the jealous Leontes and in a vein of high seriousness:

> Nor night nor day no rest: it is but weakness
> To bear the matter thus . . .
> . . . say that she were gone,
> Given to the fire, a moiety of my rest
> Might come to me again. (II iii 1)

Paulina intrudes upon him against the will of Antigonus, her husband. She brings with her the newly born girl-child whom Leontes is determined to regard as bastard. Leontes exclaims:

> How!
> Away with that audacious lady! Antigonus,
> I charged thee that she should not come about me:
> I knew she would. (II iii 41)

There is both comedy and pathos in the last four words. Then follows a three-cornered dialogue upon Antigonus' inability to rule his wife. The tone is lightened. Paulina next breaks out into accusation of Leontes and presents the child as his; he orders her to be put out of the room, but apparently no one moves, for Leontes cries:

> Traitors!
> Will you not push her out? (II iii 72)

and turns on Antigonus, jeering at him as

> ... woman-tired, unroosted
> By thy dame Partlet here.   (II iii 74)

Paulina speaks again; then Leontes: 'He dreads his wife' (II iii 79); then Paulina again; then Leontes: 'A nest of traitors!' (II iii 81). Antigonus and Paulina both speak up to repudiate the charge. Then Leontes exclaims against Paulina:

> A callat
> Of boundless tongue, who late hath beat her husband
> And now baits me!   (II iii 90)

The verse may be the verse of Leontes jealous but, in view of what has gone before, the pun ('beat', 'bait') suggests a further note of comedy. Yet he goes on to assert:

> This brat is none of mine;
> It is the issue of Polixenes:
> Hence with it, and together with the dam
> Commit them to the fire!   (II iii 92)

His jealous fury by this bold juxtaposition is shown as itself essentially comic. Paulina vehemently maintains the legitimacy of the child, pointing out its resemblance to Leontes, but her speech ends with a joke, unconscious on Paulina's part but surely not on Shakespeare's: she prays that Nature may not reproduce in the infant her father's jealousy:

> ... lest she suspect, as he does,
> Her children not her husband's.   (II iii 107)

Malone comments solemnly on this passage: 'No suspicion that the babe in question might entertain of her future husband's fidelity could affect the legitimacy of her offspring'. He thinks that Shakespeare 'in the ardour of composition' has 'forgotten the difference of sexes' – which seems rather unlikely. It is, of course, the commentators who are at fault; their critical apriorism cannot accept the close interweaving of comedy and tragedy which is so important an element in the play. The slanging match

continues, with more hard words about Antigonus' inability to
control his wife:

> *Leon.*   A gross hag!
>   And, lozel, thou art worthy to be hang'd,
>   That wilt not stay her tongue.
> *Ant.*   Hang all the husbands
>   That cannot do that feat, you'll leave yourself
>   Hardly one subject.   (II iii 108)

This is the perennial joke and the scene has reached something
like a music-hall level of seriousness. Paulina has the last word
and *exit*; Leontes turns to Antigonus again: 'Thou, traitor, hast
set on thy wife to this . . .' (II iii 131). Antigonus speaks up, and
the broil becomes general:

> *Ant.*   I did not, sir:
>   These lords, my noble fellows, if they please,
>   Can clear me in't.
> *Lords*   We can: my royal liege,
>   He is not guilty of her coming hither.
> *Leon.* You're liars all.   (II iii 141)

Leontes the tyrant has been shrewdly dealt with; as he says of
Paulina:

> > Were I a tyrant,
>   Where were her life?   (II iii 122)

He recovers rapidly, however, and his disposal of the child is
again quite serious in tone:

> > As by strange fortune
>   It came to us, I do in justice charge thee,
>   On thy soul's peril and thy body's torture,
>   That thou commend it strangely to some place
>   Where chance may nurse or end it. Take it up.
>   (II iii 179)

This is firm, dignified and solemn, without the contorted
jealousy rhythms and with no undercurrent of comedy. The
scene ends, still quite seriously, with a report of the approach of
Cleomenes and Dion newly returned from the oracle of Delphos.

The language associated with the oracle in the short scene which begins Act III introduces another plane of reality, the supernatural order, which also dominates the last scene of the play. Antigonus' vision suggests yet a further plane. It is distinguished from the play world around it by the employment of an old-fashioned rhetoric, so that the description of the vision suggests something theatrical and crude:

> . . . she did approach
> My cabin where I lay; thrice bow'd before me,
> And gasping to begin some speech, her eyes
> Became two spouts.   (III iii 23)

The ambiguity of the world of vision is stressed, for this is either a false vision (cf. Macbeth's 'fiend That lies like truth' (v v 43)) or else wrongly interpreted by Antigonus, who takes it to mean that 'Hermione hath suffer'd death' (III iii 42). Orthodox Christianity has always insisted on 'testing the spirits'; private visions must be tested by their congruency with divine revelation as interpreted by the Church. A vision might be (*a*) an objective presence, (*b*) subjective but sent from without, or (*c*) purely a projection and hallucinatory; if objective it might be angelic or diabolic or a soul out of purgatory, and if subjective but *ab extra* it might be sent by good or evil agency. In *Hamlet* and *Macbeth* Shakespeare had shown his interest in the subject, which was much debated in Elizabethan times. Antigonus' vision is apropos in further complicating the planes of reality both through its comic tone and its theological ambiguity. No doubt the audience would incline to Antigonus' interpretation, except for the extreme protestants, who did not believe it possible for the dead to return to their former haunts, since they disbelieved in an 'intermediate state', and who were not the type to indulge in a 'willing suspension of disbelief' – but most probably they were not the type to attend the theatre at all. At the end of the play, however, if they carried their minds back to this ambiguous point, the audience would necessarily modify their opinion. The vision could then be regarded as angelic, since its directions for the disposal of Perdita were providentially effective, or as diabolic, since it led to the death of Antigonus and his company, Perdita alone escaping through her childhood innocence over which the devil could have no power. Not that an audience would reason so clearly upon the matter, but their reactions would proceed against some such background of thought. The immediate dramatic purpose is, no doubt, to confirm the belief in Hermione's death and increase the effect of the *dénouement*, but the theological involvement adds to a general impression of the inadequacy of the human mind before the complex pattern of reality. We must not forget the note of burlesque; we are not to attach too much importance to the vision or to our speculations upon it – the great mystics are also sceptical about such visionary experiences.

Antigonus is summarily dismissed, 'pursued by a bear', and the most remarkable *volte-face* in the play – or perhaps in the whole of Shakespeare – now takes place. Certainly, as Dr Till-yard says, the melodramatic vision has prepared the way by dissolving the reality of Antigonus, but it is none the less remarkable to find ourselves suddenly translated to the earthy comedy of the Bohemian rustics where Antigonus, whom we have followed with a degree of sympathy, becomes a gentleman on whom the bear has not half dined. The lost ship and its crew are similarly treated and the tempest, which Professor Wilson Knight has shown to be a constant symbol of tragedy in Shake-speare, suffers a comic transvaluation.

I would you did but see how it chafes, how it rages, how it takes up the shore! but that's not to the point. O, the most piteous cry of the pour souls! sometimes to see 'em, and not to see 'em; now the ship boring the moon with her main-mast, and anon swallowed with yest and froth, as you'ld thrust a cork into a hogshead. And then for the land-service, to see how the bear tore out his shoulder-bone; how he cried to me for help and said his name was Antigonus, a nobleman. But to make an end of the ship, to see how the sea flap-dragoned it: but, first, how the poor souls roared, and the sea mocked them; and how the poor gentle-man roared and the bear mocked him, both roaring louder than the sea or weather.   (III iii 89)

There is an interesting variety within this one speech. The

tempest is at first tragic enough as it chafes and rages, the cry of the poor souls is piteous, the ship is carried to heaven, 'boring the moon with her main-mast'. Then comes a note of bathos; the tempest is compared to frothing liquor as a barrel is corked; it becomes familiar, friendly, and rather ridiculous; and from this point the sufferings of the sailors and of Antigonus are seen as trivial (the jesting 'land-service' marks the change); the sea and the bear become familiar monsters and the poor souls and the gentleman perish to the audience's laughter. This carries further the grotesque humour of Gloucester's attempted suicide in *King Lear*. There the apparent danger was purely imaginary – a parabolic suggestion that our human fears are needless, since we are in the hands of 'the clearest gods' (IV vi 73). Here the same attitude is more directly presented. Subjectively, we are shown how much depends on point of view; how the tragic becomes comic, as later the comic becomes almost tragic in the old Shepherd's lament:

> You have undone a man of fourscore three,
> That thought to fill his grave in quiet ... (IV iv 464)

Objectively, we are rendered suspicious of tragedy; *sub specie æternitatis* this being swallowed by the sea or by a bear may not be the dreadful matter we imagine it. Our silly pretensions distort the perspective; Antigonus, seized by a bear, cries out that he is a nobleman and the Clown refers to him punctiliously as 'the gentleman'. Gentlemen usually dine upon animals but now the bear will dine on the gentleman – an unusual version of 'Death the leveller'.

The general viewpoint of the scene is comic but there is a subtle mixture of attitudes, not only regarding the tragic tempest but regarding the comic rustics as well. Partly they are the stock stage types, a hitting-off of rustic simplicity, but there is a traditional rustic wisdom displayed by the Shepherd – Mr Eliot's 'uncynical disillusion':

> I would there were no age between sixteen and three-and-twenty, or that youth would sleep out the rest; for there is

nothing in the between but getting wenches with child, wronging
the ancientry, stealing, fighting ... (III iii 59)

And it is in the midst of such stuff as composes this scene that
Shakespeare is content to place a sentence central to the significance of the whole play: 'Now bless thyself: thou mettest with
things dying, I with things new-born' (III iii 116) – 'bless thyself', make the sign of the Cross, for it is through the Cross that
things dying are born again.

The sheep-shearing feast curiously blends the Florizel-
Perdita romance, the two generations of rustics, and Autolycus.
As Professor Dover Wilson has pointed out, Florizel and Perdita
are distinguished from the rustics by their costume. Perdita has
on her 'May Queen' robes and Florizel's 'swain's wearing' is rich
enough to transform Autolycus later into a 'courtier cap-a-pe'
(IV iv 761). Perhaps there is a hint here at the difference between
literary pastoral and genuine rusticity, as in the earlier contrast
between Silvius and Phebe and William and Audrey. Although
their romance has an element of tough realism, as we shall see
later, there is also a touch of comedy in the dialogue itself which
is perhaps critical of the false high seriousness of fashionable
Arcadia. In *Pandosto* Greene's Prince Dorastus has a speech on
the metamorphoses of the gods: 'The heavenly gods have sometime earthly thoughts. Neptune became a ram, Jupiter a bull,
Apollo a shepherd: they gods and yet in love...'[4] It has
often been noted that Shakespeare borrows the speech but
no one has commented on the significant changes in Florizel's
version:

> Jupiter
> Became a bull, and bellow'd; the green Neptune
> A ram, and bleated ... (IV iv 27)

'Bellow'd' and 'bleated' have a comic and satiric force reflecting
unfavourably upon the pagan deities which were treated so
seriously in contemporary pastoral.

The sheep-shearing feast is followed immediately by theatrical
plans for escape and Autolycus' satire on the court. In the fifth
act the first scene sustains the serio-comic tension in Paulina and

the second scene recounts at second hand in a burlesque version of court jargon the all-important discovery of Perdita's true identity, her restoration to Leontes and the meeting of the two kings in reconciliation. This not only saves the climax for the last scene but in itself adds another plane of reality: 'news', 'gossip', inevitably distorted in transmission. The last scene, theatrically posed, has the religious tone associated previously with the oracle; now it is carried to new heights in the reunion of Leontes and Hermione. . . .

I should like to re-emphasize one fact: all that has been considered . . . as to the treatment of time, stagecraft and 'planes of reality' has revealed not only a method of dramatic presentation but also a statement, complex and profound, of the nature of reality. This fusion of method and statement is the last degree of organic unity.

NOTES

1. 'Direct address' is the convention by which a character imparts information in direct statement to the audience; see S. L. Bethell, *Shakespeare and the Popular Dramatic Tradition* (1944) ch. v, pp. 84 ff.

2. Granville-Barker comes to a similar conclusion about the technique of *Cymbeline*; see *Prefaces to Shakespeare, Second Series* (1933) p. 243: 'it is obviously a sophisticated, not a native artlessness, the art that rather displays art than conceals it.'

3. Cf. Morton Luce's Introduction to *The Tempest* in the *Arden Shakespeare*, pp. xxx–xxxi: 'As we have seen, *The Tempest* observes the unities of place and time with a precision that must seem on the part of the author to be half combative, half humorous. This we may gather from the many pointed references to the three or four hours' limit of the action, and it is possible that after his most daring disregard of time and place in *The Winter's Tale* (which contains, by the way some equally pointed references to these particulars) the poet wished – and again half defiantly, half humorously – to show how exactly, if need were, his romantic plays could adjust themselves to the rigid conventions of the classic drama. The classic prologue or chorus may also be said to have their equivalent in *The Tempest*, as, for example, in the first part of Act I, Scene ii.' It is interesting to note that this was

written in 1901. The whole introduction deserves study; it is an unusually perceptive piece of critical writing.

    4. See *Greene's 'Pandosto' or 'Dorastus and Fawnia'*, ed. P. G.
Thomas (1907) p. 56; or *Variorum Shakespeare* (1898) pp. 343 ff. (The
latter version retains the original spelling.)

G. Wilson Knight

'GREAT CREATING NATURE' (1947)

Time as chorus functions normally with certain obvious apologies recalling Gower in *Pericles* (iv iv) and at least one touch in Gower's style: 'what of her ensues I list not prophecy' (iv chor. 25). A crucial phrase occurs at the start:

> I, that please some, try all, both joy and terror
> Of good and bad, that make and unfold error,
> Now take upon me, in the name of Time,
> To use my wings . . .   (iv chor. 1)

'Make and unfold error' links *The Winter's Tale* to the earlier comedies which, though less deeply loaded with tragic meaning, regularly hold tragic reference in close relation to 'error', and finally drive the action to a formal conclusion in which mistakes are rectified.

The Winter's Tale presents a contrast of sinful maturity and nature-guarded youth in close association with seasonal change. But there is more to notice. Shakespeare's genius is labouring to pit his own more positive intuitions, expressed hitherto mainly through happy-ending romance and comedy, against tragedy: they are to work as redeeming forces. The idyll of Florizel and Perdita will fall naturally into place: but romance in Shakespeare regularly enjoys the support, or at least the company, of humour. In Leontes Shakespeare's tragic art has reached a new compactness and intensity; and now in our next scenes, he gives us a figure of absolute comedy, Autolycus.

Richest humour offers a recognition of some happy universal resulting from the carefree stripping away of cherished values: elsewhere[1] I have compared such 'golden', or sympathetic, humour, of which Falstaff is an obvious example, with humour of the critical, moralistic, Jonsonian, sort, such as that Shakespeare touches in Malvolio. Falstaff, though utterly unmoral, yet solicits our respect, and in that recognition consists the fun. The fun itself is, moreover, in essence a lark-like thing; it will sing, or dance, and may elsewhere house itself in spring-frolic and lyrical verse, such as 'It was a lover and his lass . . .' introduced by Touchstone in *As You Like It* (v iii). Autolycus is a blend of burly comedian and lyrical jester.

He enters singing verses redolent of spring:

> When daffodils begin to peer,
>   With heigh! the doxy over the dale,
> Why, then comes in the sweet o' the year;
>   For the red blood reigns in the winter's pale.
>
> (IV ii 1)

He is spring incarnate; carefree, unmoral, happy, and sets the note for a spring-like turn in our drama, reversing the spring and winter conclusion of Shakespeare's first comedy, *Love's Labour's Lost*. His following stanzas continue with references to country linen on the hedge (cp. *Love's Labour's Lost*, v ii 914), songbirds, tooth-ache, ale, the lark and jay, 'summer songs for me and my aunts', hay-merriment: it is a glorious medley of inconsequential realistic rusticity. Suddenly he comments in prose:

> I have served Prince Florizel and in my time wore
> three-pile; but now I am out of service.   (IV ii 13)

He interrupts himself only to drop again into song – 'But shall I go mourn for that, my dear?' Like Touchstone, and Poor Tom in *King Lear*, he has seen better days, but remains happy, his thoughts slipping naturally into song. He next explains his profession of minor thief, off the high road, as 'a snapper up of unconsidered trifles' (IV ii 26).

His play with the Clown is supremely satisfying, and far more convincing than most stage trickery (e.g. Iago's of Cassio, Roderigo and Othello). The Clown is presented as a thorough gull, though not inhumanly so, as is Sir Andrew or Roderigo. Every phrase tells. As the supposedly injured man is carefully

lifted - 'O! good sir, tenderly, O!' (IV ii 76) - his purse is being
delicately manœuvred within reach; the victim's attention is
meanwhile firmly directed away from the danger-zone - 'I fear,
sir, my shoulder blade is out' (IV ii 78); and, when the business is
successfully accomplished, there is the delightful *double entendre*
'You ha' done me a charitable office' (IV ii 82). Shakespeare's last
work often recalls the New Testament, and here we have, in
Autolycus' account of his beating, robbery and loss of clothes, a
clear parody of the parable of the Good Samaritan, the pattern
being completed by the Clown's continuation, 'Dost lack any
money? I have a little money for thee' (IV ii 83), and Autolycus'
hurried and anxious disclaimer, 'No, good sweet sir: no, I beseech you, sir ... Offer me no money, I pray you! that kills my
heart' (IV iii 85). There follows Autolycus' description of himself with some rather ordinary court-satire and finally the delightful conclusion, crying out for stage-realization:

> *Clown.* How do you now?
> *Aut.* Sweet sir, much better than I was: I can stand and walk.
>   I will even take my leave of you, and pace softly towards my
>   kinsman's.
> *Clown.* Shall I bring thee on the way?
> *Aut.* No, good-faced sir; no, sweet sir.
> *Clown.* Then fare thee well: I must go buy spices for our sheep-
>   shearing.   (IV iii 119)

'Softly' is spoken with an upward lilt of the voice. Autolycus is a
sweet, smooth-voiced rogue. The Clown says his last speech to
the audience with a broad grin on his vacant face. When he is
gone, Autolycus takes one agile skip, then:

> Jog on, jog on, the footpath way
>   And merrily hent the stile-a:
> A merry heart goes all the day
>   Your sad tires in a mile-a.   (IV iii 133)

The incident circles back to its start, enclosed in melody. It is
all utterly unmoral, as unmoral as the scents of spring. This might
well be called the most convincing, entertaining, and profound

piece of comedy in Shakespeare. Such personal judgements are necessarily of doubtful interest, except to help point my argument that, so far from relaxing, Shakespeare's art is, on every front, advancing.

The sheep-shearing scene similarly sums up and surpasses all Shakespeare's earlier poetry of pastoral and romance. It is, however – and this is typical of our later plays – characterized by a sharp realism. The Clown's shopping list has already built a sense of simple cottage housekeeping and entertainment, with a suggestion of something out-of-the-ordinary in his supposed sister, Perdita:

Three pound of sugar; five pound of currants; rice. What will this sister of mine do with rice? But my father hath made her mistress of the feast, and she lays it on.   (IV ii 40)

His following reference to psalm-singing puritans sticks out awkwardly; more in place are the 'nosegays' and 'raisins o' the sun' (IV iii 43–53), especially the last. Autolycus has already sung of the 'red blood' reigning after winter (IV ii 4), and soon our merry-makers are to be 'red with mirth' (IV iii 54). We are to watch a heightening of English country festivity, touched with Mediterranean warmth, something, to quote Keats,

> Tasting of Flora and the country green,
> Dance, and Provençal song, and sun-burnt mirth.

So we move from spring to summer, under a burning sun.

The sun has not been so honoured before. We have known the moon-silvered encounters of Romeo and Juliet and glimmering tangles of the 'wood near Athens'; also the cypress shadows of *Twelfth Night* and chequered glades of Arden; but never before, not even in *Antony and Cleopatra* – a necessary step, where sun-warmth was, however, felt mainly through description, the action itself searching rather for 'gaudy' (III xi 182) or moonlit nights – never before has the sun been so dramatically awakened, so close to us, as here; and there is a corresponding advance in love poetry, compassing, though with no loss of magic, strong fertility suggestion and a new, daylight assurance:

> These your unusual weeds to each part of you
> Do give a life: no shepherdess, but Flora
> Peering in April's front. This your sheep-shearing
> Is as a meeting of the petty gods,
> And you the queen on't.   (IV iii 1)

So speaks Prince Florizel. But Perdita's answer witnesses both her country simplicity and feminine wisdom; she fears, as does Juliet, love's rashness and insecurity. Indeed, all Shakespeare's love-heroines, following the pattern laid down by Venus' prophecy in *Venus and Adonis* (1135–64), are given tragic undertones; they have an aura of tragedy about them. Florizel's love is more confident and showy (as usual in Shakespeare), but his use of mythology, as in 'Flora' above, has a new, and finely convincing, impact. He catalogues the gods who have disguised themselves for love: Jupiter as a bellowing bull, Neptune a bleating lamb and, giving highest poetic emphasis to our play's supreme deity,

> the fire-rob'd god,
> Golden Apollo, a poor humble swain
> As I seem now.   (IV iii 29)

'O Lady Fortune,' prays Perdita in a phrase reminiscent of *Pericles*, 'stand you auspicious' (IV iii 51). Though she remains doubtful, her doubts, a mixture of shyness and hard-headed feminine realism, only make the poetry more poignant. So, too, do the many homely reminders, as in the old shepherd's reminiscences of his dead wife's busy behaviour as hostess on such festival days as this, cooking, serving, and dancing in turn, bustling about, 'her face o' fire' (IV iii 60) with both exertion and refreshment. Now Perdita, following Thaisa at the court of Simonides (the repetition is close, both fathers similarly reminding their apparently shy daughters of their duties), is 'mistress of the feast' (IV iii 68; cp. 'queen of the feast' at *Pericles* II iii 17), and has to conquer her shyness.

There follows Perdita's important dialogue with Polixenes. She, rather like Ophelia in a very different context, is presenting posies according to the recipient's age and offers the two older men (Polixenes and Camillo wear white beards, IV iii 417) rosemary and rue, which, she says, keep their savour 'all the winter long' (IV iii 75): notice the recurring emphasis on age and seasons. Polixenes, however (forgetting his disguise?), appears to resent being given 'flowers of winter' (IV iii 79) and Perdita gracefully apologizes for not having an autumnal selection:

Per.   Sir, the year growing ancient,
   Not yet on summer's death, nor on the birth
   Of trembling winter, the fairest flowers o' the season
   Are our carnations, and streak'd gillyvors,
   Which some call nature's bastards: of that kind
   Our rustic garden's barren, and I care not
   To get slips of them.
Pol.   Wherefore, gentle maiden,
   Do you neglect them?
Per.   For I have heard it said
   There is an art which in their piedness shares
   With great creating nature.
Pol.   Say there be;
   Yet nature is made better by no mean
   But nature makes that mean; so, over that art,
   Which you say adds to nature, is an art
   That nature makes. You see, sweet maid, we marry
   A gentler scion to the wildest stock,
   And make conceive a bark of baser kind
   By bud of nobler race; this is an art
   Which does mend nature, change it rather, but
   The art itself is nature.
Per.   So it is.
Pol. Then make your garden rich in gillyvors
   And do not call them bastards.
Per.   I'll not put
   The dibble in earth to set one slip of them;
   No more than, were I painted, I would wish
   This youth should say, 'twere well, and only therefore
   Desire to breed by me. Here's flowers for you;

Hot lavender, mints, savory, marjoram;
The marigold, that goes to bed wi' the sun,
And with him rises weeping: these are flowers
Of middle summer, and I think they are given
To men of middle age. You're very welcome.
Cam. I should leave grazing, were I of your flock
And only live by gazing.
Per.   Out, alas!
You'd be so lean, that blasts of January
Would blow you through and through.   (IV iii 79)

Of this one could say much. Notice first, the continued emphasis
on seasons at the opening and concluding lines of my quotation;
the strong physical realism (recalling Hermione's defence) in
Perdita's use of 'breed'; and the phrase 'great creating nature' (to
be compared with 'great nature' earlier, at II ii 60).

The speakers are at cross purposes, since one is referring to
art, the other to artificiality, itself a difficult enough distinction.
The whole question of the naturalist and transcendental antinomy
is accordingly raised. The art concerned is called natural by
Polixenes in that either (i) human invention can never do more
than direct natural energy, or (ii) the human mind and therefore
its inventions are nature-born: both meanings are probably
contained. Human civilization, art and religion are clearly in one
sense part of 'great creating nature', and so is everything else.
But Perdita takes her stand on natural simplicity, growing from
the unforced integrity of her own country up-bringing, in
opposition to the artificialities of, we may suggest, the court: she
is horrified at dishonouring nature by human trickery. Observe
that both alike reverence 'great creating nature', though differing
in their conclusions. No logical deduction is to be drawn; or
rather, the logic is dramatic, made of opposing statements, which
serve to conjure up an awareness of nature as an all-powerful
presence, at once controller and exemplar. The dialogue forms
accordingly a microcosm of our whole drama.

There is a certain irony, too, in Polixenes' defence of exactly
the type of love-mating which Florizel and Perdita are planning
for themselves. Polixenes is, perhaps, setting a trap; or may be

quite unconsciously arguing against his own later behaviour. Probably the latter.

Perdita next turns to Florizel:

Per.   Now, my fair'st friend,
I would I had some flowers o' the spring that might
Become your time of day; and yours, and yours,
That wear upon your virgin branches yet
Your maidenheads growing: O Proserpina!
For the flowers now that frighted thou let'st fall
From Dis's waggon! daffodils
That come before the swallow dares, and take
The winds of March with beauty; violets dim,
But sweeter than the lids of Juno's eyes
Or Cytherea's breath; pale prim-roses
That die unmarried ere they can behold
Bright Phoebus in his strength, a malady
Most incident to maids; bold oxlips and
The crown imperial; lilies of all kinds,
The flower-de-luce being one. O! these I lack
To make you garlands of, and my sweet friend,
To strew him o'er and o'er!
Flo.   What ! like a corse?
Per. No, like a bank for love to lie and play on;
Not like a corse; or if – not to be buried,
But quick and in mine arms. Come, take your flowers:
Methinks I play as I have seen them do
In Whitsun pastorals: sure this robe of mine
Does change my disposition.   (IV iii 112)

Reference to the season-myth Proserpine is natural enough; indeed, almost an essential. You might call Perdita herself a seed sowed in winter and flowering in summer. 'Take' = 'charm', or 'enrapture'. Though Autolycus' first entry suggested spring, we are already, as the nature of our festival and these lines declare, in summer. Note the fine union, indeed identity, of myth and contemporary experience, finer than in earlier Shakespearian pastorals: Dis may be classical, but his 'wagon' is as real as a wagon in Hardy. See, too, how classical legend and folk-lore coalesce in the primroses and 'bright Phoebus in his strength', a phrase

pointing the natural poetic association of sun-fire and mature love
(as in *Antony and Cleopatra*): the sun corresponding, as it were, to
physical fruition (as the moon to the more operatic business of
wooing) and accordingly raising in Perdita, whose poetry is
strongly impregnated with fertility-suggestion (the magic here is
throughout an earth-magic, a sun-magic), a wistful aside, meant
presumably for herself. Perdita's flower-poetry reaches a royal
impressionism in 'crown imperial' and 'garland' suiting the
speaker's innate, and indeed actual, royalty. The contrasting
suggestion of 'corse' quickly merging into a love-embrace
(reminiscent of the love and death associations in *Antony and
Cleopatra* and Keats) finally serves to heighten the pressure of
exuberant, buoyant, life. The 'Whitsun pastorals', like our earlier
puritans, though perhaps historically extraneous, may be forgiven for their lively impact, serving to render the speech vivid
with the poet's, and hence, somehow, our own, personal experience.

Perdita's royalty is subtly presented: her robes as mistress of
the feast have, as she said, made her act and speak strangely.
Florizel details each of her graces (IV iii 135–43), wishing her in
turn to speak, to sing, to dance – as 'a wave o' the sea' – for ever.
He would have her every action perpetuated, the thought
recalling Polixenes' recollections of himself and Leontes as 'boy
eternal' (I ii 65). Florizel has expressed a delight in the given instant of youthful grace so sacred that it somehow deserves eternal
status; when she moves he would have her, in a phrase itself
patterning the blend of motion and stillness it describes, 'move
still, still so'. Watching her, he sees the universe completed,
crowned, at each moment of her existence:

> Each your doing,
> So singular in each particular,
> Crowns what you are doing in the present deed,
> That all your acts are queens.   (IV iii 143)

As once before, we are reminded, this time more sharply, of
Blake's 'minute particulars'. The royalistic tonings here and in
the 'crown imperial' of her own speech (IV iii 126) not merely

hint Perdita's royal blood, but also serve to stamp her actions
with eternal validity; for the crown is always to be understood as
a symbol piercing the eternity dimension. We are, it is true,
being forced into distinctions that Shakespeare, writing from a
royalistic age, need not actually have surveyed; but Florizel's
lines certainly correspond closely to those in *Pericles* imaging
Marina as a palace 'for the crown'd Truth to dwell in' and again
as monumental Patience sitting 'above kings' graves' and
'smiling extremity out of act' (*Pericles*, v i 123, 140). Perdita is
more lively; time, creation, nature, earth, all have more rights
here than in *Pericles*; but the correspondence remains close.

Perdita's acts are royal both in their own right and also
because she is, in truth, of royal birth:

> This is the prettiest low-born lass that ever
> Ran on the green-sward. Nothing she does or seems
> But smacks of something greater than herself,
> Too noble for this place.   (IV iii 156)

But this is not the whole truth. Later, after Polixenes' outburst,
she herself makes a comment more easily appreciated in our age
than in Shakespeare's:

> I was not much afeard; for once or twice
> I was about to speak and tell him plainly,
> The self-same sun that shines upon his court
> Hides not his visage from our cottage, but
> Looks on alike.   (IV iii 455)

The lovely New Testament transposition (with 'sun' for 'rain')
serves to underline the natural excellence and innate worth of
this simple rustic community; and only from some such recognition can we make full sense of the phrase 'queen of curds and
cream' (IV iii 161). We may accordingly re-group our three
royalties in terms of (i) Perdita's actual descent, (ii) her natural
excellence and (iii) that more inclusive category from which both
descend, or to which both aspire, in the eternity dimension. A
final conclusion would reach some concept of spiritual royalty

corresponding to Wordsworth's (in his *Immortality Ode*); with further political implications concerning the expansion of sovereignty among a people.

The lovers are, very clearly, felt as creatures of 'rare' – the expected word recurs (IV iii 32) – excellence, and their love, despite its strong fertility contacts, is correspondingly pure. Perdita, hearing Florizel's praises, fears he woos her 'the false way' (IV iii 151); while Florizel is equally insistent that his 'desires run not before his honour', nor his 'lusts burn hotter' than his 'faith' (IV iii 33). The statement, which appears, as in *The Tempest* later, a trifle laboured, is clearly central: Perdita, as mistress of the feast, insists that Autolycus 'use no scurrilous words in's tunes' (IV iii 215). Our first tragedy was precipitated by suspicion of marital infidelity; and our young lovers express a corresponding purity.

The action grows more rollicking, with a dance of 'shepherds and shepherdesses' (IV iii 165) in which Perdita and Florizel join. There follows Autolycus' spectacular entry as musical pedlar, preceded by a rich description (IV iii 191–201) of his rowdy-merry catches and tunes ('jump her and thump her', 'whoop! do me no harm, good man'). He enters all a-flutter with ribbons and a tray of good things and describes his absurd ballads to the awe-struck Mopsa and Dorcas. Though the words may not be scurrilous, the songs are ribald enough, one telling of a usurer's wife 'brought to bed of twenty money-bags at a burden'; and another sung originally by a fish representing a woman 'who would not exchange flesh with one that loved her' and had been metamorphosed in punishment (IV iii 265, 282). They are little burlesques of our main fertility-myth, stuck in as gargoyles on a cathedral, and the two girls' anxious enquiries as to whether the stories are true, with Autolycus' firm reassurances, serve to complete the parody. Finally Autolycus conducts and joins in a catch, followed by another dance of 'twelve rustics, habited like satyrs' (IV iii 354), given by carters, shepherds, neatherds, and swineherds. Here our rough country fun, heavily toned for fertility, reaches its climax.

But nature continues to provide poetry as refined as Florizel's image of winter purity (winter is also present in Autolycus' 'lawn as white as driven snow' at IV iii 220):

> I take thy hand; this hand,
> As soft as dove's down, and as white as it,
> Or Ethiopian's tooth, or the fann'd snow that's bolted
> By the northern blasts twice o'er.   (IV iii 374)

As in Keats' 'Bright Star' sonnet, human love is compared to the steadfast gazing on earth, or sea, of heavenly light:

> He says he loves my daughter:
> I think so too; for never gazed the moon
> Upon the water as he'll stand and read
> As 'twere my daughter's eyes ...   (IV iii 171)

This (with which we should compare the similar love imagery of *Love's Labour's Lost*, IV iii 27–42) parallels Leontes' picture of Mamillius' 'welkin eye' followed by fears for the 'centre' (i.e. of the earth), forming an association of emotional and universal stability (I ii 137, 139); and also his later contrast and identification of 'nothing' with 'the world and all that's in it' and the 'covering sky' (I ii 293–4). The universal majesty is continually imagined concretely as earth and sky facing each other, as in Leontes' 'plainly as heaven sees earth or earth sees heaven' (I ii 315); it is the universe we actually know and see, without the cosmic, spheral, idealizing emphasis of *Antony and Cleopatra* and (once) *Pericles*. So Florizel, questioned by Polixenes, calls the universe as witness to his love:

> ... and he, and more
> Than he, or men, the earth, the heavens, and all ...
>   (IV iii 383)

Should he prove false, then

> Let nature crush the sides o' the earth together
> And mar the seeds within!   (IV iii 491)

Though reminiscent of nature's 'germens' in *King Lear* (III ii 8), those 'seeds' belong especially to this, as to no other, play. The emphasis on earth's creativeness is repeated:

> Not for Bohemia, nor the pomp that may
> Be thereat glean'd, for all the sun sees or
> The close earth wombs or the profound sea hides
> In unknown fathoms, will I break my oath
> To this my fair belov'd.   (IV iii 501)

The sun, as the moon before, is thought as 'seeing'; it is the 'eye' of heaven of Sonnet xviii. The sun is constantly reverenced throughout *The Winter's Tale*, either directly (as in 'welkin eye' etc.) or 'the fire-rob'd god, golden Apollo' (IV iii 29) and his oracle. Nature here is creative, majestic, something of illimitable mystery and depth ('profound sea', 'unknown fathoms'); but it is never bookish. Nor is it dissolved into any system of elements. Earth, sea, sun and moon are felt rather as concrete realities of normal experience, nearer Renaissance commonsense than Dantesque or Ptolemaic harmonies, whilst housing strong classical-mythological powers.

As for Polixenes' brutal interruption, we recall Capulet, Egeus, York, Polonius, Lear: Shakespeare's fathers are normally tyrannical and Polixenes has, according to his lights, cause. His threats, excessive as Capulet's, drive home a contrast of social tyranny with rustic health, clinched by Perdita's admirable comment already noticed: there is court satire elsewhere (as at IV ii 94–101; IV iii 723–6). Of course, this contrast works within, without disrupting, the prevailing royalism: apart from the old shepherd, the country folk are mainly represented by three fools and a knave.

The pastoral interest slackens and significant passages become less dense as we become involved in the rather heavy machinery of getting everyone to Sicilia. Both Camillo's tortuous scheme and Autolycus' additions to it lack conviction, and we suffer rather as in *Hamlet* during Claudius' and Laertes' long discussion about the Norman, Lamond. There is, however, some purpose in the sagging action of *Hamlet*, whereas here we seem to be confronted by plot-necessity alone. About Autolycus' lengthy fooling with the Shepherd and Clown there is, however, something to say.

The dialogue not only protracts the sagging action, but rouses discomfort, Autolycus' description of the punishments awaiting the rustics, though pictorially in tone here (involving 'honey', 'wasps', midday sun, flies: iv iii 816-25), being a trifle unpleasant. Resenting Autolycus' fall from his first entry, one is tempted to dismiss the incident as an error. Autolycus is, however, being used to elaborate the vein of court satire already suggested by Polixenes' behaviour; it is almost a parody of that behaviour. The pick-pocket pedlar, now himself disguised as 'a great courtier' (iv iii 777), becomes absurdly superior and uses his new position to baffle the Clown precisely as Touchstone the courtier-fool baffles William. His elaborate description of torments is extremely cruel; but then the court – Polixenes' harshness fresh in our minds – is cruel.

But we can still disapprove the subordination of humour to satire; and yet this very subordination serves a further purpose concerned with the essence of humour itself. Autolycus is first a composite of spring music and delightful knavery; during the sheep-shearing festival he is a source of rather ribald entertainment and catchy song. Next, he goes off to sell his wares, and on his re-entry recounts his successful purse-picking, which now, however, wins less approval in view of our accumulated concern for the simple people on whom he battens as a dangerous parasite. He is later by chance forced to dress as a courtier and further looks like making a good thing out of the two rustics and their secret. He is advancing rapidly in the social scale; the fates assist him. As he says,

> If I had a mind to be honest, I see Fortune would
> not suffer me: she drops booties in my mouth.
>
> (iv iii 868)

He is now all out for 'advancement' (iv iii 873). After donning courtier's clothes, his humour takes an unnecessarily cruel turn. Something similar happened with Falstaff, who, a creature of pure humour (and also robbery) in Part i of *Henry IV*, becomes less amusing in Part ii where he has advanced socially, wears fine clothes, and is tainted by a courtier's ambition. He is himself subscribing to the very values which we thought he scorned and our source of humour to that extent weakened. The humorous parasite cannot afford to be too successful, any more than the saint. So with Autolycus: the merry robber-tramp, as he makes his way, becomes less merry. His vices become less amusing as he indulges his lust for power; as his egotism expands, a cruel strain (compare Falstaff's attitude to his recruits and Justice Shallow) is revealed; and he is at once recognized as inferior to the society on which, as a happy-go-lucky ragamuffin, he formerly preyed for our amusement. More widely, we can say that the delicate balance of unmoral humour – and no finer examples exist than the early Falstaff and Autolycus – must be provisional only; it cannot maintain the pace, cannot survive as a challenge among the summery positives here enlisted against tragedy: Falstaff was, necessarily, rejected by Prince Hal. Moreover, just as the Falstaff of *Henry IV* becomes finally the buffoon of *The Merry Wives of Windsor*, so Autolycus' last entry, when they have all arrived in Sicilia, and the Shepherd and Clown are rich and he a recognized knave, is peculiarly revealing: we see him now bowing and scraping to his former gull.[2] Meanwhile, our humorous sympathies have passed over to the Clown, rather tipsy and talking of himself as having recently become a 'gentleman born' (v ii 142–64), so providing a new and richly amusing variation in social comment.

The long scene (IV iii) accordingly has a falling movement; from exquisite pastoral and the accompanying flower-dialogue, through robust country merriment to an all but ugly humour. The romance is to survive; not so Autolycus, who is to lose dramatic dignity. No one will accuse Shakespeare of lacking humour, but it is too often forgotten that his humour works within the limits set by a prevailing 'high seriousness'.

NOTES

1. In writing of Byron in *The Burning Oracle* (1939).

2. There is a deplorable stage tradition that Autolycus should again, in this late scene, start picking the purses of the Shepherd and the Clown. The comedian will, of course, get his laughs; but for Shakespeare's opinion of such 'pitiful ambition' see Hamlet's address to the Players (III ii 50).

Harold S. Wilson

'NATURE AND ART' (1943)

THE passage in *The Winter's Tale* (IV iv 79 ff) where Polixenes and Perdita discuss the merits of such 'artificial' flowers as carnations and gillyvors[1] has been widely and justly admired. It is one of the most graceful and poetic passages in Shakspere and contains one of his keenest intellectual *aperçus*. Over and above the pastoral charm of the setting, Perdita herself, and the fragrant talk of country flowers, there is a pretty ambiguity in the action. As Furness has noted,[2] Polixenes in defending the art of grafting has unknowingly stated the relation between his royal son and the shepherd maid with his metaphor of marrying a gentler scion to the wildest stock, and Perdita cheerfully assents to the figure, if not to the application Polixenes intends; while the audience, familiar with the play and secure in the knowledge that Perdita is a true princess, after all, enjoys the further irony of the maid's accepting the partly false analogy to justify her marriage with Florizel, urged by the man who mistakenly thinks he has most interest in opposing the match.

Polixenes' defence of the carnations and gillyvors which Perdita disdains:

> *Per.*   For I have heard it said
>   There is an art which in their piedness shares
>   With great creating Nature.
> *Pol.*   Say there be;
>   Yet Nature is made better by no mean
>   But Nature makes that mean; so, over that art,
>   Which you say adds to Nature, is an art
>   That Nature makes. You see, sweet maid, we marry
>   A gentler scion to the wildest stock,
>   And make conceive a bark of baser kind

By bud of nobler race: this is an art
Which does mend Nature, change it rather, but
The art itself is Nature

is couched in terms of one of the many 'nature and art' relationships familiar in ancient and Renaissance literature. No commentator could hope to canvass the background of Shakspere's
idea completely. To exhaust even a fraction of the relevant
parallels in the literature preceding Shakspere would require
volumes, as everyone knows. Nevertheless, surprisingly few
parallels for the passage as a whole have been noted by the commentators, so far at least as I have observed;[3] and it may be
worthwhile to indicate something of their antiquity and extent.

The earlier history of the conception of 'nature' as subsuming
the arts of man has been traced by A. O. Lovejoy and George
Boas in their indispensable study, *Primitivism and Related Ideas
in Antiquity* (1935). As they have remarked, Shakspere's thought
is adumbrated though not unequivocally anticipated in a saying
attributed to Democritus: 'Nature and culture are much alike; for
culture changes a man, but through this change makes nature.'[4]
A clearer parallel for Shakspere's conception occurs in one of the
answers Plato supplies to the sophistic antithesis of 'nature' and
'art': 'Law itself . . . and art . . . exist by nature or by a cause not
inferior to nature, since, according to right reason, they are the
offspring of mind.'[5] Lovejoy and Boas have likewise noted at
length the occurrence of the conception that 'nature' comprehends 'art' in Aristotle[6] and Cicero.[7] Other such classical
antecedents of Polixenes' thought could be supplied, but probably enough have been indicated to show that the idea of 'art' as
a part of cosmic nature or as made by nature was commonplace
in antiquity. It would be likewise possible to cite a multitude of
pre-Shaksperian parallels for this commonplace from many fields
of Renaissance thought. I shall confine my citations to the field of
literary theory, with which I am most familiar, and conclude with
one which Shakspere may have had in mind when he formulated
the speech of Polixenes.

The idea of cosmic nature as guiding and controlling the

development of poetic art occurs in Petrarch: 'Nihil nisi naturae consentaneum lex poetica fingi sivit';[8] and this normative conception of 'nature' is further applied to all literary art and to human arts in general by a succession of Renaissance writers in Italy, France, and England.[9] Some discussion of the relations between 'art' and 'nature' – usually designed to justify the conceptions of the 'arts' of rhetoric or poetry and to define their limits – became a conventional part of most Renaissance treatises on literary theory. Thus Bernardino Daniello opens his *Poetica* (1536) with a discourse on this matter in which, after granting that 'every art and science has its beginnings from nature' (p. 4), he argues that the writer's 'natural' gifts should be supplemented, disciplined, and perfected by the literary 'art' with which his little book is mainly concerned. In support, he introduces an agricultural illustration in something like Polixenes' vein, if not in application to his precise contention. Many things in nature, says Daniello, are improved by human art, and not least the useful products of the soil:

For nature produces what is useful to human life mixed indiscriminately with thorns and brambles. Wherefore, if the diligent cultivator does not root out the sterile offenders from the good and useful growths, he will reap many tares and but little corn or oats. But let us look a little higher, from the products of the soil to the trees. Do we not here find, very often, something comparable? Assuredly, since, for the most part, trees are apt to degenerate and bring forth sour or insipid fruit if left to their own development. But if these are diligently and artfully grafted with the proper scions of other fruit trees, the fruits become sweet and savory....[10]

Daniello's talk on tree-grafting is not so specific and neatly turned as Polixenes'; but it shows how examples drawn from arboriculture, as from other fields, were associated with Renaissance discussions of 'art' and 'nature' well before Shakspere's time.

A French parallel for Shakspere's generalization concerning 'nature' and 'art' appears in the *Art Poétique* (1555) of Jacques

Peletier, the most judicious critic of the Pléiade group. Peletier displays an awareness, unusual for the time, of the ambiguities in the terms 'nature' and 'art' as commonly used by Renaissance theorists. He opens his discussion of these concepts with the following observation:

If one should take 'nature' in the amplest sense as that great working principle which acts universally upon everything in the world and upon all that falls within the cognizance of men, which comprehends even those things that we call 'contrary to nature' or 'supernatural'; then there is only 'nature' ... in the world ....[11]

In English literary treatises of the Renaissance the common-places of ancient and modern continental critics concerning 'art' and 'nature' regularly recur. Among these, the idea that 'nature' generates and regulates 'art' is implied in Sidney's remark about the courtly amateur among poets who, ignorant of the pre-scriptions of the learned on poetics and merely 'following that which by practise hee findeth fittest to nature, therein (though he know it not) doth according to Art though not by art'.[12] The idea that 'Nature ... is above all Arte' Shakspere could have found in Samuel Daniel's *Defence of Ryme* (1603), had he needed to.[13] More interesting, however, is the conjecture that Shakspere's remarks about 'nature' and 'art' in *The Winter's Tale* may have had some relation to the elaborate discussion of these concepts in the *Arte of English Poesie* (1589). The author of this treatise, most probably identified by the latest editors as George Puttenham,[14] is distinguished among Renaissance critics for his semantic interests and his nice discriminations in the use of words. Throughout his treatise he delights in particularizing fine distinctions of critical terminology; and he reserves for his last chapter a discourse on current uses of the terms 'nature' and 'art' and the illustration of their exact employment in criticism.[15]

By way of showing 'where arte ought to appeare, and where not, and when the naturall is more commendable than the artificiall in any humane action or workmanship', Puttenham distinguishes six different relations between 'nature' and 'art': (1) 'art' as 'an aide and coadiutor to nature, and a furtherer of her actions to good effect, or peradventure a meane to supply her wants, by reenforcing the causes wherein shee is impotent and defective'; (2) 'art' as 'not only an aide and coadiutor to nature in all her actions, but an alterer of them, and in some sort a surmounter of her skill, so as by meanes of it her owne effects shall appeare more beautiful or straunge and miraculous'; (3) 'art' as 'onely a bare immitatour of natures works, following and counterfeyting her actions and effects'; (4) 'art' as 'an encountrer and contrary to nature, producing effects neither like to hers, nor by participation with her operations, nor by imitation of her paternes, but makes things and produceth effects altogether strange and diverse, & of such forme & qualitie (nature alwaies supplying stuffe) as she never would nor could have done of her selfe'; (5) those actions which are 'so naturall & proper to man as he may become excellent therein without any arte or imitation at all'; (6) those arts and methods 'by which the naturall is in some sort relieved . . . in his imperfection, but not made more perfit then the naturall'.[16]

Among the many illustrations of these distinctions Puttenham uses, several come from agriculture. One, in particular, illustrating 'art' as an alterer and surmounter of nature's skill, might have provided the very text of the debate between Perdita and Polixenes:

And the Gardiner by his arte will not onely make an herbe, or flowr, or fruite, come forth in his season without impediment, but also will embellish the same in vertue, shape, odour and taste, that nature of her selfe woulde never have done: as to make the single gillifloure, or marigold, or daisie, double: and the white rose, redde, yellow, or carnation; a bitter mellon sweete, a sweete apple, soure; a plumme or cherrie without a stone; a peare without core or kernell, a goord or coucumber like to a horne, or any other figure he will: any of which things nature could not doe without mans help and arte.

It is precisely such 'arte' against which Perdita objects and which Polixenes so neatly justifies by pointing out the master generalization that Puttenham's discussion had overlooked.

Puttenham's treatise enjoyed a high reputation, in fashionable

literary circles especially, during Shakspere's later years, and beyond; and the solemn didacticism of its author's concluding
chapter may have drawn Shakspere's amused attention. It would
be in keeping with the quality of Shakspere's wit to play lightly
upon Puttenham's theme and provide a summary comment upon
it, delivered with the grave urbanity of a Polixenes, a comment
which should supply its main deficiency in philosophical
insight.[17]

Puttenham's principal aim in his discussion of 'nature' and
'art' was to distinguish the bases for a description of the poet's
activity and art, to analyze rather than to generalize; and this aim
he fulfilled very well. Nor would Shakspere's comment have
seemed to any thoughtful and educated contemporary, including
Puttenham himself, unfamiliar. But it represents, perhaps, as well
as any passage can, the supreme power of Shakspere to see the
main issue and to comment upon it with unequalled felicity.

Whether or not the conjectured link with Puttenham's treatise
be acceptable, we may conclude that Shakspere's thought was
commonplace both in antiquity and in the Renaissance, and that
even the horticultural illustrations Shakspere uses were familiar in
Renaissance discussions of 'nature' and 'art' long before Shakspere's time. Shakspere's originality is not in his matter but in his
art, which, as Dryden and Doctor Johnson long ago observed, is
the 'art' of 'nature' itself.

NOTES

1. On the propriety of this spelling, see *The Winter's Tale, A New Variorum Edition of Shakespeare*, ed. H. H. Furness (Philadelphia, 1898) p. 189.

2. Ibid. p. 191.

3. Sir William T. Thiselton-Dyer in *Shakespeare's England* (1916) I 514 has cited a passage from Bacon's *Sylva Sylvarum* on the cultiva-
tion of gilly-flowers and contrasts the superior insight of Shakspere in anticipating the view of recent botanists 'that nature contains the secret of its own evolution'. See also the notes to the Cambridge Shakespeare, ed. A. Quiller-Couch and J. Dover Wilson (1931). H. N. Hudson – *The Complete Works of William Shakespeare*, with . . . notes by H. N. Hudson, I. Gollancz, C. H. Herford (New York, n.d.)

– has cited parallels in Bacon and Sir Thomas Browne for 'art itself is nature'. The philosopher S. Alexander (*Bulletin of the John Rylands Library* (July 1927) pp. 256–72) has used *The Winter's Tale*, IV iv 79 ff as the text for a discourse on the use of the concepts 'nature' and 'art' in aesthetics and the criticism of the fine arts, but he is not concerned to place the Shakspere passage in its historical setting. See also note 17 below.

4. H. Diels, *Die Fragmente der Vorsokratiker* (6th ed. 1952) 2. See Lovejoy and Boas, *Primitivism*, pp. 207–8. The authors suggest that the verb-form *phusiopoiei* in Democritus's saying 'possibly comes close to: "it carries on the creative work of nature"'.

5. *Laws*, 890 D, trans. R. G. Bury (London and New York, 1926). Cf. *Primitivism*, p. 166. A different though relaxed view is contained in Pindar's often-repeated assertion that all human excellencies, including recognized arts like poetry, are, in the nature of things, innate and hereditary. (*Olympian Ode*, II 86–8, IX 100–4; *Pythian Ode*, VIII 44–5; etc.) Here the purpose is to exalt the native excellence and prerogative of a hereditary aristocracy in contrast with the acquired and therefore allegedly inferior accomplishments of the *parvenus*. The notion that all human arts and excellencies are simply or primarily a matter of 'nature' (i.e. native endowment or ability) remained current throughout antiquity – as it still is in some quarters, today – though so indiscriminate an accounting for excellent human achievements was more commonly rejected by thoughtful writers, e.g. Isocrates, *Antidosis*, 197 ff; Cicero, *De Oratore*, I 83, 90, etc.; Quintilian, *Institutio Oratoria*, II xvii 5 ff; *Per Hupsous*, II i.

6. *Primitivism*, pp. 189–90. Cf. also 'Appendix: Some Meanings of "Nature" ', p. 448 (senses 13, 14, 15).

7. Ibid. 247 ff.

8. *Rerum familiarium*, IX 4. A familiar mediaeval view, as stated, e.g., in Dante,

> natura lo suo corso prende
> Dal divino intelletto e da sua arte
>
> (*Inferno*, XI 99–100)

and often repeated through the Renaissance, is not, of course, meant to controvert the idea of cosmic nature as subsuming human arts but simply to align 'nature' in its most inclusive sense under the supreme sovereignty of God.

9. For citations, see my study of the meanings of 'nature' in Renaissance literary theory, in *Journal of the History of Ideas*, II (1941) 430 ff, senses 9, 10, 11, 12.

10. *Poetica* (1536) p. 5.

11. *Art Poétique*, p. 73.

12. G. G. Smith, *Elizabethan Critical Essays* (1904) I 203.

13. Ibid. II 359.

14. George Puttenham, *The Arte of English Poesie*, ed. Gladys Doidge Willcock and Alice Walker (1936).

15. Bk. III, ch. xxv.

16. pp. 303–6.

17. Professor Lovejoy suggests that in *The Winter's Tale*, IV iv 89–90, Shakspere is making a 'devastating comment upon the primitivism of Montaigne' (*Primitivism*, p. 207). Whether this were Shakspere's design is as impossible to prove as the relation with Puttenham's remarks suggested above. Professor Lovejoy's conjecture is in keeping with Shakspere's jocose treatment of a theme from Montaigne's essay *Des Cannibales* (1 31) in *The Tempest*, II i 147 ff. On the other hand, Shakspere would probably know Puttenham's treatise at least as well as Florio's Montaigne; and the tenor of Polixenes' remarks, with their horticultural application, is directly reminiscent of Puttenham. It is not impossible that Shakspere was recalling what he had read in both Puttenham and Montaigne.

Derek Traversi

THE FINAL SCENES (1954)

THE return to Leontes, which follows immediately on the conclusion of the pastoral scene, brings us to the last, the reconcilia-
tory movement of the play. Leontes is introduced, through the
words of Cleomenes, at the moment in which the 'saint-like
sorrow' which has prevailed in him since the revelation of
Hermione's innocence is ready to be crowned by reconciliation
with the divine powers he has offended. The years which have
passed since his last appearance, far from being an example of
careless dramatic construction, correspond to a pause, a break
necessary to the whole conception. They have been passed in a
sorrow that is in no sense merely nostalgic, a despairing regret
for the results of his folly. To Cleomenes, indeed, it appears as a
prelude to sanctity. His faults have been 'redeem'd', his trespass
balanced by a corresponding penitence, and the time has now
come when he can be called upon, without undue levity, to
'forget' his past, to accept by reassuming his full royal functions
the forgiveness which the 'heavens' are now ready to grant him.
The steeping of the action in a supernatural atmosphere, although
anticipated from the first, only now becomes fully explicit,
emerges to play its part in the resolution of the action. It follows,
not by chance, on the scene which introduced the fresh spirit of
spring-like pastoral, temporarily broken by its lack of power to
resist the bitter enmity of 'blood', but now ready to be reinforced
by the deeper experience of the 'grace'-smitten Leontes.

Leontes, however, cannot immediately accept the invitation of
his courtiers. The play at this point, as always, aims at a development, not a contrast; the past is not forgotten, but taken up,
assumed into the present, transformed by a healing action of
'grace' which only the passage of time has brought to maturity.

For Leontes, if not for those around him, the consequences of
his sin are still alive, and their memory makes it impossible for
him to act as a free man. His reply to Cleomenes, therefore, is a
refusal, but one which, whilst affirming the continuous presence
of the past, in fact transforms it, takes it up into his own deepened
understanding:

> Whilst I remember
> Her and her virtues, I cannot forget
> My blemishes in them; and so still think of
> The wrong I did myself: which was so much,
> That heirless it hath made my kingdom; and
> Destroy'd the sweet'st companion that e'er man
> Bred his hopes out of.   (v i)

The beautiful rhythmic movement of these lines, so characteristic of Shakespeare's late verse in its combination of freedom
with a close subjection to the underlying development of meaning, is perfectly contrived to relate the situation of Leontes to the
main symbolic threads of the play. They are broken, in fact, into
two parts at the words 'the wrong I did myself'; what precedes
leads up to this, the intimate recognition of a deep, self-inflicted
wound, whilst what follows at once accepts the consequences of
his own act and prepares the way for an extension beyond the
merely personal and self-accusing, indicating the response of
the speaker to a new stage in the unfolding of the temporal
pattern. The temporal process, indeed, acquires in these perfectly constructed lines a deep moral value of its own. The
memory ('I remember') of Hermione and her 'virtues' is still alive
in Leontes, makes it impossible for him to overlook his own
'blemishes in them', which it would be both sinful and insensi-
tive, even after sixteen years and in spite of the arguments of
Cleomenes, to forget; but the same passage of time which has
been powerless to efface the past has taught him that the 'wrong'
which so lives in his mind has been done less to Hermione, whose
gracious virtue has long since emerged unaffected from her trial,
than to himself. This change, not from remorse to forgetfulness,
but from despair to a more inclusive moral perspective, prepares
the way for the final reconciliation.

The development of the speech as a whole, indeed, confirms this interpretation. Once more, the rhythmic construction is of vital importance. Within the main division already referred to, the verse is characterized by the barely perceptible pauses at the end of the freely flowing lines, pauses deliberately indicated by the necessities of speech and preparing the way, step by step, for the stressed enunciation of its most important aspects. In the first part, as we have seen, the weight of memory in Leontes leads him to recall the perfections of Hermione and to weigh them against the magnitude of his faults. These have been so great ('so much': the poignancy of the apparently simple expression is stressed by its place at the end of a rhythmic unit) that, in the later lines, they are referred to as affecting not only his own happiness, but the whole of the society for whose health and proper functioning he is, as king, peculiarly responsible. They have left his kingdom 'heirless' and 'destroy'd' (once again the break after the in-conclusive 'and' in the preceding line adds power to a word itself loaded with tragic meaning) the 'sweet'st companion' –

> that e'er man
> Bred his hopes out of.

The sharp bitterness of 'destroy'd' is balanced by the intense pathos of 'sweet'st' and leads up to the final evocation, in 'bred', of fertility as the tangible expression of the deepest 'hopes' of paternity. The speech, in fact, is calculated to bring out, and relate intimately, the two characteristics which at this moment predominate in Leontes, and which give new depth to the pre-liminary utterance of Cleomenes, which they extend without, however, contradicting. The first of these is his 'saint-like sorrow', a repentance for past sins kept alive in him by the un-failing memory of Hermione, and the second is his desire for an heir to be the fulfilment, as king and father alike, of which his sin has deprived him. It is here, however, that the past more especially lives on in the present as a limiting, restraining in-fluence. A new son for Leontes can only be born from Hermione, whom he believes to be dead: can only therefore be the daughter whom, in his past folly, he condemned to die.

The exchange which follows between Leontes and his two contrasted advisers, Paulina and Dion, stresses the positions that are now awaiting resolution through the action of time. For Paulina, Hermione is unique, 'unparallel'd', and the fact that Leontes 'kill'd' her (the word strikes him with a bitterness from which he recoils, but which he recognizes as just) needs to be atoned for as an irreparable loss; for Dion, Leontes is king as well as husband and his duty to the state justifies a line of conduct which, as an individual, he would not necessarily be required to follow. His speech, indeed, set against Paulina's call to keep faith, has a meaning far beyond its value in developing the argument:

> What were more holy
> Than to rejoice the former queen is well?
> What holier than, for royalty's repair,
> For present comfort and for future good,
> To bless the bed of majesty again
> With a sweet fellow to't?   (v i)

The desire for an heir which, considered by Leontes in purely personal terms, prompted him to a keen sense of his loss, is now taken out of the purely individual sphere, acquires a fresh universality in relation to the traditional conception of royalty in its social function. Dion's words, moreover, add the essential note of sanctity ('holy . . . holier') to the emphasis on human fertility which preceded it, thus extending decisively the scope of an emotion which, on the purely personal plane, could hardly compensate the preceding tragedy. We now begin to see how the pattern of the play is to be completed. Penitence and devotion, kept alive in Leontes by his memory and by Paulina's stressing of his responsibility for his loss, can be raised to the level of sanctity, on a plane in which the personal and royal motives become one continuous reality, and the functions of 'blood', no longer the cause of jealousies and divisions which have exhausted their tragic consequences with the passage of time, are seen as a source of life to the unified and gracious personality.

The necessary prelude to reconciliation, meanwhile, is a further projection of the past into the present, a poignant deepening of Leontes' love for Hermione. This is apparent when he says of her:

> I might have look'd upon my queen's full eyes;
> Have taken treasure from her lips,

and when Paulina takes up and emphasizes the sensation of spiritual wealth in her reply –

> And left them
> More rich for what they yielded;

the lover's gift of himself in emotional fullness becomes, typically, a cause of deeper enrichment. Here, indeed, as in so many of the later plays, fullness and riches are typical attributes of the Shakespearean state of grace. Again, when Leontes abjures all other loves as he remembers the eyes of his former queen –

> Stars, stars,
> And all eyes else dead coals! –

the intensity of his emotion suggests how the typically Shakespearean sense of the constant pressure of 'devouring time' is in the process of being overcome. The answer, of course, is not that of the philosopher, but of the artist. It consists in opposing to the action of time, sensibly apprehended, the value of Leontes' experience, intensifying it as a sensation of boundless wealth, until time itself is felt to be only a necessary element in the creation of this rich intuition. Time, as at certain moments of *Antony and Cleopatra*, has become irrelevant; in *The Winter's Tale*, it has simply served to shape the fullness of grace. Only, whereas in *Antony* the achievement of transcendent, vital justification is purely personal, balanced against aspects of corruption and egoism which threatens it continually with collapse, Leontes' love for Hermione, here recalled, kept alive in a spirit of penitence and growing self-understanding, exists in a symbolic framework more ample than itself, which gives it meaning and universality of context. Hermione lives in Leontes' mind as a 'sainted spirit', and his state is still that of an 'offender', 'soul-vex'd', exposed to the alternatives personified in Paulina and

Dion, awaiting a resolution which cannot be merely that suggested by personal feeling. When Leontes, in a spirit of religious
dedication ('so be blest my spirit!'), accepts Paulina's request that
he should not marry again without her consent, and when she
deliberately makes him face the full implications of this –

> That
> Shall be when your first queen's again in breath;
> Never till then –

we realize that we are moving in a world essentially different
from that of *Antony and Cleopatra*, less limited to the merely
personal, more universal and symbolic in its implications. The
restored fulfilment of Leontes' love is to take place against a
background more ample than anything in that love itself. The
past, far from being forgotten, will need to live again in the
present as a formative influence, the feeling of the individual will
find its proper context in the social obligations of the king, and
both will be subject together to a common dedication to the ends
of 'grace'. There could be no better indication of the essential
novelty of Shakespeare's purpose in these, the last plays of his full
maturity.

The situation of Leontes having been thus clarified, the action
proceeds by stages to prepare the way for the final resolution.
The first step is the entry of the Gentleman announcing the
approach of Florizel with his 'princess'. His evocation of –

> ... the most peerless piece of earth, I think,
> That e'er the sun shone bright on,

both contributes to the effect of 'value' which is essential to
Perdita's symbolic function, and calls forth from Paulina, watch-
ful as ever for the rights of Hermione, a reproof steeped in the
sense of tragic mutability:

> O Hermione,
> As every present time doth boast itself
> Above a better gone, so must thy grave
> Give way to what's seen now!

The inexorable passage of time is here stated once more as a persistent background to the main action. Not finally valid, not even – we may say – at this stage a main theme of the play, it is none the less present as a persistent base, a reality which gives humanity and pathos to the symbolic situation and is clearly associated with Hermione's sixteen years' concealment, still to be revealed. The Gentleman's admission – 'the one I have almost forgot' – points in the same direction. Hermione as a mere memory cannot live, affirm her being against fresh realities, except in the fixed, absolute devotion of Paulina, which itself imposes upon Leontes an abstraction from the current world that will be, in the long run, impossible to maintain; only her final 'resurrection', and the fact that her youthful perfection lives, spiritually and physically, in the person of her daughter, will make the final triumph over mutability possible. Meanwhile, the stress is already laid upon Perdita's perfection conceived in terms of a call to spiritual devotion:

> This is a creature,
> Would she begin a sect, might quench the zeal
> Of all professors else;

and we are told of her that –

> Women will love her, that she is a woman
> More worth than any man; men, that she is
> The rarest of all women.

'Worth', 'rarity'; these are words which exercise a familiar attraction in the last plays, from *Pericles* onward. They call forth from the regenerate Leontes a response of gracious tenderness which finds issue, even before he has seen Florizel and his companion, in a summons to his 'embracement'.

Before the actual entry of the newcomers, Paulina is given another opportunity, brief but intensely used, to relate the past to the present and to foreshadow their association in a spirit of all-embracing richness. In so doing, she brings the sorrowful past, still alive in her afflicted master, more closely into contact with the germinating growth of the future. Mamillius, 'jewel of children', would have been, had he lived, of the same age as the prince now about to enter. The fact, and the manner of stating it, at once associates the idea of treasure once more with that of youth, and comes home to Leontes with a pain not less intense for the temporal remoteness of its cause:

> Prithee, no more; cease; thou know'st
> He dies to me again when talk'd of.

Sorrow and reconciliation, life and death are being bound together, firmly and tenderly, in the expanding content of the play.

The actual entry of the fugitives brings us finally to the first great episode in the pattern of reconciliation which we are now engaged in tracing through its successive stages. Leontes' speech, welcoming them, is worthy, in its rich, symbolic beauty, of the occasion:

> Your mother was most true to wedlock, prince;
> For she did print your royal father off,
> Conceiving you: were I but twenty one,
> Your father's image is so hit in you,
> His very air, that I should call you brother,
> As I did him, and speak of something wildly
> By us perform'd before. Most dearly welcome!
> And your fair princess, – goddess! – O, alas!
> I lost a couple, that 'twixt heaven and earth
> Might thus have stood begetting wonder, as
> You, gracious couple, do! and then I lost,
> All mine own folly, the society,
> Amity, too, of your brave father, whom,
> Though bearing misery, I desire my life
> Once more to look on him.   (v i)

The opening words, raising once more the theme of 'wedlock' and fidelity – and was not Leontes' sin against Hermione in the first place a revelation of the lack of such faith? – go on to stress the 'royalty' both of Polixenes and his son, thus reaffirming the special dignity which is part of the complete effect; the emphasis upon conception, birth, we have seen already to presage the growth of renewed life. The thought, however, raises in the speaker memories of his own past. Seeing before him the 'image' of Polixenes reflected in his son, he is reminded of the times when his former friend was his 'brother', joined to him by a union the youthful intimacy of which was broken through actions by themselves 'wildly ... perform'd before'. Leontes' past experience, in fact, though not forgotten, is falling, as it were, into perspective, completed by the present which is dominated by what is at once an image of the past repeating itself and a new birth.

In its double nature as reflection of the past revived and the present newly born, this vision of Florizel is as welcome to Leontes as the 'fair princess' whose true identity is still unknown to him, but whose perfect beauty, symbol of an inner state of perfection, leads him to address her as nothing less than 'goddess'. In the light of this vision of a new generation of lovers, Hermione and Perdita appear in turn as memories of superhuman rarity:

> I lost a couple, that 'twixt heaven and earth
> Might thus have stood begetting wonder, as
> You, gracious couple, do.

This imaginative transfiguration of humanity reminds us once more, in its intensity, of *Antony and Cleopatra*, though here – as we have suggested before – it stands no more as a mere expression of personal sentiment, subject to a process of change and disillusionment which its intensity can only in part, and precariously, ignore, but is rather incorporated into a symbolic vision that transcends the purely personal; the fact that the couple now before him are seen as 'gracious' reinforces the effect with the most inclusive conception of the whole play. Unlike Cleopatra, moreover, Leontes is not content to isolate himself from his own past. On the contrary, his sense of this harmonious, transcendent vision gains its force by being set against his memory of the passion-driven act that originally destroyed its forerunner. Against the rebirth still unachieved in his mind is set a sense of loss, proceeding from his own 'folly' and implying the breaking of the link, essentially *social* (the word 'society' is not used accidentally), of 'amity' that bound him to the father whose features are now so hauntingly repeated in his son. Thus poised between past and present, aware of age and anticipating a certain rebirth, Leontes' is the state of one who, although 'bearing misery' in the shape of sorrow for acts still felt to be beyond repair, desires life in so far as it may bring him to reconciliation. To the spirit of this speech, Florizel's reply, with its mention of an 'infirmity' in Polixenes which is felt to be the natural consequence of 'worn times' and to correspond to Leontes' own age, is an affirmation of continued relationship. The attitude of the speaker's father to his former friend is still one of loving devotion:

> ... whom he loves,
> He bade me say so, more than all the sceptres
> And those that bear them living.

If the idea of royalty is an important element in the symbolic conception of *The Winter's Tale*, it is still secondary to the depth of human feeling. It is, indeed, the latter, incarnate in the figures of their respective children, that confers true poetic validity upon the final reconciliation.

To this expression of emotion, Leontes replies with a spontaneous overflow of feeling. Polixenes is his 'brother', related to him by a tie that is felt to be even stronger than that of friendship, that implies a unity of blood; in a play in which the most intimate relationships of the family play so great a part, this insistence upon fraternity, repeated from the speech previously quoted, is not an accident. The traditional conception of brotherhood in royalty is bound, in fact, to a deeper, more intimate relationship which is close to the heart of the play. Prompted by this resurgence of emotion, the memory of his past behaviour stirs anew in Leontes, like the new birth which it indeed is –

> ... the wrongs I have done thee stir
> Afresh within me –

and the salutations of Florizel, so '*rarely* kind' (the choice of adverb again has something to contribute to the total effect), prompts his 'behind-hand slackness' to a response. This competition in generosity of emotion, feeling vieing with feeling in an effect of cumulative harmony, recalls the spirit of the exchanges between Duncan and the loyal Banquo in the early scenes of *Macbeth*. The response, in turn, is associated with the rebirth of the seasons with which so much in the spirit of the play has been conceived:

> Welcome hither,
> As is the spring to the earth.

The fresh kindling of positive emotion in Leontes is in this way related to the natural movement of the seasons, and the link that binds developed understanding to this renewed access of feeling is further stressed just below in the reference to the 'ungentle' storms and 'fearful usage' through which Perdita, 'this paragon', has passed to make this moment possible; to it corresponds properly the speaker's own admission that he is still, at least in his own eyes, 'a man not worth her pains'.

The following exchange between Florizel and Leontes, after a reference to the 'prosperous south-wind friendly' which has brought the fugitives to Bohemia and which contrasts, in its own passing fashion, with earlier references to the elements in tempest, leads up to a direct expression of welcome, in which once more the unmistakable note of poetic symbolism is present:

> The blessed gods
> Purge all infection from our air whilst you
> Do climate here! You have a holy father,
> A graceful gentleman; against whose person,
> So sacred as it is, I have done sin:
> For which the heavens, taking angry note,
> Have left me issueless; and your father's blest,
> As he from heaven merits it, with you
> Worthy his goodness. What might I have been,
> Might I a son and daughter now have look'd on,
> Such goodly things as you. (v i)

Practically every expression in this speech can be paralleled in Shakespeare's later writing, of which it is in some sense a kind of condensed fulfilment. The reference to the 'blessed gods', taking

up the providential note that has been present in the play at least
since the intervention of the oracle (III i), leads up to a prayer
that the air may be 'purged' of 'all infection' during the visitor's
stay; we are reminded again of the spirit of Banquo's description
of Macbeth's castle at Inverness (I vi), and the unusual choice of
the verb 'climate', for 'sojourn', weds the elements more closely
to the spiritual state that is being conveyed. The 'infection', of
course, has connections with the passion that destroyed Leontes'
peace at the outset; it recalls Polixenes' reference (I ii) to the
'infected jelly' into which his 'best blood' should have been transformed, had Leontes' suspicion been true. From this opening
welcome, it is natural for Leontes to look back from Florizel
before him to his father, the friend of his youth, in whom he sees
holiness and a suggestion of 'grace' – he calls him 'holy' father
and 'graceful gentleman' – combined; and against the memory of
this 'sacred' person there rises in his mind the sense of the wrong
inflicted upon him, now given its full moral weight as an offence
against the right ordering of life, as 'sin'. The movement of the
imagery, first connecting pure 'air' with the action of the 'gods',
and then leading up through the idea of purification implied in
'*purge* all infection' to that of sin, which is moral disease calling –
as in the case of the Doctors in *Macbeth* and *Lear* who ministered
less to the ills of the flesh than to the infirmities of the spirit – for
its appropriate purgation, is characteristic; so is the counter-
process which links 'holy' and 'graceful', culminating in the
direct assertion of the religious value of just kingship:

> . . . against whose person
> So *sacred* as it is, I have done sin.

The state of Leontes preparatory to the final reconciliation,
combining the memory of wrong inflicted in the past with a
present depth of penitence for the 'sin' the full enormity of
which he has now come to understand, receives here its full
expression.

The complete content of the speech, however, has still to be
completed in its later lines. The idea of sin leads naturally to that
of the divine displeasure which has lain so heavily for sixteen

years upon the speaker, and which has accompanied him from
maturity to old age:

> For which the heavens, taking angry note,
> Have left me issueless.

The anger of the heavens, indeed, implies something more than a
mere figurative reference to the divine displeasure, more closely
knit into the play's symbolic structure and more directly related
to its human vicissitudes. It bears, in 'angry', a clear sense of
threatening storm-clouds, and thus connects the speech with the
symbolic theme of tempest through which, in all the late plays,
sin has to be led, through atonement in accepted suffering, to
final reconciliation; the very rhythm of the lines is one which
seems at this time to have been significant to Shakespeare, who
repeated it, or something very similar, in the lines from Ariel's
great speech in *The Tempest*:

> . . . . for which foul deed
> The powers, delaying, not forgetting, have
> Incensed the seas and shores, yea, all the creatures
> Against your peace.

'Sin' for 'foul deed', the 'heavens' for 'the powers', 'taking angry
note' for 'delaying, not forgetting': the movement of the thought
as conveyed by poetic rhythm deliberately devised to lay stress
upon the presence of weighty and inevitable judgement is surely
similar enough to point to a significant unity of conception, and
the similarity is furthered by the fact that, as Leontes has been
left 'issueless', so Alonso was 'bereft' of his son. To deprive the
offender, at least in his own belief, of natural fulfilment in the
shape of issue is, indeed, the normal reaction of the 'heavens' in
these plays to sin, the unbridled action of passion breaking down
the limits of sweet reason; and it is no accident that Leontes, thus
left childless, as he still believes, through his own action, sees
Florizel's father, his lost companion, as 'blest', in response to his
merits, by the 'heavens' with an heir 'worthy his goodness'. The
speech ends on a note of nostalgia for what the speaker has lost, in
terms which themselves look forward to the final effect.

The moment of reconciliation, however, is not yet due for development. Progress towards it is interrupted, not for the first time, by an unwelcome entry; as always, the achievement of final unity has to be gained, not in passivity, but in a series of re-actions, of which this is the last and the most inclusive, against the continued pressure of the forces making for disruption. A Lord enters with the news, well-nigh incredible to those ad-dressed, that Polixenes is at hand in chase of his son, who has cast off his princely 'dignity' and filial 'duty' alike to attach himself to 'a shepherd's daughter'. The accusation, though not, of course, finally valid, needs, given the symbolic formulations on which the action rests, to be taken seriously enough to amount to a new turn in the development of the play. Once more, as formerly in the pastoral scene, the entry of Polixenes is associated with the bitterness of age and frustrated mortality; he is said to be threatening the shepherds with 'diverse deaths in death', and the re-entry of the tragic note is given universal meaning in the momentary bitterness of Perdita's phrase, 'the heaven sets spies upon us'. It seems, indeed, that the same heaven which Leontes has recently invoked as the key to loving reconciliation has now set itself against the celebration of her contract to Florizel. The changed position of Leontes, however, is the key to the next stage in the unfolding of the complete story. Accepting what is, indeed, an essential part of the play's conception, for which royalty is sacred and the bonds that bind child to father in duty necessary to lasting reconciliation, he expresses his sorrow that Florizel seems to have broken a relationship to which he was 'tied in duty', and that the object of his choice seems not to be so *rich* (the very choice of the word carries its own weight) in moral 'worth' and princely standing as in the beauty which she so un-deniably possesses. Beauty, however, is by now an external attribute of merit, and Florizel is able to set against the thought of affliction a counter-assertion of the value of his love:

> Though Fortune, visible an enemy,
> Should chase us with my father, power no jot
> Has she to change our loves.

'Fortune', as always, is in herself blind, the enemy of personal bonds that reach out after timelessness; but the relationship itself which feels this enmity is already, in the last resort, beyond her power. In asserting this, Florizel appeals to Leontes' own memory of his lost youth –

> Remember since you owed no more to time
> Than I do now –

and the appeal, joined to the sight of a 'precious mistress' in whom Leontes, though still unaware of the truth, obscurely senses the continuation of his own youth, is strong enough to coincide with the understanding born of experience and moral maturity and leads him to take up the task of mediation. Paulina's protest that his eye, in admiring Perdita, 'hath too much youth in't', is countered by his assertion that, in praising her, it is of his lost wife that he is thinking –

> I thought of her,
> Even in these looks I made.

Florizel's 'desires' appear to him, in the light of this, as in no sense contrary to 'honour', and the friendship which binds him to father and son alike is such that he, who was formerly the cause of division and tragedy, can now become the instrument of restored harmony. With that end in mind, he proceeds to his meeting with Polixenes.

The following scene (v ii) is one of those episodes, characteristic of Shakespeare's later manner, in which incidents apparently trivial, even seemingly marginal to the main story, are woven by the conscious elaboration of style into a developing symbolic fabric. Its grave and involved prose is seen, in fact, on closer reading, not to be mere decoration, but to belong to the spirit of the play, in forming which it plays its own distinctive part. It opens, of course, with the Gentleman's account of the finding, sixteen years ago, of the child Perdita, as related by the Shepherd; and the manner of the telling, far from being an excursion into literary artifice, is admirably calculated both to maintain the necessary 'legendary' quality of the episode, the sense of remoteness in time, and to further the symbolic unity of the whole conception. The Gentleman's first speech insists on the idea of finding ('the manner how he found it': 'I heard the shepherd say, he found the child'), and introduces the sense of 'amazedness', of having been present at the birth of high issues as yet most imperfectly understood; his second utterance introduces us fully into the emotional atmosphere of this finding, which is one of miracle and spiritual significance:

... they seemed almost, with staring on one another, to tear the cases of their eyes; there was speech in their dumbness, language in' their very gesture; they looked as they had heard of a world ransomed, or one destroy'd: a notable passion of wonder appeared in them; but the wisest beholder, that knew no more but seeing, could not say if the importance were joy or sorrow; but in the extremity of the one, it must be.   (v ii)

The resemblance of the phrase 'to tear the cases of their eyes' with certain repeated images from *King Lear* is perhaps too tenuous to be insisted on, but it is just worth noting that the two aspects of sight, physical and spiritual, are closely related in that play, and that here too the Gentleman feels himself to be present at events whose meaning is more than material, events of whose significance he has barely more than a glimpse. The element of wonder, essential to the whole episode, is implicit in the speechlessness that itself, translated into gesture, became charged with half-revealed significance in the eyes of the bystander; those present at this finding, and in a position to appreciate its full meaning, were rapt into contemplation, stricken with a silence beyond the possibilities of speech. The basis of their wonder, fundamentally religious, is indicated in the following reference to 'a world *ransomed*', with its gravely Christian implications, and in the contrast implied by 'destroyed'; the 'passion of wonder' which overcame the central figures, as recorded by this minor observer, is allied to their sense of the spiritual qualities involved in this miraculous rebirth of a dead past. The likeness of joy to sorrow, especially evident here to those who have no key to the full meaning of the action to which they are witnesses, is, of course, familiar in Shakespeare's late plays; and so is the sense of the 'extremity' which must accompany either emotion, a feeling of being poised on the edge of an experience which may be related either in terms of life or death, but which is unquestionably near the limits of human understanding. The confirmation, brought by the second Gentleman, that 'the oracle is fulfilled', itself takes us back sixteen years and recalls the entry into the action of an explicitly religious sanction; the result now is a 'wonder' which, though not incompatible with a certain gentle scepticism ('ballad-makers cannot be able to express it'), is a proper prelude to the final resolution.

The entry of the Third Gentleman, the first direct eye-witness of the scene, builds up still further the symbolic effect. The prose, at once carefully elaborated and finely evocative, is, once more, a factor of primary importance. Even such a phrase as 'if ever truth were pregnant by circumstance' has its further function in contributing to the general sense of fertility, of significant birth set in the process of time; and the terms of the description of the child which immediately follows are related less to anything immediately seen than to the communication of an underlying content:

... the majesty of the creature in resemblance of the mother, the affection of nobleness which nature shows above her breeding, and many other evidences proclaim her with all certainty to be the king's daughter.

The 'majesty' of Perdita, conceived as a reflection of that of Hermione, is evidently related to one of the main concepts of the play. 'Nobleness', too, exercises a function in associating the civilized, courtly graces with the universal simplicities of life as their crown and goal. The 'nobleness' of Perdita is bestowed upon her by 'nature', and stands out in contrast to her supposed humble 'breeding'. One of the main results of the final integration will be to bridge the gap between pastoral simplicity and the civilized graces, bringing them together in a harmonious unity.

The description thus conveyed leads up to the meeting between the two kings, and with it to the healing of the first of the great breaches which the effects of passion had introduced into the early action. Once again, the words of the Gentleman are charged with symbolic undertones:

There might you have beheld one joy crown another, ... that it seemed sorrow wept to take leave of them, for their joy waded in tears.

Once more, the apparently contrary emotions of joy and sorrow have become fused, so that the one, far from undoing its opposite, reinforces it, becomes an element in its full expression. Each new joy is the 'crown' of its predecessor, so that emotion itself is related to the inclusive effect of 'majesty'; at the same time, this joy expresses itself in tears, in a sorrow which 'wept to take leave of them' in the moment of being replaced by the joy of new discovery. In Leontes, 'the joy of his found daughter' is balanced against the 'loss', still present in his memory, of her mother; and the happiness of his reunion with Polixenes expresses itself immediately, in the typical manner of these plays, in a request for 'forgiveness' in respect of his earlier sin. The wrapping of this description in carefully elaborated forms of expression, coupled with the stressing of its similarity to an old 'tale', contributes to removing the action from common modes of feeling, and thus to the creation of the necessary symbolic atmosphere.

The reconciliation having been thus described, the Gentleman proceeds to recall once more the tempest from which Perdita was saved by the shepherd; the 'instruments' which 'aided to expose' her 'were even then lost when it was found'. This new variation upon the theme of loss and finding reflects once more what is now in effect the prevailing rhythm of the action; and Paulina, too, at the moment of 'locking' the princess to her heart in embrace, clings to her with a depth of emotion which is intensified by her having learnt in the same moment of her husband's end, and, above all, by the 'danger of losing' which gives a fresh keenness to the positive emotions of the play. By so doing, she concludes an act 'worth the audience of kings and princes' in its dignity; 'for by such' – not accidentally – 'it was acted'.

The following account of Perdita's grief for Hermione's

supposed death – expressed in prose in which, for once, the artificiality of elaboration seems to be insufficiently integrated into a true artistic effect* – leads up to the first mention of the 'statue' in Paulina's keeping, and so anticipates the last stage in the final resolution. The statue, be it noted, is celebrated as a work of art which could 'beguile nature', had it only the attribute of eternity which would enable it to create 'breath'. In point of fact, the statue will, of course, come to life, raising the imitation of 'art' to the life of nature, in much the same way as the pastoral simplicities have been perfected in their courtly setting. The conversation finishes by referring explicitly to the birth of 'some new grace', an anticipation at once of the final reconciliation and a contribution to its emotional completeness. The whole has been an admirable example of the manner in which the artificiality of conventional Elizabethan prose has been turned to a purpose which transcends its apparent limitations. The action, having been transferred to the court, requires a courtly style to set against the pastoral simplicities which preceded its final stages; but this style needs to be rich without being artificial, to secure an exploration of emotion that is not merely conventional, approaching it from a vast number of viewpoints and bringing these together in implied comparisons whose complexity is more than conventional. For the operation of artistic intuition, gathering up dissimilarities and fusing them into a superior unity which is, in this case, the entry into a new, richer life, this peculiar prose is a most suitable instrument.

The last part of the scene, having thus created its effect of harmony, returns by way of contrast to the unassimilated simplicities of life. In this way, the effect of excessive simplification is once more avoided, and common vitality given a place of its own in the complete pattern. Autolycus, significantly, refers immediately after the departure of the courtiers to 'the dash of my former life in me'; he, at least, is not ready to be assimilated to any symbolic scheme, however noble and compelling in its vision,

---

* Note, for example, such a phrase as 'one of the *prettiest* touches of all and that which *angled for mine eyes, caught the water though not the fish* . . .', where the decorative purpose clearly prevails.

and the contrast between the 'dash' of unregenerate humanity and
the theme of 'grace' is clearly deliberate. The following mention
of the sea-sickness of the shepherd's daughter contributes
similarly to this sense of contrast. His exchange with the Shepherd and the Clown, who now appear for the last time, introduces
in turn a comment, gently pointed with irony, upon the claims to
the civilized graces implied in the aristocratic conception behind
the word 'gentleman'. The Clown, indeed, takes up a familiar
Shakespearean theme when he associates the aristocratic ideal
with that of external appearance: 'See you those clothes? say you
see them not, and think me still no gentleman born: you were
best say these robes are not gentleman born'. The spirit of the
play is very different, of course, from that which inspired in *King
Lear* the crucial confronting of the pride implied in rich raiment
with the reality of 'unaccommodated man', but it comes still
from the same experience. The contrast is now between inherent
aristocracy, a true graciousness born, in the last analysis, of
nature, but perfected by 'grace', and the superficial assumption of
the external features of rank. The naïvety with which the Clown
is ready to equate the two serves at once as a contrast and a
criticism, bringing out the true value of the main conception and
qualifying it with a saving irony.

A similar effect is produced, just below, by the telling association of simple pretension with true, and equally simple grief,
implied in 'so we wept, and there was the first gentleman-like
tears that ever we shed'. The note of relativity is maintained in
the Clown's following question to Autolycus: 'Thou wilt amend
thy life?' to which the latter gives an off-hand consent which not
even the Shepherd accepts as other than it is: 'You may say it' –
that Autolycus is now as 'honest a true fellow as any is in
Bohemia' – 'but not swear it'. Most telling of all comes, at the
end of the scene, the Clown's farewell to Autolycus, with which
the latter, enigmatic to the last, leaves the action:

If it be ne'er so false, a true gentleman may swear it in the behalf
of his friend: and I'll swear to the prince thou art a tall fellow of
thy hands and that thou wilt not be drunk; but I know thou art
no tall fellow of thy hands and that thou wilt be drunk: but I'll

swear it, and I would thou wouldst be a tall fellow of thy hands.

(v ii)

The Clown's desire stands out, in a contrast at once comic and pathetic, against a reality that cannot be assimilated completely to any symbolic design, however gracious and inclusive. As he swears on behalf of Autolycus, he knows that his oath is in fact unfounded, that its object will continue to exist on the margin of the new life, enhancing its beauty by contrast but giving it also a sense of relativity, of pathos, which not even its splendid realization in terms of poetic integration can entirely overcome; his realistic knowledge is balanced against his desire that things should be otherwise than they are, and the episode concludes on a note, between comic and resigned, that has its part in the complete conception. Seeing 'the kings and the princes' as 'our kindred', with a pretentiousness that is absurd, comic, but not entirely devoid of pathos, his attitude stands out alike against the spirit of the main court action and against the comment implied in the constant scepticism of Autolycus.

The transformation towards which the whole action has been pointing is completed, given visible dramatic expression, in the final scene (v iii). In it, the Shakespearean experience, different in kind and quality from anything else in English poetry, reaches a complete integration. The fetters of the plot are dissolved; or rather, the plot itself, conceived as an extension of the poetic development which we have traced through the course of the play, is at last finally assimilated to the interplay of imagery. The words of the reconciled parties at the foot of Hermione's 'statue' are as significant in their sequence as in their thematic content and plain sense; they proceed by an antiphonal building-up towards the final, inclusive harmony. This sequence is given continuity, external projection by the various successive stages of the plot, by the process of Leontes' slow awakening to the fact that Hermione herself is before him, and by the almost imperceptible stages of her coming to life, which itself corresponds to the definitive birth of the new 'grace' out of the long winter of his penance. In this final scene, plot finally assumes its full status as the crown of an intricate development of poetic resources. Technique becomes the free and adequate instrument of experience, and the development of imagery which we have traced through the pattern of this play is given an adequate external consummation, seen as logically complete.

Compared with this general impression, irresistibly conveyed by the very movement of the action towards its conclusion, the analysis of detail becomes of secondary importance, almost unnecessary in view of the degree of clarity finally achieved. The distinctive Shakespearean use of imagery, however, although more closely identified than ever before with the flow of dramatic incident, is still pervasively present. The opening exchange between Leontes and Paulina echoes, this time on a level of full mutual sincerity, the relationship between royal bounty and devoted service which characterizes the early scenes of *Macbeth*. To Leontes' salutation of the 'grave and good' Paulina and to his thanks for the 'great comfort' he has received from her in his past trials, she replies with a simple rejoinder:

> All my services
> You have paid home;

and goes on to describe as 'a surplus of your grace', impossible to repay in like measure, his royal condescension in visiting her house.* The introduction is brought to a close, just before Paulina unveils the niche to reveal Hermione, with the statement that the queen's 'dead likeness', like her 'peerless life', has a unique quality:

* For the conception, though not of course for the spirit, compare the following from *Macbeth*:
> All our service,
> In every point twice done, and then done double,
> Were poor and single business to contend
> Against those honours deep and broad wherewith
> Your majesty loads our house.   (I vi)

Leontes' final comment, 'We honour you with trouble', can also be paralleled in Duncan's:
> The love that follows us sometimes is our trouble,
> Which still we thank as love.

> Excels whatever yet you look'd upon
> Or hand of man hath done.

For this reason, as a work of art which yet excels art, Paulina has kept her treasure 'lonely, apart', a 'lively' mocking of life, as close to its original as sleep is to death.

Leontes' first reaction to the revelation of the motionless 'statue' is one of 'silence' and 'wonder'. His first words, recalling his past treatment of Hermione, are a request that she should 'chide' him; his second utterance contrasts his sense of sin explicitly with the perfection he remembers and associates his memory of that perfection significantly with a new birth:

> ... for she was as tender
> As infancy and grace.

It is, indeed, a rebirth whose successive stages we are now witnessing, a rebirth the impression of which is strengthened in Leontes by his acute sense of the passage of time; for the Hermione he sees is 'wrinkled' as the wife of his memories never was, and Paulina has to explain that this is due to the artist's skill in taking into account the years which have passed since her 'death'. The relation of the time-theme to those of rebirth and reconciliation is thus retained to the last as a necessary part of the complete effect.

The first reaction of Leontes to the restored image of his 'dead' wife is, significantly, one of profound disquiet. The sight is now as 'piercing' to his soul, as full of memories of the follies he has committed, as her life, by himself destroyed, might have been to his 'good comfort'. In Perdita, on the other hand, the vision produces the first move towards reconciliation. She kneels and, like all the children of these plays in like situation, implores her parent's 'blessing'. Her prayer, moreover, is addressed to her 'that ended when I but begun', binding together – as in *Pericles* – mother and daughter in the single process of re-created life which this play aims at conveying. It is, in fact, the triumph of this continuity, a triumph as natural and inevitable as life itself, that we are witnessing. When Leontes is 'transported' by the contrary emotions which assail him, when, in spite of the grief which the

sight of the 'statue' has roused in him, he begs that the deceptive
life-likeness, as he still considers it, may not be taken from him:

> Make me to think so twenty years together,

and echoes the idea so emphatically, a little later, in his exclama-
tion 'No, not these twenty years', he is once more suggesting that
time can stand still as he contemplates his love. This can only be
justified by the power of the poetic process, which shows that
this conception of love is one of life and value, incommensurate
with time, which has now become only a condition of it. It is not
an accident that Hermione's slow re-awakening – slow both to
ease the intolerable shock to Leontes' own senses and to reflect
the successive stages of his own full awakening to reality – is
from now on surrounded by symbols explicitly religious. The
'statue' itself is said to be placed in a 'chapel', and the war
between Leontes' contradictory feelings is envisaged as one in
which good and evil spirits are at odds for possession of his soul.
Above all, and most explicitly, Paulina stresses that, as a prelude
to Hermione's 'descending' –

> It is required
> You do awake your faith;

the solemnity of the expression, and the subsequent calling upon
music, here as ever the indication of harmony, forces us to give
due weight to the underlying sense of the action. Without 'faith',
indeed, the awakening of the 'statue' will appear a mere prodigy,
an external marvel, not the logical crown of a long and rich
spiritual process that it in fact is.

Paulina's final call to Hermione removes any doubt as to the
true scope of the 'resurrection' we are about to witness:

> 'Tis time, descend; be stone no more; approach;
> Strike all that look upon with marvel. Come,
> I'll fill your grave up; stir, nay, come away,
> Bequeath to death your numbness, for from him
> Dear life redeems you.   (v iii)

The first line, broken into short phrases, intense, insistent, is as much the evocation to a descending spirit as a call to Hermione to leave her pedestal. Her restoration to Leontes is to be hailed as a 'marvel' of more than physical content, as the miracle of life spiritually re-born. The sense of temporal impermanence overcome is indeed present in the reference to the filling up of the grave, the returning of former 'numbness' to death, and – most plainly of all – in the assertion of the *redemption* by 'dear life' from the bonds of mortality. Finally, and to dissipate the remaining fears of those around her, Paulina insists that such 'spells' as she has exercised are 'lawful', and the actions of Hermione herself consistently 'holy'; the adjective confirms, if further confirmation were needed at this stage, the essentially religious nature of the action we are witnessing.

With Leontes and Hermione finally embraced, to the wonder of those who surround them, it only remains for the play to be rounded off by the gesture, also typical of these comedies, by which the family unity is finally restored, and in which the father bestows his blessing. First Paulina restores Perdita to her mother, confirming the daughter's own instinct and laying emphasis on the symbolic meaning carried by her name:

> Kneel
> And pray your mother's blessing. Turn, good lady;
> Our Perdita is found;

and secondly, Hermione, in terms barely less familiar, makes it her first act in her new state to beseech the gods to 'look down' and pour their 'graces' upon her daughter's head. With the marrying of Paulina to Camillo, ratified by 'us, a pair of kings', Leontes and Polixenes newly rejoined in amity, the pattern of reconciliation is finally complete. It would be hard to find, even in Shakespeare, a more profound purpose more consistently carried out to its proper artistic conclusion.

Northrop Frye

RECOGNITION IN *THE WINTER'S TALE* (1963)

IN structure *The Winter's Tale*, like *King Lear*, falls into two main parts separated by a storm. The fact that they are also separated by sixteen years is less important. The first part ends with the ill-fated Antigonus caught between a bear and a raging sea, echoing a passage in one of Lear's storm speeches. This first part is the 'winter's tale' proper, for Mamillius is just about to whisper his tale into his mother's ear when the real winter strikes with the entrance of Leontes and his guards. Various bits of imagery, such as Polixenes' wish to get back to Bohemia for fear of 'sneaping winds' blowing at home and Hermione's remark during her trial (reproduced from *Pandosto*) that the emperor of Russia was her father, are linked to a winter setting. The storm, like the storm in *King Lear*, is described in such a way as to suggest that a whole order of things is being dissolved in a dark chaos of destruction and devouring monsters, and the action of the first part ends in almost unrelieved gloom. The second part is a tragicomedy where, as in *Cymbeline* and *Measure for Measure*, there is frightening rather than actual hurting. Some of the frightening seems cruel and unnecessary, but the principle of 'all's well that ends well' holds in comedy, however great nonsense it may be in life.

The two parts form a diptych of parallel and contrasting actions, one dealing with age, winter, and the jealousy of Leontes, the other with youth, summer, and the love of Florizel. The first part follows Greene's *Pandosto* closely; for the second part no major source has been identified. A number of symmetrical details, which are commonplaces of Shakespearian design, help to build up the contrast: for instance, the action of each part begins with an attempt to delay a return. The two parts are related in two ways, by sequence and by contrast. The cycle of nature, turning through the winter and summer of the year and through the age and youth of human generations, is at the center of the play's imagery. The opening scene sets the tone by speaking of Mamillius and of the desire of the older people in the country to live until he comes to reign. The next scene, where the action begins, refers to Leontes' own youth in a world of pastoral innocence and its present reflection in Mamillius. The same cycle is also symbolized, as in *Pericles*, by a mother-daughter relationship, and Perdita echoes Marina when she speaks of Hermione as having 'ended when I but began'. In the transition to the second part the clown watches the shipwreck and the devouring of Antigonus; the shepherd exhibits the birth tokens of Perdita and remarks, 'Thou mettest with things dying, I with things new-born'. Leontes, we are told, was to have returned Polixenes' visit 'this coming summer', but instead of that sixteen years pass and we find ourselves in Bohemia with spring imagery bursting out of Autolycus's first song, 'When daffodils begin to peer'. If Leontes is an imaginary cuckold, Autolycus, the thieving harbinger of spring, is something of an imaginative cuckoo. Thence we go on to the sheep-shearing festival, where the imagery extends from early spring to winter ever-greens, a vision of nature demonstrating its creative power throughout the entire year, which is perhaps what the dance of the twelve satyrs represents. The symbolic reason for the sixteen-year gap is clearly to have the cycle of the year reinforced by the slower cycle of human generations.

Dramatic contrast in Shakespeare normally includes a superficial resemblance in which one element is a parody of the other. Theseus remarks in *A Midsummer Night's Dream* that the lunatic, the lover, and the poet are of imagination all compact. Theseus, like Yeats, is a smiling public man past his first youth, but not, like Yeats, a poet and a critic. What critical ability there is in that family belongs entirely to Hippolyta, whose sharp comments are a most effective contrast to Theseus's amiable bumble. Hippolyta objects that the story of the lovers has a consistency to it that lunacy would lack, and everywhere in

Shakespearian comedy the resemblance of love and lunacy is based on their opposition. Florizel's love for Perdita, which transcends his duty to his father and his social responsibilities as a prince, is a state of mind above reason. He is advised, he says, by his 'fancy':

> If my reason
> Will thereto be obedient, I have reason;
> If not, my senses, better pleased with madness,
> Do bid it welcome.

Leontes' jealousy is a fantasy below reason, and hence a parody of Florizel's state. Camillo, who represents a kind of middle level in the play, is opposed to both, calling one diseased and the other desperate. Both states of mind collide with reality in the middle, and one is annihilated and the other redeemed, like the two aspects of law in Christianity. As the Gentleman says in reporting the finding of Perdita, 'They looked as they had heard of a world ransomed, or one destroyed'. When Leontes has returned to his proper state of mind, he echoes Florizel when he says of watching the statue,

> No settled senses of the world can match
> The pleasure of that madness.

The play ends in a double recognition scene: the first, which is reported only through the conversation of three Gentlemen, is the recognition of Perdita's parentage; the second is the final scene of the awakening of Hermione and the presenting of Perdita to her. The machinery of the former scene is the ordinary *cognitio* of New Comedy, where the heroine is proved by birth tokens to be respectable enough for the hero to marry her. In many comedies, though never in Shakespeare, such a *cognitio* is brought about through the ingenuity of a tricky servant. Auto- lycus has this role in *The Winter's Tale*, for though 'out of service' he still regards Florizel as his master, and he has also the rascality and the complacent soliloquies about his own cleverness that go with the role. He gains possession of the secret of Per- dita's birth, but somehow or other the denouement takes place without him, and he remains superfluous to the plot, consoling himself with the reflection that doing so good a deed would be inconsistent with the rest of his character. In *The Winter's Tale* Shakespeare has combined the two traditions which descended from Menander, pastoral romance and New Comedy, and has consequently come very close to Menandrine formulas as we have them in such a play as *Epitripontes*. But the fact that this conventional recognition scene is only reported indicates that Shakespeare is less interested in it than in the statue scene, which is all his own.

In *Measure for Measure* and *The Tempest* the happy ending is brought about through the exertions of the central characters, whose successes are so remarkable that they seem to many critics to have something almost supernatural about them, as though they were the agents of a divine providence. The germ of truth in this conception is that in other comedies of the same general structure, where there is no such character, the corresponding dramatic role is filled by a supernatural being – Diana in *Pericles* and Jupiter in *Cymbeline*. *The Winter's Tale* belongs to the second group, for the return of Perdita proceeds from the invisible providence of Apollo.

In *Pericles* and *Cymbeline* there is, in addition to the recognition scene, a dream in which the controlling divinity appears with an announcement of what is to conclude the action. Such a scene forms an emblematic recognition scene, in which we are shown the power that brings about the comic resolution. In *The Tempest*, where the power is human, Prospero's magic presents three emblematic visions: a wedding masque of gods to Ferdinand, a disappearing banquet to the Court Party, and 'trumpery' (IV i 186) to entice Stephano and Trinculo to steal. In *The Winter's Tale* Apollo does not enter the action, and the emblematic recognition scene is represented by the sheep-shearing festival. This is also on three levels. To Florizel it is a kind of betrothal masque and 'a meeting of the petty gods'; to the Court Party, Polixenes and Camillo, it is an illusion which they snatch away; to Autolycus it is an opportunity to sell his 'trumpery' (IV iv 608) and steal purses.

An emblematic recognition scene of this kind is the dis-

tinguishing feature of the four late romances. As a convention, it
develops from pastoral romance and the narrative or mythological
poem. The sheep-shearing festival resembles the big bravura
scenes of singing-matches and the like in Sidney's *Arcadia*, and
The Rape of Lucrece comes to an emblematic focus in the tapestry
depicting the fall of Troy, where Lucrece identifies herself with
Hecuba and Tarquin with Sinon, and determines that the second
Troy will not collapse around a rape like the first one. In the
earlier comedies the emblematic recognition scene is usually in
the form of burlesque. Thus in *Love's Labour's Lost* the pageant
of Worthies elaborates on Don Armado's appeal to the pre-
cedents of Solomon, Samson, and Hercules when he falls in love;
but his appeal has also burlesqued the main theme of the play.
The allegorical garden episode in *Richard II* represents a similar
device, but one rather different in its relation to the total dramatic
structure.

In any case the controlling power in the dramatic action of *The
Winter's Tale* is something identified both with the will of the
gods, especially Apollo, and with the power of nature. We have
to keep this association of nature and pagan gods in mind when
we examine the imagery in the play that reminds us of religious,
even explicitly Christian, conceptions. At the beginning Leontes'
youth is referred to as a time of paradisal innocence; by the end
of the scene he has tumbled into a completely illusory knowledge
of good and evil. He says:

> How blest am I
> In my just censure, in my true opinion!
> Alack, for lesser knowledge! How accurs'd
> In being so blest!

Or, as Ford says in *The Merry Wives*, 'God be praised for my
jealousy!' The irony of the scene in which Leontes is scolded by
Paulina turns on the fact that Leontes tries to be a source of
righteous wrath when he is actually an object of it. Hermione's
trial is supposed to be an act of justice and the sword of justice is
produced twice to have oaths sworn on it, but Leontes is under
the wrath of Apollo and divine justice is his enemy. The op-

posite of wrath is grace, and Hermione is associated throughout
the play with the word grace. During the uneasy and rather
cloying friendliness at the beginning of the play Hermione pro-
nounces the word 'grace' conspicuously three times, after which
the harsh dissonances of Leontes' jealousy begin. She also uses
the word when she is ordered off to prison and in the only speech
that she makes after Act III. But such grace is not Christian or
theological grace, which is superior to the order of nature, but a
secular analogy of Christian grace which is identical with nature
– the grace that Spenser celebrates in the sixth book of *The Faerie
Queene.*

   In the romances, and in some of the earlier comedies, we have
a sense of an irresistible power, whether of divine or human
agency, making for a providential resolution. Whenever we have
a strong sense of such a power, the human beings on whom it
operates seem greatly diminished in size. This is a feature of the
romances which often disappoints those who wish that Shakespeare had simply kept on writing tragedies. Because of the heavy
emphasis on reconciliation in *Cymbeline,* the jealousy of Posthumus is not titanic, as the jealousy of Othello is titanic; it
expresses only a childish petulance about women in general:
'I'll write against them, Despise them, curse them.' Similarly
Leontes (as he himself points out) falls far short of being a somber
demonic tyrant on the scale of Macbeth, and can only alternate
between bluster and an uneasy sense of having done wrong:

> Away with that audacious lady! Antigonus,
> I charg'd thee that she should not come about me.
> I knew she would.

This scaling down of the human perspective is in conformity
with a dramatic structure that seems closely analogous to such
Christian conceptions as wrath and grace. But the only one of
the four romances in which I suspect any explicit – which means
allegorical – references to Christianity is *Cymbeline. Cymbeline*
was king of Britain at the birth of Christ, and in such scenes as
the Jailer's speculations about death and his wistful 'I would we
were all of one mind, and that mind good', there are hints that

some far-reaching change in the human situation is taking place
off-stage. The play ends on the word 'peace' and with Cymbeline's promise to pay tribute to Rome, almost as though,
as soon as the story ended, another one were to begin with
Augustus Caesar's decree that all the world should be taxed.

No such explicit links are appropriate to *The Winter's Tale*,
though it is true that the story does tell of a mysterious disappearing child born in the winter who has four father-figures
assigned to her: a real one, a putative one who later becomes her
father-in-law, a fictional one, Smalus of Libya in Florizel's tale,
and a shepherd foster-father. This makes up a group of a shepherd and three kings, of whom one is African. The first part of
The Winter's Tale is, like *Cymbeline*, full of the imagery of superstitious sacrifice. Leontes, unable to sleep, wonders if having
Hermione burnt alive would not give him rest. Antigonus offers
to spay his three daughters if Hermione is guilty, though he
would prefer to castrate himself. Mamillius, whom Leontes
thinks of as a part of himself, becomes the victim necessary to
save Leontes, and the exposing of Perdita is attended by a
sacrificial holocaust. Not only is Antigonus devoured by a bear,
but the ship and its crew were 'Wrecked the same instant of their
master's death and in the view of the shepherd; so that all the
instruments which aided to expose the child were even then lost
when it was found'. In contrast, the restoring of Perdita to her
mother is an act of sacramental communion, but it is a secular
communion, and the 'instruments' aiding in it are the human arts.
The main characters repair to Paulina's house intending to 'sup'
there, and are taken into her chapel and presented with what is
alleged to be a work of painting and sculpture. Hermione, like
Thaisa in *Pericles*, is brought to life by the playing of music, and
references to the art of magic follow. Art, therefore, seems part
of the regenerating power of the play, and the imagination of the
poet is to be allied with that of the lover as against that of the
lunatic.

Apart from the final scene, at least three kinds of art are mentioned in the play. First, there is the art of the gardener who,
according to Polixenes' famous speech, may help or change

nature by marrying a gentler scion to the wildest stock but can do so only through nature's power, so that 'the art itself is nature'. This is a sound humanist view: it is the view of Sidney, who contrasts the brazen world of nature with the golden world of art but also speaks of art as a second nature. Sidney's view does not necessitate, but it is consistent with, his ridiculing of plays that show a character as an infant in one act and grown up in the next, and that mingle kings and clowns in the same scene. It is also the view of Ben Jonson who, recognizing a very different conception of nature in Shakespeare's romances, remarked good-humoredly that he was 'loth to make nature afraid in his plays, like those that beget tales, tempests, and suchlike drolleries'. We note that Polixenes' speech entirely fails to convince Perdita, who merely repeats that she will have nothing to do with bastard flowers:

> No more than, were I painted, I would wish
> This youth should say 'twere well, and only therefore
> Desire to breed by me. . . .

– a remark which oddly anticipates the disappearance of the painted statue of Hermione into the real Hermione. It also, as has often been pointed out, fails to convince Polixenes himself, for a few moments later we find him in a paroxysm of fury at the thought of his own gentle scion marrying the wild stock of a shepherd's daughter. Whatever its merits, Polixenes' view of art hardly seems to describe the kind of art that the play itself manifests.

Secondly, there is the kind of art represented by Julio Romano, said to be the painter and sculptor of Hermione's statue, a mimetic realist who 'would beguile Nature of her custom, so perfectly is he her ape'. But it turns out that in fact no statue has made of Hermione, and the entire reference to Romano seems pointless. We do not need his kind of art when we have the real Hermione, and here again, whatever Romano's merits, neither he nor the kind of realism he represents seems to be very central to the play itself. The literary equivalent of realism is plausibility, the supplying of adequate causation for events. There is little plausibility in *The Winter's Tale*, and a great deal of what is repeatedly called 'wonder'. Things are presented to us, not explained. The jealousy of Leontes explodes without warning: an actor may rationalize it in various ways; a careful reader of the text may suspect that the references to his youth have touched off some kind of suppressed guilt; but the essential fact is that the jealousy suddenly appears where it had not been before, like a second subject in a piece of music. 'How should this grow?' Polixenes asks of Camillo, but Camillo evades the question. At the end of the play Hermione is first a statue, then a living woman. The explanations given do not satisfy even Leontes, much less us. He says:

> But how, is to be question'd; for I saw her,
> As I thought, dead, and have in vain said many
> A prayer upon her grave.

As often in Shakespeare, further explanations are promised to the characters, but are not given to the audience: Paulina merely says, 'it appears she lives'.

Thirdly, though one blushes to mention it, there is the crude popular art of the ballads of Autolycus, of which one describes 'how a usurer's wife was brought to bed of twenty money-bags at a burden'. 'Is it true, think you?' asks Mopsa, unconsciously using one of the most frequently echoed words in the play. We notice that Shakespeare seems to be calling our attention to the incredibility of his story and to its ridiculous and outmoded devices when he makes both Paulina and the Gentlemen who report the recognition of Perdita speak of what is happening as 'like an old tale'. The magic words pronounced by Paulina that draw speech from Hermione are 'Our Perdita is found', and Paulina has previously said that the finding of Perdita is 'monstrous to our human reason'. And when one of the Gentlemen says 'Such a deal of wonder is broken out within this hour that ballad-makers cannot be able to express it', we begin to suspect that the kind of art manifested by the play itself is in some respects closer to these 'trumpery' ballads than to the sophisticated idealism and realism of Polixenes and Romano.

My late and much beloved colleague Professor Harold S. Wilson has called attention to the similarity between Polixenes' speech and a passage in Puttenham's *Arte of English Poesie* (1589), which in discussing the relation of art and nature uses the analogy of the gardener and the example of the 'gillyvor' (see p. 151 f). Puttenham also goes on to say that there is another context where art is 'only a bare imitator of nature's works, following and counterfeiting her actions and effects, as the Marmoset doth many countenances and gestures of man; of which sort are the arts of painting and carving'. We are reminded of Romano, the painter and carver who is the perfect 'ape' of nature. The poet, says Puttenham, is to use all types of art in their proper place, but for his greatest moments he will work 'even as nature her self working by her own peculiar virtue and proper instinct and not by example or meditation or exercise as all other artificers do'. We feel that Puttenham, writing before Shakespeare had got properly started and two centuries earlier than Coleridge, has nonetheless well characterized the peculiar quality of Shakespeare's art.

The fact that Leontes' state of mind is a parody of the imagination of lover and poet links *The Winter's Tale* with Shakespeare's 'humor' comedies, which turn on the contrast between fantasy and reality. Katharina moves from shrew to obedient wife; Falstaff from the seducer to the gull of the merry wives; the King of Navarre and his followers from contemplative pedants seeking authority from books to helpless lovers performing the tasks imposed on them by their ladies. Similarly when Florizel says that his love for Perdita

> cannot fail but by
> The violation of my faith; and then
> Let nature crush the sides o' th' earth together
> And mar the seeds within! . . .

– he is supplying the genuine form of what Camillo describes in parallel cosmological terms:

> you may as well
> Forbid the sea for to obey the moon,
> As or by oath remove or counsel shake
> The fabric of his folly, whose foundation
> Is piled upon his faith.

Puttenham begins his treatise by comparing the poet, as a creator, to God, 'who without any travail to his divine imagination made all the world of nought'. Leontes' jealousy is a parody of a creation out of nothing, as the insistent repetition of the word 'nothing' in the first act indicates, and as Leontes himself says in his mysterious mumbling half-soliloquy:

> Affection, thy intention stabs the centre!
> Thou dost make possible things not so held,
> Communicat'st with dream – how can this be?
> With what's unreal thou coactive art,
> And fellow'st nothing.

A humor is restored to a normal outlook by being confronted, not directly with reality, but with a reflection of its own illusion, as Katharina is tamed by being shown the reflection of her own shrewishness in Petruchio. Similarly Leontes, in the final scene, is 'mocked with art', the realistic illusion of Romano's statue which gradually reveals itself to be the real Hermione.

In the artificial society of the Sicilian court there are Mamillius, the hopeful prince who dies, and the infant Perdita who vanishes. In the rural society of Bohemia there are the shepherdess Perdita who is 'Flora Peering in April's front', and Florizel who, as his name suggests, is her masculine counterpart, and the Prince Charming who later reminds Leontes strongly of Mamillius and becomes Leontes' promised heir. Perdita says that she would like to strew Florizel with flowers:

> like a bank for love to lie and play on,
> Not like a corse; or if, not to be buried,
> But quick and in mine arms.

The antithesis between the two worlds is marked by Polixenes, who is handed 'flowers of winter' and who proceeds to destroy the festival like a winter wind, repeating the *senex iratus* role of Leontes in the other kingdom. But though he can bully Perdita, he impresses her no more than Leontes had impressed Hermione. Perdita merely says:

> I was not much afeard; for once or twice
> I was about to speak and tell him plainly
> The selfsame sun that shines upon his court
> Hides not his visage from our cottage but
> Looks on alike.

There is a faint New Testament echo here, but of course to Perdita the god of the sun would be Apollo, who does see to it that Polixenes is outwitted, though only by the fact that Perdita is really a princess. As always in Shakespeare, the structure of society is unchanged by the comic action. What happens in *The Winter's Tale* is the opposite of the art of the gardener as Polixenes describes it. A society which is artificial in a limited sense at the beginning of the play becomes at the end still artificial, but natural as well. Nature provides the means for the regeneration of artifice. But still it is true that 'The art itself is nature', and one wonders why a speech ending with those words should be assigned to Polixenes, the opponent of the festival.

The context of Polixenes' theory is the Renaissance framework in which there are two levels of the order of nature. Art belongs to human nature, and human nature is, properly speaking, the state that man lived in in Eden, or the Golden Age, before his fall into a lower world of physical nature to which he is not adapted. Man attempts to regain his original state through law, virtue, education, and such rational and conscious aids as art. Here nature is a superior order. In poetry this upper level of nature, uncontaminated by the sin and death of the fall, is usually symbolized by the starry spheres, which are now all that is left of it. The starry spheres produce the music of the spheres, and the harmony of music usually represents this upper level of nature in human life.

Most Shakespearian comedy is organized within this framework, and when it is, its imagery takes on the form outlined by

G. Wilson Knight in *The Shakespearean Tempest* (1932). The tempest symbolizes the destructive elements in the order of nature, and music the permanently constructive elements in it. Music in its turn is regularly associated with the starry spheres, of which the one closest to us, the moon, is the normal focus. The control of the tempest by the harmony of the spheres appears in the image of the moon pulling the tides, an image used once or twice in *The Winter's Tale*. The action of *The Merchant of Venice*, too, extends from the cosmological harmonies of the fifth act, where the moon sleeps with Endymion, to the tempest that wrecked Antonio's ships. In *Pericles*, which employs this imagery of harmony and tempest most exhaustively, Pericles is said to be a master of music, Cerimon revives Thaisa by music, Diana announces her appearance to Pericles by music, and the final recognition scene unites the music and tempest symbols, since it takes place in the temple of Diana during the festival of Neptune. Music also accompanies the revival of Hermione in the final scene of *The Winter's Tale*. All the attention is absorbed in Hermione as she begins to move while music plays; and we are reminded of Autolycus and of his role as a kind of rascally Orpheus at the sheep-shearing festival: 'My clown . . . would not stir his pettitoes till he had both tune and words; which so drew the rest of the herd to me that all their other senses stuck in ears. . . . No hearing, no feeling, but my sir's song, and admiring the nothing of it.' Here again Autolycus seems to be used to indicate that something is being subordinated in the play, though by no means eliminated.

In another solstitial play, *A Midsummer Night's Dream*, the cosmology is of this more conventional Renaissance kind. In the middle, between the world of chaos symbolized by tempest and the world of starry spheres symbolized by music, comes the cycle of nature, the world of Eros and Adonis, Puck and Pyramus, the love-god and the dying god. To this middle world the fairies belong, for the fairies are spirits of the four natural elements, and their dissension causes disorder in nature. Above, the cold fruit-less moon of Diana, whose nun Hermia would have to be, hangs over the action. While a mermaid is calming the sea by her song

and attracting the stars by the power of harmony, Cupid shoots
an arrow at the moon and its vestal: it falls in a parabola on a
flower and turns it 'purple with love's wound'. The story of
Pyramus is not very coherently told in Peter Quince's play, but
in Ovid there is a curious image about the blood spurting out of
Pyramus in an arc like water out of a burst pipe and falling on the
white mulberry and turning it purple. Here nature as a cycle of
birth and death, symbolized by the purple flower, revolves under-
neath nature as a settled and predictable order or harmony, as it
does also in a third solstitial play, *Twelfth Night*, which begins
with an image comparing music to a wind blowing on a bank of
violets.

But in *The Winter's Tale* nature is associated, not with the
credible, but with the incredible: nature as an order is subordinated to the nature that yearly confronts us with the impossible
miracle of renewed life. In Ben Jonson's animadversions on
Shakespeare's unnatural romances it is particularly the functional
role of the dance, the 'concupiscence of jigs', as he calls it, that he
objects to. But it is the dance that most clearly expresses the
pulsating energy of nature as it appears in *The Winter's Tale*, an
energy which communicates itself to the dialogue. Such words as
'push' and 'wild' (meaning rash) are constantly echoed; the play
ends with the words 'Hastily lead away', and we are told that the
repentant Leontes

> o'er and o'er divides him
> 'Twixt his unkindness and his kindness; th' one
> He chides to hell and bids the other grow
> Faster than thought of time.

Much is said about magic in the final scene, but there is no
magician, no Prospero, only the sense of a participation in the
redeeming and reviving power of a nature identified with art,
grace, and love. Hence the final recognition is appropriately that
of a frozen statue turning into a living presence, and the appropriate Chorus is Time, the destructive element which is also the
only possible representative of the timeless.

Nevill Coghill

SIX POINTS OF STAGE-CRAFT (1958)

IT is a critical commonplace that *The Winter's Tale* is an ill-made play: its very editors deride it. A recent apologist, S. L. Bethell, after posing the question 'Why is his dramatic technique crude and apparently incoherent?'[1] answers with the bold suggestion that Shakespeare was trying to be funny: instancing several examples in the Florizel-Perdita-Camillo-Autolycus-Shepherd-Clown sequences of IV iv, he concludes: '. . . surely this is a deliberately comic underlining of a deliberately crude technique. Considering now the play as a whole, are we not justified in suspecting a quite conscious return to naïve and outmoded technique, a deliberate creaking of the dramatic machinery?'[2]

These conjectures may seem valid in the study, but have no force on the stage. Shakespeare's stage-craft in this play is as novel, subtle and revolutionary as it had been a few years before in *Antony and Cleopatra*, but in an entirely different way: just as he had then found the technical path to an actual and life-sized world – to the drums and tramplings of the Roman Empire – so, in *The Winter's Tale* he hit upon a means of entry into the fabulous world of a life standing (as Hermione says) in the level of dreams (III ii 78).

Stage-craft is a word for the mechanics in the art of telling a story, through actors, on some sort of stage, *with a certain effect*. It must inventively use the facilities available to it. No one was more inventive than Shakespeare: deftness and dexterity of this kind mark all his work, and his surprises (so often, afterwards, felt to be 'inevitable') recall those in Beethoven, of whose last quartets the composer Balfour Gardiner said once to me, with a sigh of envy, 'Ah, the desolating old monkey! Never without a fresh rabbit to pull out of his hat!'

Six main charges of creaking dramaturgy have been made against *The Winter's Tale*, severally, by Bethell and the Cambridge editors. Let us consider them one by one, with this thought in mind, that if Shakespeare has demonstrably told his story in certain rather unusual ways, he may well have had some special, and perhaps discernible, intention in doing so: the careful consideration of how a contrivance works may often guide us to an understanding of its purpose.

1. THE SUPPOSED SUDDENNESS OF THE JEALOUSY OF LEONTES

In *Pandosto* (we shall use Shakespeare's names) Leontes' jealousy is made slow and by increase plausible. Shakespeare weakens the plausibility of it as well by ennobling Hermione – after his way with good women – as by huddling up the jealousy in its motion so densely that it strikes us as merely frantic and – which is worse in drama – a piece of impossible improbability. This has always and rightly offended the critics. . . . (Sir Arthur Quiller-Couch).[3]

Then suddenly with no more hint of preparation – and no hint at all on the psychological plane – Leontes' jealousy comes full upon him (S. L. Bethell).[4]

In an appendix devoted to this subject Bethell adds the conjecture that if Shakespeare had intended Leontes to be jealous from the start he would have brought him on alone 'to deliver an appropriate soliloquy'.[5] This would indeed have been 'a naïve and outmoded technique', one at least as old-fashioned as that which, long before, had so brilliantly opened *Richard III*. But in *The Winter's Tale* Shakespeare went about his business with new subtlety of dramatic invention. To understand it we must begin at the opening scene, a dialogue between Archidamus and Camillo, asking ourselves certain questions in dramaturgy.

What is the reason for this dialogue? What information does it convey? What is it supposed to do to an audience? At first sight it seems to resemble the opening scenes of *King Lear* and *Antony and Cleopatra*: just as Kent and Gloucester prepare us for the

division of Lear's kingdom and introduce the Bastard, just as
Philo and Demetrius announce Antony's dotage and prepare us
to see him enter as a strumpet's fool, so Archidamus and Camillo
prepare us to witness a kingly amity between Sicilia and Bohemia,
his guest, and to introduce us to Mamillius. There is no other
point in the little scene:

> *Cam.* Sicilia cannot show himself over-kind to Bohemia. They
> were trained together in their childhoods; and there rooted
> betwixt them then such an affection, which cannot choose but
> branch now ... they have seemed to be together, though absent,
> shook hands, as over a vast, and embraced, as it were, from the
> ends of opposed winds. The heavens continue their loves!
> *Arch.* I think there is not in the world either malice or matter
> to alter it. You have an unspeakable comfort of your young
> prince Mamillius. ...   (1 i 23–38)

Now whereas Kent and Gloucester, Philo and Demetrius, prepare the audience for what it is about to see (technique of
gratifying expectation raised), Camillo and Archidamus prepare
it for what it is about *not* to see (technique of the prepared surprise): directed to expect a pair of happy and affectionate friends,
the audience is startled by seeing exactly the opposite: the two
monarchs enter separately, and one, perceived to be the other's
host, wears a look of barely controlled hostility that may at any
moment blacken into thundercloud. The proof of this is in the
dialogue, which contains all the stage-directions necessary;
Polixenes leads in with his elaborate lines:

> Nine changes of the watery star hath been
> The shepherd's note since we have left our throne
> Without a burthen: time as long again
> Would be fill'd up, my brother, with our thanks;
> And yet we should, for perpetuity,
> Go hence in debt: and therefore, like a cipher,
> Yet standing in rich place, I multiply
> With one 'We thank you' many thousands moe
> That go before it.   (1 ii 1–9)

Polixenes is an artist in the language of court compliment, at

once flowery and formal, like Jacobean embroidery. All the
flourish of his opening lines conveys no more information than
this: '*I am visiting the King and have been here nine months.*' His
closing lines, however, make it certain that he is standing beside
Hermione (she is perhaps upon his arm?) and addressing her.
With self-deprecating paronomasia, and a bow no doubt, he pays
her compliment:

> And therefore, *like a cipher,*
> *Yet standing in rich place.* . . . .

To a visiting King there can be no richer place than next to the
Queen. This Queen, however, has something specially remarkable about her: she is *visibly pregnant,*[6] and near her hour, for a
day later we hear the First Lady tell Mamillius:

> The queen your mother rounds apace.   (II i 16)

This fact about her has been grasped by the audience at her first
entry, because they can see it is so; they hear the visiting King say
he has been there nine months; who can fail to wonder whether
the man so amicably addressing this expectant mother may not
be the father of her child? For what other possible reason can
Shakespeare have contrived the conversation so as to make him
specify nine changes of the inconstant moon? These things are
not done by accident; Shakespeare has established a complex
situation with the same inerrant economy, swiftness and originality that he used to open *Hamlet* or *Macbeth.*

How then is Leontes to bear himself? Again the clue lies in the
dialogue, in the calculated contrast between the flowery language
of Polixenes and the one-syllabled two-edged utterances of his
host. To the airy conceits of his boyhood's friend, Leontes replies
with ironic brevity, sprinkled with equivocation:

> Stay your thanks awhile;
> And pay them when you part.   (I ii 8)

To these lines Dover Wilson offers the illuminating note:
'Though very gracious on the surface, this remark, Leontes' first,
is ominous . . . "Praise in departing", a proverbial expression,

meaning "wait till the end before praising" ' (*W.T.* p. 131). The
équivoques of Leǫntes continue to alternate with the flourishes of
Polixenes, mannerly on the surface, menacing beneath:

> We are tougher, brother
> Than you can put us to't.   (I ii 15)
>
> Tongue-tied, our queen? speak you.   (I ii 27)

'Our queen' are cold vocables for married love and 'tongue-tied'
is a familiar epithet for guilt. It is clear that Leontes, as in the
source-story which Shakespeare was following, has long since
been jealous and is angling now (as he admits later) with his
sardonic amphibologies, to catch Polixenes in the trap of the
invitation to prolong his stay, before he can escape to Bohemia
and be safe. All this, as Dover Wilson's note points out, is easy
for an actor to suggest, facially and vocally, and it is the shock we
have been prepared to receive by the conversation of Archidamus and Camillo. We have witnessed a little miracle of stage-
craft.

11. EXIT PURSUED BY A BEAR

The stage-craft is justifiably described as crude or naïve. We have
the frequently remarked *Exit, pursued by a bear* ... (S. L.
Bethell).[7]

Now let us take Antigonus and the deep damnation of his taking
off. The child Perdita is laid on the seashore. . . . All we have
now to do as a matter of stage-workmanship is to efface Antigonus. But why introduce a bear? The ship that brought him is
riding off the coast of Bohemia and is presently engulfed with all
her crew. The clown sees it all happen. Then why, in the name
of economy, not engulf Antigonus with the rest – or better still,
as he tries to row aboard? If anyone asks this editor's private
opinion, it is that the bear-pit in Southwark ... had a tame animal
to let out, and the management took the opportunity to make a
popular hit (Sir Arthur Quiller-Couch, *W.T.* p. xx).

Let us note the mild self-contradiction contained in the above; if
the appearance of a bear at this point would make 'a popular hit'

it would be a very good piece of stage-workmanship, supposing it to be consistent with the story to be told, as it demonstrably is.

... nor can it be disputed that tame bears (very tame) were seen upon the stage at this period. The popular *Mucedorus*, for example, was revived in 1610 or 1611, and a new scene was written ... in which the clown, in attempting to escape from a white bear, is actually made to tumble over her on the stage. ... After this it can hardly be doubted that Antigonus was pursued by a polar bear in full view of the audience at the Globe (J. Dover Wilson, *W.T.* pp. 156–7).

Now the polar bear is an extremely dangerous beast, even if bred in captivity, and albino brown bears are of the utmost rarity, though it is true a pair was born at Berne in 1575. A brown bear could, of course, be painted white, but brown bears are cross and unreliable;[8] even if they were as mild as milk they could not be counted on for a well-timed knock-about routine such as is needed with Antigonus. On the other hand it is easy, even for a modest acrobat, to personate a bear, with an absolutely calculated degree of comic effect: he has only to be able to walk on all fours without flexing his knees and rise thence on to his 'hind legs' for an embrace. There is of course no difficulty in making a bear-costume. Real bears are neither so reliable, so funny, nor so alarming as a man disguised as a bear can be; the practical aspects of production make it certain that no Harry Hunks or Sackerson was borrowed for *The Winter's Tale* from the bear-pit next door. We are back, ther , at Q's question '*Why introduce a bear?*'

If we appreciate the problem in dramaturgy that faced Shake-speare at this turn in his story, the answer is clear enough: it was a *tour de force*, calculated to create a unique and particular effect, at that point demanded by the narrative mood and line of the play. It is at the moment when the tale, hitherto wholly and deeply tragic, turns suddenly and triumphantly to comedy. One may modulate in music from one key to another through a chord that is common to both; so, to pass from tragedy to comedy, it may not be unskilful to build the bridge out of material that is both tragic and comic at the same time.

Now it is terrifying and pitiful to see a bear grapple with and carry off an elderly man to a dreadful death, even on the stage; but (such is human nature) the unexpectedness of an ungainly animal in pursuit of an old gentleman (especially one so tedious as Antigonus) can also seem wildly comic; the terrible and the grotesque come near to each other in a *frisson* of horror instantly succeeded by a shout of laughter; and so this bear, this unique and perfect link between the two halves of the play, slips into place and holds.

There are those who will say this is a piece of far-fetched, sub-jective interpretation; but that is how the scene works on the stage, as Shakespeare foresaw that it would; he deliberately underlined the juxtaposition of mood, achieved by the invention of the bear, in the speeches he put into the mouth of the Clown, grisly and ludicrous, mocking and condoling, from one sentence to another:

O, the most piteous cry of the poor souls! Sometimes to see 'em, and not to see 'em; now the ship boring the moon with her main-mast, and anon swallowed with yeast and froth, as you'ld thrust a cork into a hogshead. And then for the land-service, to see how the bear tore out his shoulder-bone; how he cried to me for help and said his name was Antigonus, a nobleman. But tó make an end of the ship, to see how the sea flap-dragoned it: but, first, how the poor souls roared, and the sea mocked them; and how the poor gentleman roared and the bear mocked him, both roaring longer than the sea or weather. . . . I have not winked since I saw these sights: the men are not yet cold under water, nor the bear half dined on the gentleman: he's at it now.

(III iii 88–110)

If Shakespeare did not mean it that way, why did he write it that way? So far from being crude or antiquated, stage-craft such as this is a dazzling piece of *avant-garde* work; no parallel can be found for what, at a stroke, it effects: it is the transformation of tragedy into comedy: it symbolizes the revenge of Nature on the servant of a corrupted court: it is a thundering surprise; and yet those Naturals that are always demanding naturalism cannot complain, for what could be more natural than a bear? That this scene is a kind of dramaturgical hinge, a moment of planned structural antithesis, is certain from the dialogue; we are passing from tears to laughter, from death to life:

> Now bless thyself: thou mettest with things dying,
> I with things new-born.   (III iii 115)

III. FATHER TIME

In this play of ours, having to skip sixteen years after Act 3, he desperately drags in Father Time with an hour-glass . . . which means on interpretation that Shakespeare, having proposed to himself a drama in which a wronged woman has to bear a child, who has to be lost for years and restored to her as a grown girl, simply did not know how to do it, save by invoking some such device (Sir Arthur Quiller-Couch, *W.T.* p. xix).

Time the Chorus is not central at all but a necessary mechanism of the plot . . . . (S. L. Bethell)[9]

Both critics essentially regard Time as a mechanism for over-leaping sixteen years and therefore necessary to the plot. But in fact, if that is all he is there for, he is redundant. His choric soliloquy makes three plot-points: first, that we are to slide over sixteen years, second, that Leontes has shut himself away in penitence for his great sin, and, third, that we are about to hear of Florizel and Perdita. As all these points are clearly made in the scene immediately following (between Camillo and Polixenes, IV ii), Time and his speech, so far as mere plot is concerned, could be cut without much loss; but the loss to the theme and quality of the play would be enormous, for Time is absolutely central to both and if he were not a character in the play, it would be necessary to invent him. His function is as follows: he shows us we are being taken beyond 'realism' into the region of parable and fable, adumbrated in the title of the play. Time stands at the turn of the tide of mood, from tragedy to comedy, and makes a kind of pause or poise at the play's centre; coming to us from an unexpected supernatural or mythological region, yet he encourages us (in spite of that solemnity) to enter with confidence, by the easy-going familiarity of his direct address, into that mood of comedy initiated by the no less unexpected bear. The same unique imagination envisaged both Time and bear for the great moment necessary to the narrative and to the theme it bears, when the hour-glass turns and the darkness passes. To take a further step in the defence of Time's presence in the play will perhaps lead me into the subjective interpretations I believe myself so far to have avoided; but the risk must be taken. Few will deny that the central theme is the sin of Leontes, which has its wages in the death, and seeming death or dispersion of all that he loves; but, under the guidance of Paulina, this sin is long and truly repented, and the self-inflicted wound, given, as Camillo says, by one who is 'in rebellion with himself', is healed. But repentance and healing both take *time*; Time is the tester:

> I, that please some, try all.   (IV i I)

Time is at the heart of the play's mystery; why should his visible presence offend? We do not take offence at Time with his hour-glass in a Bronzino or a Van Dyck; why then in Shakespeare? He who holds too tenaciously in the study of Shakespeare to 'realism' and the Unities, has left the punt and is clinging to the pole.

IV. THE CRUDE SHIFTS TO CLEAR STAGE IN THE FLORIZEL-PERDITA-CAMILLO-AUTOLYCUS SEQUENCE

The stage-craft is justifiably described as crude or naïve . . . there is a patch of astonishingly awkward management towards the end of Act IV Scene IV, beginning at the point where Camillo questions Florizel and learns he is determined to 'put to sea' with Perdita (IV iv 509). Then we have:

> Flo.   Hark, Perdita (*drawing her aside*)
> (*To Camillo*) I'll hear you by and by.
> Cam.   He's irremovable,
>   Resolved for flight. Now were I happy, if
>   His going I could frame to serve my turn. (IV iv 514-17)

The conversation of Florizel and Perdita is required only to cover Camillo's explanation of his motives and this explanation is given to the audience in soliloquy, with more than a tinge of direct address (S. L. Bethell).[10]

There is nothing in the least awkward, crude or naïve about this stage-craft. As for direct address, its use has been among the chief glories of drama from Aeschylus to T. S. Eliot; let us, then, in considering Shakespeare, for a moment free ourselves of the limitations of the proscenium arch and its attendant fads, one of which is the denigration of soliloquy. It will be safer, too, to eliminate the stage-directions offered in the extract quoted, for they do not appear in Folio; we may have to replace them, but with a difference.

Next, let us consider the context. Perdita has said nothing for thirty lines; her last speech was one of sad resignation to fate:

> How often have I told you 'twould be thus!
> How often said, my dignity would last
> But till 'twere known!   (IV iv 484–6)

Now she stands anxiously by, listening to her headstrong lover at odds with one who is (to her) an elderly stranger of grave authority, a friend and servant of the dreaded King himself; the Prince is wildly asserting that he is ready to be wiped out of the succession for her sake; she hears him end brusquely with a less than civil defiance of Camillo's kindly counsel:

> What course I mean to hold
> Shall nothing benefit your knowledge, nor
> Concern me the reporting.   (IV iv 513–15)

Camillo replies with a mixture of rebuke and pleading:

> O my lord!
> I would your spirit were easier for advice,
> Or stronger for your need.

What if we suppose that Perdita, in sympathy with the caution of Camillo, makes some impulsive gesture towards him, at this point, to show her feelings? And why should not such a gesture be the cue for Florizel to swing round on her with his 'Hark, Perdita' (as who should say, in a mood of bravado, 'Now you listen to me, my girl!'), and take her a few steps upstage for a brief private colloquy, to divulge to her the plan he is keeping so secret from Camillo? To whom, over his shoulder, he throws:

I'll hear you by and by.

This would lead very simply and convincingly to Camillo's

He's irremovable,
Resolved for flight. . . .

Stage-directions such as these I have suggested are certainly no less authorized by the text than those in the extract quoted by Bethell; candid consideration may even judge them more in harmony with the line and feeling of the scene; and so, nearer to Shakespeare's intention. Be that as it may, no audience would be aware of any awkwardness or difficulty.

But Bethell does not base his case on a single instance:

A little later the device is repeated; Camillo has disclosed his plan and ends:

For instance, sir,
That you may know you shall not want, one word. (*They talk aside*)
(*Re-enter Autolycus*)
Aut. Ha, ha! what a fool Honesty is! etc.   (IV iv 604)

At the end of his speech we have another stage-direction: *Camillo, Florizel, and Perdita come forward.* There is no natural occasion for this 'talk aside' since all three are engaged in it; its only purpose is to allow Autolycus his direct address to the audience on the gullibility of rustics. Worst of all is the device to allow Camillo a last explanation to the audience in an aside. Florizel exclaims:

O Perdita, what have we twain forgot!
Pray you a word. (*They converse apart*)
We never hear what they have forgot. . . . (S. L. Bethell).[11]

Let us take these points one by one, first eliminating all the stage-directions quoted by Bethell, for they are the inventions of editors. We can invent our own if we need them. Folio reads (Camillo speaking):

That you may know you shall not want: one word,
                    Enter Autolycus
Aut. Ha, ha, what a Foole Honestie is?

There is a colon in Camillo's line (transformed by Bethell into a comma). What is it there for? It is there to indicate a sudden pause; the cautious Camillo, in mid-sentence, has *heard* the approach of Autolycus, laughing, like a Jaques (*As You Like It,* II, vii). He stops, looks round behind him, sees the intruder, frowns, and draws his companions aside to conclude their highly secret colloquy in a corner, leaving the centre of the stage to the still laughing Autolycus. There is nothing very awkward or archaic in that.

Next comes the question what it is that Florizel and Perdita have forgotten; no doubt Bethell is right in supposing this a simple dodge to give Camillo a soliloquy, but no producer would find the smallest difficulty in masking that basic fact, and no audience would even be aware that he had done so; Shakespeare left many such stage-directions to our common sense. At this point upon common sense we must rely, for there are no pointers in Folio, which reads:

Flo. O *Perdita*: what haue we twaine forgot?
    Pray you a word.

'Pray you a word' clearly must be addressed, not to Perdita, but to Autolycus, so as to draw him away as well, and leave Camillo isolated for his direct address. Therefore what they have forgotten concerns Autolycus too.

Now we have just witnessed a hasty exchange of garments between Florizel and Autolycus; nothing is easier than to suppose that Florizel, having left something that he and Perdita value in the garments he has given to Autolycus, and suddenly remembering, takes the rogue aside with Perdita to recover it. What could this 'something' be? Perhaps the betrothal flowers she had given her lover earlier in the scene, or some fairing bought from Autolycus – it does not matter what, *so long as the audience sees and recognizes it*; for if the audience can see what it is

that the lovers have forgotten, there is no reason why they should
be told what it is.

v. THE MESSENGER-SPEECHES IN v ii

But the greatest fault of all, to our thinking – worse even than
the huddling up in Act 1 – is the manner in which the play mis-
handles Leontes' recognition of Perdita. . . . If, having promised
ourselves a mighty thrill in the great master's fashion, we really
prefer two or three innominate gentlemen entering and saying
'Have you heard?' 'You don't tell me!' 'No.' 'Then you have lost
a sight' – why that is the sort of thing we prefer and there is no
more to be said (Sir Arthur Quiller-Couch, *W.T.* p. xxiii).

It *is* the sort of thing we prefer; in practice this scene is among the
most gripping and memorable of the entire play. Whoever saw
the production of it by Peter Brook at the Phoenix Theatre in
1951–2 will remember the excitement it created. I know of at
least two other productions of the play in which this scene had the
same effect, and generated that mounting thrill of expectation
needed to prepare us for the final scene. No doubt Shakespeare
could have handled the matter just as rousingly in the way sighed
for by Q, if he had so wished. Instead he decided on a messenger-
speech scene for several voices (an unusual experiment) and
made a masterpiece of it.

Bethell holds a different view from Q and believes that Shakespeare used this technique so as to have a last fling at court
jargon. His comment on the scene runs thus: 'This can only be
burlesque; Shakespeare had always enjoyed a thrust at such
affectation, and a straight line runs from Don Armado through
Osric to these gentlemen in *The Winter's Tale*.'[12] But there is no
such 'straight line'. Don Armado is a fantastical foreigner and his
language reflects it; Osric, the subtlest of Claudius' emissaries,
emits a smoke-cloud of words with the intent to blind Hamlet (as
he successfully does) into thinking him of no account; whereas
he is the bearer of his death-warrant.[13] The Three Gentlemen of
The Winter's Tale are neither Armados nor Osrics; they talk the
same dialect of early seventeenth-century refinement and wit as is

used by Archidamus and Camillo in Act i, scene i, and by Polixenes (though he speaks it in verse) in Act i scene ii.

There may be a case to be made against the Metaphysicals and their wit, but I do not believe that Shakespeare was here making it; we, if we admire Donne and Crashaw, should not gird at the conceits of the Three Gentlemen. Let us consider their situation; never in the memory of court-gossip has there been so joyful and so astounding a piece of news to spread; they are over the edge of tears in the happy excitement and feel a noble, indeed a partly miraculous joy, for the oracle has been fulfilled; so far as they can, they temper their tears with their wit. What could be a more delightful mixture of drollery and tenderness, or more in the best 'Metaphysical' manner than

One of the prettiest touches of all and that which angled for mine eyes, caught the water though not the fish, was when, at the relation of the queen's death, with the manner how she came to't bravely confessed and lamented by the king, how attentiveness wounded his daughter; till, from one sign of dolour to another, she did, with an 'Alas,' I would fain say, bleed tears, for I am sure my heart wept blood. . . .   (v ii 89)

Could Donne have found a better hyperbole than 'wounded', or Crashaw a more felicitous conceit for eyes and tears?

VI. THE STATUE SCENE

Of all Shakespeare's *coups de théâtre*, the descent of Hermione from her pedestal is perhaps the most spectacular and affecting; it is also one of the most carefully contrived and has indeed been indicted for its contrivance: 'Hermione's is not a genuine resurrection . . . The very staginess of this "statue" scene acknowledges the inadequacy of the dramatic means' (S. L. Bethell).[14] These dramatic means (Bethell seems to argue) are inadequate to certain religious ends he senses in the play. I had hoped in this essay to avoid those private, still more those metaphysical interpretations, to which even the best of us are liable; but since, by drawing attention to the fineness of Shakespeare's stage-craft in this scene, I may be aggravating the charge of staginess, let it be

admitted certainly that Hermione is not a Lazarus, come from
the dead, come back to tell us all; that she is *believed* dead is one
of those errors which Time makes and unfolds (IV i 2). The
spiritual meaning of the play in no way depends on her being a
Lazarus or an Alcestis. It is a play about a crisis in the life of
Leontes, not of Hermione, and her restoration to him (it is not a
'resurrection') is something which happens not to her, but to
him. He had thought her dead by his own hand ('She I kill'd',
v i 7) and now finds her unexpectedly alive in the guardianship of
Paulina. (So a man who believed himself to have destroyed his
soul by some great sin might, after a long repentance under his
Conscience, find that that very Conscience had unknown to him
kept his soul in being and could at last restore it to him alive and
whole.) That is the miracle, it seems to me, for which Shakespeare so carefully prepared.

It had to be a miracle not only for Leontes, but for the
audience. His first dramaturgical job, then, was to ensure that the
audience, like Leontes, should *believe her dead.* For this reason
her death is repeatedly reasserted during the play by a number of
characters, and accepted by all as a fact. Shakespeare's next care
was to give credentials to the statue. The audience must accept it
as a statue, not as a woman; so the Third Gentleman names its
sculptor, an actual man, Giulio Romano; a novel trick to borrow
a kind of authenticity from the 'real' world of the audience, to
lend solidity to the imaginary world of the play; it seems to
confer a special statueishness. For the same reason Paulina warns
Leontes that the colour on it is not yet dry.

But above all Shakespeare stretched his art in creating for his
'statue' a long stillness. For eighty lines and more Hermione must
stand, discovered on her pedestal, not seeming to breathe; that is,
for some four long minutes. Those among the audience who may
think her a living woman, encouraged by Paulina's promise to
'make the statue move indeed', must be *reconvinced against hope
that she is a statue* if the miracle is really to work excitingly for
them. So when at last Hermione is bidden to descend Shakespeare
does not allow her to budge; against all the invocations of Paulina,
he piles up colons, twelve in five lines; it is the most heavily

punctuated passage I have found in Folio. It can be no other than his deliberate contrivance for this special effect; only at the end of the long, pausing entreaty, when the suspense of her motion-lessness has been continued until it must seem unendurable, is Hermione allowed to move:

> Musick; awake her: Strike:
> 'Tis time: descend: be Stone no more: approach:
> Strike all that looke vpon with meruaile: Come:
> Ile fill your Graue vp: stirre: nay, come away:
> Bequeath to Death your numnesse: (for from him,
> Deare Life redeemes you) you perceiue she stirres. . . .

There is nothing antiquated or otiose in stage-craft such as this.

NOTES

1. S. L. Bethell, *The Winter's Tale: a Study* (1946) p. 47. This important work is a contribution to the imaginative and philosophical understanding of the play; although in my essay I have only quoted from it to disagree, the disagreements are largely of a technical kind on relatively minor matters.

2. Ibid. pp. 49–50.

3. Sir Arthur Quiller-Couch and John Dover Wilson, *The Winter's Tale* (1931, reprinted 1950) p. xvi. This work hereafter will be referred to as *W.T.*

4. Bethell, op. cit. p. 78.

5. Ibid. p. 122.

6. A point also noted by Miss M. M. Mahood in her *Shakespeare's Word Play* (1957) p. 147, in discussing the first line spoken by Polixenes.

7. Bethell, op. cit. p. 48.

8. I am indebted to Mr R. B. Freeman, Reader in Taxonomy, University College, London, for reference to Marcel A. J. Couturier, *L'Ours brun, Ursus arctos L.* (1954), published by the author at 45 Rue Thiers, Grenoble, Isère, from which this information about bears is taken.

9. Bethell, op. cit. p. 89.

10. Ibid. pp. 48–9.

11. Ibid. pp. 48–9.

12. Ibid. p. 42.

13. I accept the account of Osric's character put forward by Richard Flatter in his *Hamlet's Father* (1949) pp. 119–20.

14. Bethell, op. cit. p. 103.

M. M. Mahood

THE WINTER'S TALE (1957)

AT this late hour, it would be a work of supererogation to defend the last plays of Shakespeare against the charges of dullness and incompetence which were once frequent in criticism. On a superficial level, there is little to distinguish such a play as *The Winter's Tale* from the fashionable romances of Beaumont and Fletcher; but as recent writers have demonstrated,[1] Shakespeare's poetry in these last plays is too intense to be read superficially. Each image, each turn of phrase, each play upon a word's meanings, compels us to feel that Shakespeare's total statement adds up to much more than the fairy-tale events of the plot. Yet in the theatre the impetus of the action itself leaves us no time to ponder this deeper significance which remains at or very near the unconscious level, and so inseparable from our theatrical excitement and wonder at Leontes' jealousy, Perdita's preservation, and the return to life of Hermione.

Shakespeare packs meaning into *The Winter's Tale* in a way that might be instanced by the opening words of the second scene. Polixenes, the visiting king, is anxious to get home:

> Nine Changes of the Watry-Starre hath been
> The Shepheards Note, since we haue left our Throne
> Without a Burthen.

After the naturalistic prose dialogue with which the play began, this orotund phrase achieves one of those swift changes in the pressure of realism – here from contemporary Court life to the world of the Player King – which is typical of the dramatic climate of these last plays. But the image accomplishes much more than that. The moon's nine changes imply the themes of pregnancy (helped, perhaps, by 'Burthen'), of sudden changes of fortune, and of madness, which are all to become explicit in the course of the same scene. The whole image is the first of many taken from country things and the pastoral life, which persist throughout the Sicilian scenes of the play and so help to bridge the 'great gap' of time and place over which we pass later to the shepherd kingdom of Bohemia. And the leading theme of these scenes in Bohemia, the summer harmony of heaven and earth, is prepared here by mention of the 'watery star' that draws the tides.

For instances of wordplay which, in their economy, match these uses of imagery, we may go back to the opening dialogue between Camillo and Archidamus. Although there are not very many puns in *The Winter's Tale*, the few that are used generate a superb energy. This opening dialogue, for instance, seems no more than the explanatory chat between two minor characters which is part of the competent dramatist's stock-in-trade; but some enquiry into its play of meanings shows it to be much more than this. 'If you shall chance (Camillo)', Archidamus begins, 'to visit Bohemia, on the like occasion whereon my seruices are now on-foot, you shall see (as I haue said) great *difference* betwixt our *Bohemia* and your *Sicilia*.' This *difference* we shall soon discover to be 'contention' as well as 'dissimilarity'; for *Bohemia* and *Sicily* stand eponymously for the kings as well as the kingdoms – as, after a brief exchange of civilities, Camillo's words indicate:

Sicilia cannot show himselfe ouer-kind to *Bohemia*: They were *trayn'd* together in their Child-hoods; and there rooted betwixt them then such a affection, which cannot chuse but *braunch* now.

(I i 23–8)

Trained, used of fruit trees as well as of the education of children, introduces an image of two plants united in such a way as to propagate new growth, and this anticipates the talk in Act IV of grafting a noble scion upon the wildest stock, which is symbolic both of the union of court and country in Perdita's upbringing as a shepherd's daughter and of the reunion of the two kings through the marriage of Perdita and Florizel. But *branch*, besides meaning 'throw out new shoots from the family tree', has the sense of 'divide'; and 'Sicilia cannot show himself over-kind' is ambiguous. On the one hand the undertones of the scene prepare us for the fertility legend of a child healing an old man and so bringing prosperity to the land; on the other hand, the secondary meanings of *difference* and *branch*, together with Camillo's ominous insistence upon Mamillius's 'promise', prepare us for the estrangement of the kings and the death of Mamillius which must intervene before a child, Perdita, 'Physicks the Subject; makes old hearts fresh'.

Some of the most richly ambiguous wordplay in all Shakespeare occurs at the beginning of this estrangement, in Leontes' violent seizure of jealousy against Polixenes. It is possible, of course, to read long-standing suspicion into all Leontes' speeches to Polixenes and Hermione, from the first appearance of the three characters. But this impairs the dramatic contrast between the happiness and harmony of the three characters when Polixenes has agreed to stay, and Leontes' subsequent outburst of passion:

> Too hot, too hot:
> To mingle friendship farre, is mingling bloods.
> I haue Tremor Cordis on me: my heart daunces,
> But not for ioy; not ioy. (I ii 109–12)

Unlike the Age of the Enlightenment, with its demand for logically clear motivation of character, the pre-Locke and the post-Freud epochs share an acceptance of the seemingly incalculable in human behaviour. The Elizabethans might have put Leontes' outburst down to demonic possession; we should call it a libidinous invasion. The effect in either case is the same – a sudden outburst of normally suppressed feelings, which struggle for their release in savage wordplay. Leontes' puns erupt like steam forcing up a saucepan lid, and by the end of some hundred lines he has fairly boiled over with 'foul imaginings'. There are the conscious puns which release his obscene and aggressive tendencies in

> We must be *neat*; not *neat*, but *cleanly*, Captaine:
> And yet the Steere, the Heyfer, and the Calfe,
> Are all call'd *Neat*,   (I ii 124–6)

and in –

> Let what is *dear* in Sicily, be *cheape*:
> Next to thy selfe, and my young Rouer, he's
> *Apparant* to my heart,   (175–7)

where *apparent* means 'seen-through, obvious' as well as 'heir-apparent'. There are unconscious puns on words which remain unspoken: *die*, for example, in 'and then to sigh, as 'twere The Mort o'th'*Deere*' and perhaps *stews* in 'his Pond fish'd by his next Neighbor'. And there are the innuendoes which Leontes reads into Camillo's innocent use of such words as *business* (216) and *satisfy* (232). At one point this kind of wordplay becomes threefold, in that it reveals Shakespeare's intentions as well as Leontes' disturbance of mind:

> Goe *play* (Boy) *play*: thy Mother *playes*, and I
> *Play* too; but so *disgrac'd* a part, whose *issue*
> Will hisse me to my Graue.   (187–9)

Only the first *play* is used in a single sense. We might paraphrase Leontes' *double-entendres* thus: 'Go and amuse yourself; your mother is also pretending to play by acting the kind hostess, but I know that she is a real daughter of the game and up to another sport which makes me act the contemptible role of the deceived husband. So for the moment I'm playing her like a fish ("I am angling now") by giving her line.' This ironic wordplay of Leontes is sustained through *disgraced*, meaning both 'ungraceful' and 'shameful', and *issue* meaning 'exit', 'result' and perhaps also 'Polixenes' bastard child that Hermione now carries'. But *play*, *disgraced* and *issue* have other functions besides that of rendering Leontes' paroxysm true to life. Shakespeare counters each of Leontes' puns by further meanings which relate the word to the larger context of the play's thought and action. The meaning 'make-believe' is added in this way to all the senses of *play*. Leontes is play-acting in his outburst; it is characteristic of such obsessions as his that the sufferer is deluded yet half knows he is under a delusion – as when we know we are in a nightmare but cannot wake from it. Only the make-believe of Hermione, in playing at being a statue, and the make-believe of Perdita in playing the part of a shepherd's daughter, can restore Leontes to a sane discrimination between illusion and reality. *Disgraced* also has further meanings for the play as a whole: Leontes is without the grace of Heaven in sinning against Hermione; but because the irony of wordplay has a negative as well as a positive force, the word also foreshadows Hermione's symbolic role of Heavenly Grace which never deserts Leontes. *Issue* can, positively, mean Mamillius, whose death drives Leontes to a mortified existence; or it can be Leontes' 'action' (a meaning peculiar to Shakespeare) in defying the oracle and so driving Mamillius to *his* grave. It can also mean the legal issue of Hermione's trial. Perhaps its strongest ironic meaning is 'child', taken negatively; Perdita will, in fact, restore him to life. Perdita is preserved from a death of exposure, Leontes is reclaimed from his life-in-death of grief, and Hermione is called upon to bestow to death her numbness, and all this is in accordance with the oracle of Apollo since 'to the Lord God belong the issues of death'.

II

We can quote the Geneva Bible with no sense of incongruity. The presiding deity of the play may be Apollo, but the Christian scheme of redemption is a leading element, though not by any means the only element, in its pattern of ideas. *Grace*, with *gracious* a keyword of the play, is frequently used in its theological sense of 'the divine influence which operates in men to regenerate and sanctify' (*N.E.D.* II 6b). As Everyman, Humanity, Polixenes is able to recall a primeval innocence when he was 'Boy eternal':

> We were as twyn'd Lambs, that did frisk i'th'Sun,
> And bleat the one at th'other: what we chang'd,
> Was Innocence, for Innocence: we knew not
> The Doctrine of ill-doing, nor dream'd
> That any did: Had we pursu'd that life,
> And our weake Spirits ne're been higher rear'd

With stronger blood, we should haue answer'd Heauen
Boldly, not guilty; the Imposition clear'd,
Hereditarie ours. (I ii 67–75)

In the dialogue which follows, the word *grace* is used three times
by Hermione, the implication being that she acts the role of
regenerative grace to Leontes now he has exchanged Innocence
for Experience. But immediately there follows Leontes' rejection
of this grace in his outburst against Hermione. 'You'le be found,
Be you beneath the Sky' is his threat to Hermione and Polixenes;
the words are strong dramatic irony, since it is Leontes himself
who is sinning in the sight of Heaven, the single Eye of Apollo
made actual to us by the sight images of Leontes' talk with
Camillo in the first act – 'your eye-glasse Is thicker then a
Cuckolds Horne' (I ii 268); 'a Vision so apparent' (270); 'to
haue nor Eyes' (275); 'and all Eyes Blind with the Pin and Web,
but theirs' (290); 'Canst with thine eyes at once see good and
euill' (303); 'Seruants true about me, that bare eyes' (309); 'who
may'st see Plainely, as Heauen sees Earth, and Earth sees
Heauen' (314). The small but vitally important scene between
Cleomenes and Dion, as they return from Delphos at the
beginning of Act III, stresses this awesome aspect of the Destroyer Apollo, whose oracle is 'kin to Ioues Thunder'; and their
hope that the *issue* of their visit will be *gracious* is not immediately fulfilled. Apollo keeps jealous guard over the fortunes
of the gracious Hermione, and her belief that 'Powres Diuine
Behold our humane Actions' is vindicated when, his oracle
defied, Apollo at once smites Leontes with the death of Mamillius: 'Apollo's angry, and the Heauens themselues Doe strike at
my Iniustice.'

Leontes' change of heart, from a proud defiance of the God
to guilt, despair and finally a sober repentance, is marked by two
instances of wordplay. At the beginning of the trial scene he
announces that justice shall have 'due course, Euen to the Guilt,
or the *Purgation*'. In the legal sense, human justice will proceed
to find Hermione guilty or give her the chance 'of clearing [her]
self from the accusation or suspicion of crime and guilt'; in the
theological sense, Apollo's justice will establish Leontes' guilt

and will also purify him from it by the repentance vowed at the
end of the scene:

> once a day, Ile visit
> The Chappell where they lye, and teares shed there
> Shall be my *recreation*.

Recreation and *re-creation*: the pun is a promise that Leontes is to
become 'man new made' at the end of the play, for Apollo offers
him grace in the sense of time for amendment (*N.E.D.* II 7) and
also hope for the eventual grace of pardon (*N.E.D.* II 8). The
King takes to himself the words of Hermione:

> I must be patient, till the Heauens looke
> With an aspect more fauorable,   (II i 105–6)

and her withdrawal symbolises Everyman's patient hope in the
return of grace. In the major tragedies of Shakespeare, patience
had been a stoical virtue, the capacity to endure. Here it is a
Christian virtue, the ability to possess one's soul in patience,
which is rewarded when Hermione reappears literally as Patience
on a monument, 'smiling' (in the words of *Pericles*) 'extremity
out of act'.

Meanwhile Perdita has 'grown in grace'; as with Tuesday's
child, the word has a theological as well as a physical meaning.
At the sheep-shearing feast, Leontes' grace of repentance and
Hermione's grace of patient forgiveness are kept in mind by
Perdita's graceful presentation of flowers to the disguised
Polixenes and Camillo:

> Reuerend Sirs,
> For you, there's Rosemary, and *Rue*, these keepe
> Seeming, and sauour all the Winter long:
> *Grace*, and Remembrance be to you both,
> And welcome to our Shearing.   (IV iii 73–7)

The theological language of the play's first part is revived and
intensified when the action returns to Sicily at the beginning of
Act V. The restoration of both the wife and the daughter is
spoken of as a regeneration for Leontes. 'Now blesse thy selfe:'
the old shepherd had said at the finding of Perdita, 'thou met'st

with things dying. I with things new borne'; and the theme is
repeated when one courtier tells another how Leontes was reunited with Camillo: 'they look'd as they had heard of a World
ransom'd, or one destroyed.' The ritual-like solemnity of the last
scene completes this regeneration. 'It is requir'd', commands
Paulina, 'You doe awake your Faith'; and to music such as
accompanied the awakening of Lear and Pericles, Faith, in the
person of Hermione, steps off her plinth into Leontes' arms:

> You Gods looke downe,
> And from your sacred Viols poure your graces
> Vpon my daughters head.   (v iii 121–3)

III

So *The Winter's Tale* is a morality play; but its morality is wider,
wiser and more humane than that of a Puritan inner drama of sin,
guilt and contrition. Something is omitted in the attempt made
here to allegorise the play. We have had to leave out the sunburnt
mirth of the scenes in Bohemia, the Clown, Mopsa, and the rogue
Autolycus who made such an impression on Simon Forman
when he saw the play in 1611. Worse still, Perdita is really unnecessary if we read *The Winter's Tale* as a kind of *Grace
Abounding*, and we are forced to ask why Shakespeare could not
have symbolised the spiritual health of the lapsed and forgiven
soul by a single figure like Dante's Beatrice or Blake's Jerusalem.

A clue to the answer may perhaps be found if we return to
Leontes' outburst in Act I. After 'Goe play (Boy) play', Leontes
abandons the ordinary sense of 'to sport or frolic' for bitterly
ironic meanings; and in this wordplay, and the act of dismissing
Mamillius, is revealed Leontes' inability to keep himself young,
to become as a child again. Polixenes understands the value of
play, and Florizel's 'varying child-nesse' keeps him from a
spiritual winter. Mamillius also has the power to make old hearts
fresh; the sight of him can take twenty-three years off his father's
life, and he has a *welkin* eye – the adjective suggesting something
providential and life-giving, and not merely 'clear and blue like
the sky'. In spite of this, Leontes cannot recapture the non-moral

vision of childhood, the state of the 'Boy eternal' who had not as
yet the knowledge of good and evil. At the beginning of the last
act, Cleomenes pleads with Leontes to forgive himself; but this is
just what Leontes cannot do until Perdita's return. For if Hermione represents the grace of heaven towards Leontes, Perdita
stands for his self-forgiveness, for his recapture of the child's non-
moral acceptance of things as they are in Nature. In this way,
Perdita plays a role of Nature complementary to Hermione's role
of Grace. This moral intransigence in Leontes may have very
deep roots. J. I. M. Stewart hints at the transference, in the king's
outburst of delusional jealousy, of his guilt at an adolescent
relationship with Polixenes for which he cannot forgive himself.[2]
Whatever the cause of his fury, his bawdy use of *play* in 'thy
Mother playes' suggests the moral rigidity born of a moral uncertainty; he cannot see Hermione's real need to play, to the
extent perhaps of a harmless flirtation with Polixenes. So a tension is established between two forms of *play*: play as sport, a
holiday freedom, and play as Leontes' imprisoning delusion that
Hermione is unfaithful to him. Unable to play in the sense of
refreshing himself from the non-moral and instinctive life of
childhood, Leontes begins to play in the sense of constructing an
intensely moral drama in which he enacts the role of the deceived
husband. In the opening scene of Act II, these two forms of play,
the natural and the unnatural, are literally juxtaposed. On one
side of the stage, Mamillius at play produces make-believe
shudders with his ghost story; on the other, Leontes' delusion –
'I have drunke, and seene the spider' – communicates a real
horror to the audience who are to see him, in the grip of his
involuntary make-believe, turn Mamillius's winter's tale into
earnest. 'What is this? Sport?' Hermione asks as Mamillius is
snatched from her; and once again Leontes perverts the meaning
of the most innocent word:

> Away with him, and let her sport her selfe
> With that shee's big with, for 'tis Polixenes
> Ha's made thee swell thus.   (II i 59)

The contrast between these two kinds of play is kept up in

Leontes' insistence that his delusion is fact:

> No: if I mistake
> In those Foundations which I build vpon,
> The Centre is not bigge enough to beare
> A Schoole-Boyes Top.[3]   (II i 99–102)

So deluded, he is beyond the reach of reason as it is voiced in the well-ordered rhetoric of Camillo or that of Hermione in her formal self-defence at the trial. Hermione is forced to admit that she and Leontes move in different worlds:

> You speake a Language that I vnderstand not:
> My Life stands in the leuell of your Dreames,
> Which Ile lay downe.   (III ii 81–3)

With much more irony than he intends, Leontes replies: 'Your Actions are my Dreames.' Nothing can in fact destroy his confusion of nightmare and reality except the real-life disaster of Mamillius's death.

For two and a half acts of the play the audience has shared an overcharged moral atmosphere, as it has witnessed Leontes' protest against his supposedly impaired honour, shared Paulina's moral indignation at Leontes' treatment of Hermione, and experienced with the whole Court a sense of heavenly retribution in the death of Mamillius. Now in the ensuing few scenes, this tension is relaxed and we are transported into a world on holiday. By its remoteness from the real Hermione of the trial scene, Antigonus's vision of Hermione begins the distancing of Sicily and Sicilian attitudes; and the shift from a courtly to a country outlook starts with the old shepherd's grumbles about the hunt and the coarse kindness with which he dismisses Perdita's begetting as 'behinde-doore worke: they were warmer that got this, then the poore Thing is heere'. There is a matter-of-fact acceptance of Nature as it is in the Clown's account of the shipwreck and of Antigonus's encounter with the bear. If his vivid descriptions of both seem callous, they are in fact only honest; hogsheads have more reality for him than have Sicilian courtiers, and he sees Antigonus's fate from the bear's point of view. The creature must have its dinner, and 'they are neuer *curst* but when they are hungry'; his use of the word to imply 'fierce' without any moral nuance contrasts with Leontes' use of it when in the grip of his delusion:

> How blest am I
> In my iust Censure? in my true Opinion?
> Alack, for lesser knowledge, how *accurs'd*
> In being so blest?   (II i 35–8)

In *King Lear* a vision of Nature's cruelty, of man as one of the most savage beasts of prey, was opposed to the traditional notion of Nature as harmony, fecundity and order. In *The Winter's Tale*, however, Nature is neither morally good nor bad; a bear's appetite and a waiting-gentlewoman's lapse are accepted as the way of the world. Animal images are used by Leontes, in the first part of the play, with all the revulsion of Othello's 'goats and monkeys!' but Antigonus's stud language shows up, by a kind of grotesque parody, the folly of thus regarding everything in Nature as subject to moral judgment; and the scenes in Bohemia restore the child's or the peasant's freedom from morbid pre-occupations about good and evil. The wordplay reveals the same change of attitude. *Blood*, for example, when used in the first part of the play, often carries a connotation of 'lust' – its primary meaning in a play like *Othello*. Now, in Autolycus's song about 'the red blood raigns in the winters pale', it represents a passion as natural and inevitable as the sap that rises in spring, to be accepted as philosophically as the old shepherd endures the ways of 'these boylde-braines of nineteene, and two and twenty'. For all his classical name, Autolycus is an English coney-catcher, and his daffodil and doxy belong less to the classical Arcadia[4] than to Herrick's Devonshire, where Christianity has absorbed much of an older cult, and if there is a Puritan he too sings psalms to hornpipes. According to Blake's paradox, the return of spiritual vision by which what now seemed finite and corrupt would appear infinite and holy was to be accomplished by 'an improvement of sensual enjoyment'; and such enjoyment is felt throughout the scenes in Bohemia. The sensuous blend of the colourful, the fragrant, the sweet and the spicy in the Clown's shopping list contrasts sharply with the painful sensibility of some images in the first part of the play – for instance, Leontes' rebuke to Antigonus:

> Cease, no more:
> You smell this businesse with a sence as *cold*
> As is a dead-mans nose,   (II i 149–51)

where the wordplay, by suggesting the touch of death, achieves a *frisson* worthy of a winter's tale.

By the time Autolycus, who has overheard the Clown's list, has caught this particular coney in a travesty of the Good Samaritan story, the holiday mood is complete.[5] Like Florizel we

> Apprehend
> Nothing but iollity: the Goddes themselues
> (Humbling their Deities to loue) haue taken
> The shapes of Beasts vpon them. Iupiter,
> Became a Bull, and bellow'd: the green Neptune
> A Ram, and bleated: and the Fire-roab'd-God
> Golden Apollo, a poore humble Swaine,
> As I seeme now.   (IV iii 24–31)

These lines, based on a section of Greene's *Pandosto* which Shakespeare did not utilise in any other way, have a particular aptness to the holiday mood of this feast. Even the Gods are at play. Jupiter and Neptune become the horned animals in which Leontes saw only the symbol of human bestiality and cuckoldry, and their bellowing and bleating evoke the laughter which is lacking in Leontes, who cannot play. Greene's phrase: 'Neptune became a ram, Jupiter a Bull, Apollo a shepherd' may have recalled to Shakespeare the story told in the second book of the *Metamorphoses* of Apollo's love for the nymph Chione, whom in jealousy he slew with his dart, but whose child he reared to be the lifegiving Aesculapius; a parallel to his dual role of destroyer and preserver in *The Winter's Tale*. Apollo's metamorphosis into the shepherd 'humbling his Deity to love' is not incompatible with the presentation of Apollo as the supreme and just God in the first part of the play; it suggests just such a union of Heaven and earth as is implied by Milton's

> Or if Vertue feeble were,
> Heav'n it self would stoop to her.

But in these scenes of the play the reconciliation of heaven and earth is not theological but natural, the fructification of nature by the sun that shines alike upon the good and the evil. In the scenes of sixteen years before, heaven had been at destructive variance with earth in the 'dangerous vnsafe Lunes I' th' King', in Apollo's thunderbolt, and in the storm's conflict of sea and sky. Now the imagery stresses their harmony:

> for neuer gaz'd the Moone
> Vpon the water, as hee'l stand and reade
> As 'twere my daughters eyes.   (IV iii 172–4)

And in proof of his constancy, Florizel protests that not

> for all the Sun sees, or
> The close earth wombes, or the profound seas, hides
> In vnknowne fadomes, will I breake my oath
> To this my faire belou'd.   (IV iii 502–5)

The image persists after the lovers' voyage to Sicily. Perdita seems to Leontes at his first sight of her

> the most peereless peece of Earth, I thinke,
> That ere the Sunne shone bright on,   (V i 94–5)

and he tells how he

> lost a couple, that 'twixt Heauen and Earth
> Might thus haue stood, begetting wonder, as
> You (gracious Couple) doe,   (V i 132–4)

where both the natural and the spiritual union are implied in 'begetting' and 'gracious'. This awareness of the bridal of the earth and sky lends irony to Florizel's bitter assertion (V i 206) that the stars will kiss the valleys before he and Perdita will be able to marry. The stars do kiss the valleys through those heavenly influences in which most Jacobeans firmly believed;

heaven is matched with earth in the life of growth, in the Bohemian shepherds' acceptance of nature's ways, of which Perdita is the symbol.

For Perdita, dressed as the queen of the feast, and acting the part of hostess to her father's guests, represents the natural rightness of play, the renewing power of youth which Leontes once had, and lost, in Mamillius. In her presentation of flowers, time runs back to fetch the age of gold, from winter herbs to August's carnations and striped gillyflowers, to the June marigold that goes to bed with the sun (another symbol of the union of heaven and earth), and so back to the spring flowers she would give Florizel. The great flower passage is full of what Herrick calls a 'cleanly wantonness': the violets are as sweet as the breath of Venus, the primroses lovesick, the oxslip inviting, and the daffodils *take* the air in a triple sense – enchant, seize, and come out for exercise and pleasure – which suggests all the tentative and yet bold grace of the flower. The daffodil flings itself on the winds of March with that enchanting blend of abandon and modesty that is found in Perdita's wish to strew Florizel with these flowers

> like a banke, for Loue to lye, and *play* on:
> Not like a Coarse: or if: not to be buried
> But quicke, and in mine armes. Come, take your flours,
> Me thinks I *play* as I haue seene them do
> In Whitsun-Pastorals: Sure this Robe of mine
> Do's change my disposition. (IV iii 130–5)

The first *play* here has the same connotation as 'thy Mother playes', but it is used with an innocent sexuality which represents that acceptance of the ways of nature that Perdita is to restore to her father. This restoration can be made only when Perdita plays one further role, that of the Libyan princess. For no sooner has she cast aside her disguise with 'Ile queene it no inch further' than Camillo arranges to see her 'royally appointed, as if The Scene you play, were mine' and Perdita acquiesces with: 'I see the Play so lyes That I must beare a part.' Her part, and that of Florizel also, is to enable Leontes to forgive himself. Looking on

them both, the old king feels time unravel until he can understand
and accept the excesses of his own youth:

> Were I but twentie one,
> Your Fathers Image is so hit in you,
> (His very ayre) that I should call you Brother,
> As I did him, and speake of something wildly
> By vs perform'd before. . . .
> . . . You haue a holy Father
> A gracefull Gentleman, against whose person
> (So sacred as it is) I haue done sinne,
> For which, the Heauens (taking angry note)
> Haue left me Issue-lesse: and your Father's bless'd
> (As he from Heauen merits it) with you,
> Worthy his goodnesse.   (v i 126–30, 170–6)

The irony of this is not only that Leontes' daughter and son-in-
law stand before him as he speaks, but that he should call
Polixenes 'gracefull'. In fact Polixenes, in breaking the match
between Florizel and Perdita, has shown a lack of that imaginative vision, symbolised by the two lovers, which Leontes has now
acquired and which makes him the lovers' advocate, sympathetic
to Florizel's plea:

> Remember, since you ow'd no more to Time
> Then I do now.   (v i 219–20)

The reunion of Leontes with Perdita concludes this aspect of
the play as a defence and justification of play itself. Because
Shakespeare is here concerned with recreation as re-creation,
much of the play itself seems trifling, a kind of vaudeville: the
comic turns of Autolycus, the dances, the Clown's part, the
ballads. We must not look closely for wisdom in this fooling; its
purpose is to remind Everyman – Leontes and the audience –
of his need for folly.

IV

Besides this theme of spiritual renewal through the double operation of Grace and Nature, other meanings of the two words are
at work in *The Winter's Tale*. It shares with Shakespeare's other

late romances a dramatic contrast between Nature and the Graces
of Art. Moreover, the theme of spiritual renewal is closely paralleled by one of social reinvigoration. The question of True
Nobility, which Shakespeare had already raised in *All's Well*, is
made a concern of *The Winter's Tale* by Shakespeare's play on
several words with restrictive social meanings, of which *grace* is
one. Leontes carries the title of the King's Grace (*N.E.D.* II 9),
but he is none the more gracious, in the sense of being comely or
blessed, on that account. Autolycus, a sometime hanger-on of the
court, pretends to be outraged because the Shepherd should 'offer
to haue his Daughter come into *grace*', but we have already been
told that she has 'growne in *grace*' and have taken it to mean her
natural dignity of bearing as well as her goodness and beauty.
Again, in the use of the word *breeding* there is interplay between
the widest meaning of 'begetting', the more limited social meaning of 'a good upbringing' and the most restricted meaning of
'good manners'. Polixenes, slighted by Leontes, is left 'to consider what is *breeding*, That changes thus his Manners', and in
Florizel's 'She's as forward, of her *Breeding*, as She is i'th' reare'
our *Birth*' there is an additional wordplay on *birth*: Perdita's
only inferiority is in fact in her age, for she has not only royal
birth, but also the natural good breeding of the old shepherd
whose head is nothing turned when he finds himself in high
society: 'we must be *gentle*, now we are Gentlemen'. The glories
of our *blood* and *state* are vanity, because the vaunted blue blood
turns out to be the ordinary red stuff in everyone's veins, and
however stately our dignity, every man must belong to one or
other of the estates which make up the state of society; and
Shakespeare makes subtle use of all these meanings in the course
of the play.[6] Lastly there is his use of *free* to mean 'of gentle birth'
or 'of noble or honorable character' or 'at liberty'. Hermione in
prison remains in her innocence as *free* as the child of whom she
is delivered; to Paulina's suggestion that she take the new-born
child to the king, Emilia replies:

> Most worthy Madam,
> your honor, and your goodnesse is so euident,

> That your *free* vndertaking cannot misse,
> A thriuing *yssue*,   (II ii 42–5)

and Paulina protests to the Court that the Queen is

> A gracious innocent soule,
> More free, then he is iealous.   (II ii 29–30)

In these two scenes which close the second act, the point is driven home that the truest courtesy is not a veneer of the court. Leontes' court is a beargarden and the scenes enacted there are farce on the brink of tragedy.[7] Hermione in contrast keeps court in prison with all the ceremony of innocence and so associates herself, before the trial scene, with the gracious ceremonial of Apollo's devotees, as Dion describes them:

> I shall report,
> For most it caught me, the Celestiall Habits,
> (Me thinkes I so should terme them) and the reuerence
> Of the graue Wearers. O, the Sacrifice,
> How ceremonious, solemne, and vn-earthly
> It was i'th'Offring?   (III i 3–8)

At the end of the play, the ceremony which should surround the King's Grace is restored to Leontes; his visit to Paulina is spoken of by her as a surplus of his Grace.

Before this renewal can be achieved, however, the royal grace must replenish itself from the life of nature. When the old shepherd chides Perdita for her tardiness in welcoming his guests, and compares her reserve with his old wife's joviality, Shakespeare seems at first hearing to be restating the Elizabethan certainty that blood will tell; Florizel and Perdita are merely pretended shepherd and shepherdess, two figures by Fragonard superimposed on a scene by Breughel. Yet if Perdita is full of grace in every meaning of the word, she owes that upbringing to the two old peasants. Polixenes' praise of the custom of grafting 'a gentler Sien, to the wildest stocke' is vivid dramatic irony, not only because he is shortly going to repudiate his theory when his son seeks to marry a shepherdess, but because Perdita's upbringing has been just such a fruitful grafting. The child of a father who has cut himself off from a wholesome rural way of living and thinking is returned by Apollo to the education of Nature, in order that ultimately court and cottage may flourish together under the sun of his favour who 'Lookes on alike'.

NOTES

1. Especially S. L. Bethell, *The Winter's Tale: a Study* (1947); G. Wilson Knight, *The Crown of Life* (1947); F. R. Leavis, 'The Criticism of Shakespeare's Late Plays', in *Scrutiny*, x; E. M. W. Tillyard, *Shakespeare's Last Plays* (1938); and D. A. Traversi, *Shakespeare: The Last Phase* (1955).

2. J. I. M. Stewart, *Character and Motive in Shakespeare* (1948) pp. 30–7.

3. This is, I think, echoed in *Comus* when the Elder Brother declares that 'evil on it self shall back recoyl. . . .'

> if this fail,
> The pillar'd firmament is rott'nness
> And earths base built on stubble.

Comus has in common with Shakespeare's last plays more than the family likeness of a pastoral. It has been suggested by J. E. Crofts that Sabrina's role in the masque is very much that of a nature spirit such as Perdita. The Lady remains frozen in a Puritanical disapproval until the nymph releases her.

4. Shakespeare may have changed round the Sicily and Bohemia of his source in order to avoid the literary associations of Sicilian shepherds.

5. S. L. Bethell, in *The Winter's Tale: a Study*, discusses very fully the fade-out of Sicilian attitudes. The Biblical parallel, pointed out by G. Wilson Knight (*The Crown of Life*, p. 101) is given support by Autolycus's recall of how he once compassed a motion (that is, staged a puppet show) of the Prodigal Son.

6. See especially IV iii 148; ibid., 413, 439, 442.

7. The complexity of Paulina accords with this. She is both magnificent and ludicrous. She has moreover a third aspect, that of guardian angel to Hermione and Leontes. She is very like Julia in *The Cocktail Party* – a play which is also about redemption, the eye of God and the need for ordinary mortals not to take themselves too seriously.

Louis MacNeice

AUTOLYCUS

In his last phase when hardly bothering
To be a dramatist, the Master turned away
From his taut plots and complex characters
To tapestried romances, conjuring
With rainbow names and handfuls of sea-spray
And from them turned out happy Ever-afters.

Eclectic always, now extravagant,
Sighting his matter through a timeless prison
He ranged his classical bric-à-brac in grottos
Where knights of Ancient Greece had Latin mottoes
And fishermen their flap-jacks* – none should want
Colour for lack of an anachronism.

A gay world certainly though pocked and scored
With childish horrors and a fresh world though
Its mainsprings were old gags – babies exposed
Identities confused and queens to be restored;
But when the cracker bursts it proves as you supposed –
Trinket and moral tumble out just so.

Such innocence – In his own words it was
Like an old tale, only that where time leaps
Between acts three and four there was something born
Which made the stock-type virgin dance like corn
In a wind that having known foul marshes, barren steeps,
Felt therefore kindly towards Marinas,† Perditas.

    * See *Pericles*.   † Pericles' daughter.

Thus crystal learned to talk. But Shakespeare balanced it
With what we knew already, gabbing earth
Hot from Eastcheap* – Watch your pockets when
That rogue comes round the corner, he can slit
Purse strings as quickly as his maker's pen
Will try your heart-strings in the name of mirth.

O master pedlar with your confidence tricks,
Brooches, pomanders, broad sheets and what-have-you
Who hawk such entertainment but rook your client
And leave him brooding, why should we forgive you
Did we not know that, though more self-reliant
Than we, you too were born and grew up in a fix?

* Falstaff's haunt.

QUESTIONS

1. What were the main changes made by Shakespeare in dramatising Greene's *Pandosto* and why did he make them?

2. At what point, before or during the play, did Leontes become jealous?

3. What light, if any, does the imagery throw on the meaning of the play?

4. Why does Shakespeare call attention to the improbabilities of the plot?

5. Why was the scene in which Leontes recognises his daughter merely reported?

6. What evidence is there that Shakespeare revised the play after 1611?

7. 'Shakespeare's powers of characterisation had weakened when he came to write the plays of the Final Period.' Do you agree?

8. How would you defend Shakespeare's violation of the unities of Time and Place?

9. Write detailed character-sketches of the following with detailed references to the text: Leontes; Hermione; Polixenes; Paulina; Autolycus.

10. Compare Perdita with Marina and Miranda.

11. What are the main differences between a performance of the play in Shakespeare's theatre and a modern production?

12. Describe how you would produce (*a*) the sheep-shearing scene, (*b*) the statue scene.

13. The following is the speech by Bellaria at her trial in Greene's novel; discuss the use Shakespeare made of it.

If the divine powers be privy to human actions (as no doubt they are) I hope my patience shall make fortune blush, and my unspotted life shall stain spiteful discredit. For although lying report hath sought to appeach mine honour, and suspicion hath intended to soil my credit with infamy, yet where virtue keepeth the fort, report and suspicion may assail, but never sack. But how I have led my life before Egistus' coming, I appeal to the gods and to thy conscience. What hath passed betwixt him and me, the gods only know, and I hope will presently reveal. That I loved Egistus I cannot deny; that I honoured him I shame not to confess: to the one I was forced by his virtues, to the other for his dignities. But, as touching lacivious lust, I say Egistus is honest, and I hope myself to be found without spot. For Franion, I can neither accuse him nor excuse him, for I was not privy to his departure. And that this is true which I have here rehearsed, I refer myself to the divine oracle.

14. Comment on the meaning and style of the following passages:

(a)
                  Gone already!
Inch-thick, knee-deep, o'er head and ears a fork'd one!
Go, play, boy, play: thy mother plays, and I
Play too, but so disgraced a part, whose issue
Will hiss me to my grave: contempt and clamour
Will be my knell. Go, play, boy, play. There have been,
Or I am much deceived, cuckolds ere now;
And many a man there is, even at this present,
Now while I speak this, holds his wife by the arm,
That little thinks she has been sluiced in's absence
And his pond fish'd by his next neighbour, by
Sir Smile, his neighbour: nay, there's comfort in't
Whiles other men have gates and those gates open'd,
As mine, against their will. Should all despair
That have revolted wives, the tenth of mankind
Would hang themselves. Physic for't there is none;
It is a bawdy planet, that will strike
Where 'tis predominant; and 'tis powerful, think it,

From east, west, north and south: be it concluded,
No barricado for a belly; know't;
It will let in and out the enemy
With bag and baggage: many thousand on's
Have the disease, and feel't not. How now, boy!

(*b*)   *Paul.* What studied torments, tyrant, hast for me?
What wheels? racks? fires? what flaying? boiling?
In leads or oils? what old or newer torture
Must I receive, whose every word deserves
To taste of thy most worst? Thy tyranny
Together working with thy jealousies,
Fancies too weak for boys, too green and idle
For girls of nine, O, think what they have done
And then run mad indeed, stark mad! for all
Thy by-gone fooleries were but spices of it.
That thou betray'dst Polixenes, 'twas nothing;
That did but show thee, of a fool, inconstant
And damnable ingrateful: nor was't much,
Thou wouldst have poison'd good Camillo's honour,
To have him kill a king; poor trespasses,
More monstrous standing by: whereof I reckon
The casting forth to crows thy baby-daughter
To be none or little; though a devil
Would have shed water out of fire ere done't:
Nor is't directly laid to thee, the death
Of the young prince, whose honourable thoughts,
Thoughts high for one so tender, cleft the heart
That could conceive a gross and foolish sire
Blemish'd his gracious dam: this is not, no,
Laid to thy answer: but the last, – O lord,
When I have said, cry 'woe!' – the queen, the queen,
The sweet'st, dear'st creature's dead, and vengeance
                                                              for't
   Not dropp'd down yet.

(*c*)   *Cam.* I should leave grazing, were I of your flock,
      And live only by gazing.
      Per.   Out, alas!
      You'ld be so lean, that blasts of January

Would blow you through and through. Now, my
                             fair'st friend,
I would I had some flowers o' the spring that might
Become your time of day; and yours, and yours,
That wear upon your virgin branches yet
Your maidenheads growing: O Proserpina,
For the flowers now, that frighted thou let'st fall
From Dis's waggon! daffodils,
That come before the swallow dares, and take
The winds of March with beauty; violets dim,
But sweeter than the lids of Juno's eyes
Or Cytherea's breath; pale primroses,
That die unmarried, ere they can behold
Bright Phoebus in his strength – a malady
Most incident to maids; bold oxlips and
The crown imperial; lilies of all kinds,
The flower-de-luce being one! O, these I lack,
To make you garlands of, and my sweet friend,
To strew him o'er and o'er!

Flo.   What, like a corse?
Per. No, like a bank for love to lie and play on;
Not like a corse; or if, not to be buried,
But quick and in mine arms. Come, take your flowers:
Methinks I play as I have seen them do
In Whitsun pastorals: sure this robe of mine
Does change my disposition.

SELECT BIBLIOGRAPHY
(Books from which extracts are taken are omitted.)

B. Evans, *Shakespeare's Comedies* (Oxford U.P., 1960).

H. Northrop Frye, *A Natural Perspective* (Columbia U.P., New York and London, 1965).

F. D. Hoeniger, 'The Meaning of *The Winter's Tale*', in *University of Toronto Quarterly*, xx (1950).

D. G. James, *Scepticism and Poetry* (Allen & Unwin, 1937; Barnes and Noble, 1960).

F. R. Leavis, *The Common Pursuit* (Chatto & Windus, 1952; New York U.P., 1952).

C. Leech, 'The Structure of the Last Plays', in *Shakespeare Survey 11* (Cambridge U.P., 1958).

K. Muir, *The Last Periods of Shakespeare, Racine and Ibsen* (Liverpool U.P., 1961; Wayne State U.P., 1961).

Fitzroy Pyle, *Winter's Tale: A Commentary on the Structure* (Routledge & Kegan Paul, 1969).

A. Quiller-Couch, *Shakespeare's Workmanship* (Cambridge U.P., 1918).

P. N. Sie l. 'Leontes, a jealous Tyrant', in *Review of English Stuaü* (1950), pp. 302–7.

Lytton Strachey, 'Shakespeare's Final Period', in *Books and Characters* (Chatto & Windus, 1906).

NOTES ON CONTRIBUTORS

S. L. BETHELL, formerly of the University College of South Wales, Cardiff; author of *Shakespeare and the Popular Dramatic Tradition, The Winter's Tale: a Study*, etc. (died 1954).

NEVILL COGHILL, formerly Merton Professor of English Literature in the University of Oxford, and author of *Shakespeare's Dramatic Skills*, etc.

INGA-STINA EWBANK, Professor of English at Bedford College, University of London, and author of *Their Proper Sphere*.

NORTHROP FRYE (University of Toronto), author of *The Anatomy of Criticism* and of a book on Shakespeare's last period, *A Natural Perspective*.

G. WILSON KNIGHT, Professor Emeritus of the University of Leeds; author of *The Wheel of Fire* and many other works of interpretation.

LOUIS MACNEICE, poet, critic, radio dramatist and translator (died 1963).

M. M. MAHOOD (University of Canterbury), author of *Poetry and Humanism* and *Shakespeare's Word Play*.

ERNEST SCHANZER (University of Munich), editor of the New Penguin edition of *The Winter's Tale* and author of *Shakespeare's Problem Plays* (died 1976).

DONALD A. STAUFFER, author of *Shakespeare's World of Images* and of a book on Yeats.

E. M. W. TILLYARD (formerly Master of Jesus College, Cambridge), author of many books, chiefly on Milton and Shakespeare (died 1962).

DEREK TRAVERSI, author of *Approach to Shakespeare* and three other Shakespearian studies.

HAROLD S. WILSON (formerly of the University of Toronto), author of *On the Design of Shaksperian Tragedy*.

INDEX